THE PSYCHOANALYTIC STUDY
OF SOCIETY

Volume 11

THE PSYCHOANALYTIC STUDY
OF SOCIETY

Volume 11

Essays in honor of Werner Muensterberger

Edited by
L. BRYCE BOYER
SIMON A. GROLNICK

 THE ANALYTIC PRESS
1985

Distributed by
LAWRENCE ERLBAUM ASSOCIATES, PUBLISHERS
Hillsdale, New Jersey   London

Distributed solely by

Lawrence Erlbaum Associates, Inc., Publishers
365 Broadway
Hillsdale, New Jersey 07642

ISBN 0-88163-032-2
ISSN 0079-7294

Printed in the United States of America
10 9 8 7 6 5 4 3 2 1

Editors

Contributors

Renato J. Almansi, M.D. Clinical Professor of Psychiatry, New York University; Training Analyst (Emeritus), The Psychoanalytic Institute, New York University; Associate Editor, *American Imago.*

Leon Balter, M.D. Associate Clinical Professor of Psychiatry, Albert Einstein College of Medicine.

Yoram Bilu, Ph.D. Lecturer, Departments of Sociology, Anthropology, and Psychology, Hebrew University, Jerusalem.

L. Bryce Boyer, M.D. Associate Director, Residency Training, Herrick Hospital, Berkeley.

Ruth M. Boyer, Ph.D. Professor, Humanities and Science, and Chairperson, Textile Department, California School of Arts and Crafts, Oakland.

George A. De Vos, Ph.D. Professor of Anthropology, University of California, Berkeley.

Gilbert H. Herdt, Ph.D. Assistant Professor of Anthropology, Stanford University.

Géza Róheim, Ph.D. Lecturer, New York Psychoanalytic Institute; deceased.

Howard F. Stein, Ph.D. Associate Professor of Medical Anthropology, Department of Family Medicine, University of Oklahoma Health Sciences Center, Oklahoma City; Editor, *The Journal of Psychoanalytic Anthropology.*

Robert J. Stoller, M.D. Professor of Psychiatry, UCLA School of Medicine, Los Angeles.

Contents

Bibliography of Werner Muensterberger

BOOKS

Ethnologische Studien an Indonesischen Schöpfungsmythen: Ein Beitrag zur Kultur-Analyse Südostasiens. (In German: *Anthropological Studies in Indonesian Creation Myths: A Contribution to Cultural Analysis of Southeast Asia.)* The Hague: Nijhof, 1939.

Primitieve Kunst en Cultuur. (In Dutch: *Primitive Art in Culture.)* 4 Vols. Arnhem: van Loghum Slaterus, 1940–1941. (Published under the auspices of the Royal Colonial Institute [now Royal Institute for the Tropics].)

(with Hella S. Haasse) *Lyriek der Naturvolken.* (In Dutch: *Lyrics of Primitive People.)* Arnhem: van Loghum Slaterus, 1947.

Vincent van Gogh. Drawings, Pastels, Studies. New York: Beechhurst Press, 1946. (Also British, Dutch, French, and Swedish editions.)

Sculpture of Modern Man. New York: Harry N. Abrams, 1955. (Also British, Dutch, French, and German editions.)

Universality of Tribal Art. Geneva: Barbier-Müller, 1979.

EDITORSHIPS

Róheim, Géza, Editor; Muensterberger, Warner, Assistant Editor. *Psychoanalysis and the Social Sciences,* Vol. 3. New York: International Universities Press, 1951.

Muensterberger, Warner, and Axelrad, Sidney. *Psychoanalysis and the Social Sciences,* Vols. 4 and 5. New York: International Universities Press, 1955, 1958.

Muensterberger, Warner, and Axelrad, Sidney. *The Psychoanalytic Study of Society,* Vols. 1 through 4. New York: International Universities Press, 1960, 1962, 1964, 1967.

Muensterberger, Warner, and Esman, Aaron H. *The Psychoanalytic Study of Society,* Vols. 5 and 6. New York: International Universities Press, 1972, 1975.

Muensterberger, Werner, Esman, Aaron H., and Boyer, L. Bryce. *The Psychoanalytic Study of Society,* Vol. 7. New Haven: Yale University Press, 1976.

Muensterberger, Werner, and Boyer, L. Bryce, Editors; Rose, Gilbert J., Associate Editor. *The Psychoanalytic Study of Society,* Vol. 8. New Haven: Yale University Press, 1979.

Muensterberger, Werner, and Boyer, L. Bryce, Editors; Grolnick, Simon A., Associate Editor. *The Psychoanalytic Study of Society,* Vol. 9. New York: Psychohistory Press, 1981.

Muensterberger, Werner, Boyer, L. Bryce, and Grolnick, Simon A. *The Psychoanalytic Study of Society,* Vol. 10. Hillsdale, N.J.: The Analytic Press, 1984.

EDITED BOOKS

Wilbur, George B., and Muensterberger, Warner. *Psychoanalysis and Culture. Essays in Honor of Géza Róheim.* New York: International Universities Press, 1951.

Muensterberger, Warner (with the assistance of Posinsky, S. H.). *Magic and Schizophrenia,* by Géza Róheim. New York: International Universities Press, 1955.

Muensterberger, Warner. *The Panic of the Gods and Other Essays,* by Géza Róheim. New York: Harper Torchbooks, 1972. Paris: Payot, 1976.

Muensterberger, Werner, and Nichols, Christopher. *The Riddle of the Sphinx,* by Géza Róheim. New York: Harper Torchbooks, 1974.

Muensterberger, Warner. *Children of the Desert. The Western Tribes of Central Australia,* Vol. 1, by Géza Róheim. New York: Basic Books, 1974.

Muensterberger, Warner. *Man and his Culture. Psychoanalytic Anthropology After* Totem and Taboo. New York: Taplinger, 1969. Paris: Payot, 1973. Munich: Kindler Verlag, 1974.

Grolnick, Simon A., and Barkin, Leonard, in collaboration with Muensterberger, Werner. *Between Reality and Fantasy.* New York: Jason Aronson, 1978.

ARTICLES AND BOOK CHAPTERS

De Oorsprong van het Masker. *Onze Aarde,* 1937, 9:321ff. (In Dutch: The Origin of the Mask.)

De Religieuze Betekenis van de Afrikaansche Kunst. *Onze Aarde,* 1938, 10:198ff. (In Dutch: The Religious Meaning of African Art.)

Die Ornamente an Dayak-Tanzschilden und Ihre Beziehung zu Religion und Mythologie. *Cultureel Indie,* 1939, 1:337-343. (In German: The Ornaments on Dayak Dance Shields and Their Relation to Religious and Mythological Concepts.)

Het Raadsel van het Paascheiland. *Leven en Werken* (monthly of the Radio University of the Netherlands), 1940, 4. (In Dutch: The Riddle of Easter Island.)

The Importance of Mentawei Research. Appendix to F. Pfotenhauer, A Film Expedition to the Mentawei Islands. *Cultureel Indie,* 1940, 2:104.

Nias en Marquesas: Proeve van een Ethnologisch Onderzoek over het Cultur-Contact. *Koninklijik Nederlands Aardrijkskundig Genootschap Tijdschirft,* 1940, 2nd series, 57:728-739. (In Dutch: Nias and Marquesas: A Possibility of Culture Contact.)

Melanesische Sporen in Noord-Sumatra? *Cultureel Indie,* 1940, 2:93ff. (In Dutch: Melanesian Influences in North Sumatra?)

Praehistorische Schilderingenen Plastiek en Ethnologische Parallellen. *Mensch en Maatschappij,* 1940, 16:155-160. (In Dutch: Prehistorical Plastic Representations and Anthropological Parallels.)

On the Sacred Stools of the Sepik Area, New Guinea. *International Archiv für Ethnographie,* 1943, 43:242-246.

Over Primitieve Kunst en over den Korwar-stijl in Indonesië en Oceanië. *Cultureel Indie,* 1945, 7:63-74. (In Dutch: On Primitive Art and on the Korwar Style in Indonesia and Oceania.)

Ethnologie und Ich-Forschung. In: *Die Psychohygiene: Grundlagen und Ziele* (Festgabe an Heinrich Meng). Eds.: Federn, Paul, and Meng, Heinrich. Bern: Verlag Hans Huber, 1949, pp. 145-153. (In German: Anthropology and Ego Research.)

Oral Trauma and Taboo. A Psychoanalytic Study of an Indonesian Tribe. *Psychoanalysis* and the Social Sciences, 1950, 2:129–172. Ed.: Géza Róheim. New York: International Universities Press. .

Some Elements of Artistic Creativity among Primitive Peoples. In: Beiträge zur Gesellungs- und Völkerwissenschaft (Thurnwald Festschrift). Berlin: Gebr. Mann, 1950, pp. 313ff.

Orality and Dependence: Characteristics of Southern Chinese. Psychoanalysis and the Social Sciences, 1951, 3:37–70. Ed.: Géza Róheim. New York: International Universities Press.

Roots of Primitive Art. In: Psychoanalysis and Culture. Eds.: Wilbur, George B., and Muensterberger, Werner. New York: International Universities Press, 1951, pp. 371–398.

Über einige Beziehungen zwischen Individuum und Umwelt, unter Berücksichtung der Pomo-Indianer. Sociologus, 1951, 1:127–137. (In German: On Some Relationships between Individual and Environment, with Special Consideration of the Pomo Indians.)

The Use of Psychoanalytic Concepts of Anthropology. International Journal of Group Psychotherapy, 1951, 1:200–207.

Über einige psychologische Fundamente der menschlichen Gesellschaftsbildung. Psyche, 1953, 6:683–698. (In German: On Some Psychological Elements of Human Social Formation.)

Foreword to Hungarian and Vogul Mythology, by Géza Róheim. Locust Valley, N.Y.: J. J. Augustin, 1954.

Observations on the Collapse of Leadership. Psychoanalysis and the Social Sciences, 1955, 4:158–165. Eds.: Muensterberger, Warner, and Axelrad, Sidney. New York: International Universities Press.

On the Bio-psychological Determinants of Social Life. In Memoriam Géza Róheim. Psychoanalysis and the Social Sciences, 1955, 4:7–25. Eds.: Muensterberger, Warner, and Axelrad, Sidney. New York: International Universities Press.

Perversion, Cultural Norm and Normality. In: Perversions: Psychodynamics and Therapy. Eds.: Lorand, Sandor, and Balint, Michael. New York: Random House, 1956, pp. 55–67. (Italian edition, 2 printings, 1959: Perversioni Sessuali, pp. 65–79. Milan: Parenti.)

Man's Need to Change. Persona Grata (University of St. Thomas, Houston, Texas), 1960, pp. 14–20.

The Adolescent in Society. In: Adolescents: Psychoanalytic Approach to Problems and Therapy. Eds.: Lorand, Sandor, and Schneer, Henry I. New York: Paul B. Hoeber, Inc., 1961, pp. 346–368.

The Creative Process: Its Relation to Object Loss and Fetishism. The Psychoanalytic Study of Society, 1962, 2:161–185. Eds.: Muensterberger, Warner, and Axelrad, Sidney. New York: International Universities Press. (Translated into German as Der schöpferische Vorgang. Seine Beziehung zu Objektverlust und Fetishismus. Jahrbuch der Psychoanalyse. Beiträge der Theorie und Praxis, 1967, 4:11–42.)

Vom Usprung des Todes. Eine psychoanalytisch-ethnologische Studie zur Todesangst. Psyche, 1963, 17:169–185. (In German: The Origin of Death. A Psychoanalytical and Ethnological Study of the Fear of Death.)

Remarks on the Function of Mythology. The Psychoanalytic Study of Society, 1964, 3:94–97. Eds.: Muensterberger, Warner, and Axelrad, Sidney. New York: International Universities Press.

(with Ira A. Kishner) Hazards of Culture Clash: A Report on the History and Dynamics of a Psychotic Episode in a West African Exchange Student. The Psychoanalytic Study of Society, 1967, 4:99–123. Eds.: Muensterberger, Warner, and Axelrad, Sidney. New York: International Universities Press.

Symposium, with Mitscherlisch, Alexander, Hacker, Frederick J., Horkheimer, Max, and Spiegel, John. Individuelle and Soziale Psychopathologie und Ihre Wechselwirkungen. Jahrbuch der Psychoanalyse, 1968, 5:49–68. (In German: Individual and Social Psychopathology and Their Reciprocal Interactions.)

Psyche and Milieu. *Jahrbuch der Psychoanalyse,* 1968, 5:89–106. (In German: Psyche and Environment.)

On the Cultural Determinants of Individual Development. In: *Man and his Culture. Psychoanalytic Anthropology After* Totem and Taboo. Ed.: Muensterberger, Werner. New York: Taplinger, 1969, pp. 11–30.

Psyche and Environment: Sociocultural Variations in Separation and Individuation. *Psychoanalytic Quarterly,* 1969, 38:191–216.

Anthropology and Art. In: *Roots of Primitive Art.* Ed.: Otten, M. New York: Museum of Natural History Press, 1971.

Art and Aesthetics in Primitive Societies. In: *Art and Aesthetics in Primitive Societies.* Ed.: Jopling, C. F. New York: Dutton, 1971.

The Sources of Belief: A Reappraisal of Géza Róheim's Theory of Religious Origins. Introduction to *The Panic of the Gods and Other Essays,* by Géza Róheim. Ed.: Muensterberger, Werner. New York: Harper Torchbooks, 1972, pp. ix–xxiii.

(with Christopher Nichols) Róheim and the Beginnings of Psychoanalytic Anthropology. Introduction to *The Riddle of the Sphinx,* by Géza Róheim. Ed.: Muensterberger, Werner, and Nichols, Christopher. Trans.: Money-Kyrle, R. New York: Harper Torchbooks, 1974, pp. ix–xxviii.

Other Realities: Psychoanalytic Research Among Primitive Peoples. Introduction to *Children of the Desert. The Western Tribes of Central Australia,* Vol. 1, by Géza Róheim. Ed.: Muensterberger, Werner. New York: Basic Books, 1974, pp. ix–xix.

Some Reflections on Multiple Mothering, Cross-Culturally. *Psychosocial Process,* 3:57–71. (Amended and translated into German as Versorgung durch mehrere Mütter — interkulturelle Betrachtungen. *Psyche,* 1980, 34:677–693.)

Between Reality and Fantasy. In: *Between Reality and Fantasy.* Ed.: Grolnick, Simon A., and Barkin, Leonard, in collaboration with Muensterberger, Werner. New York: Jason Aronson, 1978, pp. 3–14.

Versuch einer transkulturellen Analyse: Der Fall einers Chinesischen Offiziers. *Psyche,* 1982, 36:865–887. (In German: Research into Transcultural Analysis: The Case of a Chinese Officer.)

The Past in the Present. In: *Visible Religion,* Vol. 3. Ed.: Kippenberg, H. Leiden: Brill, in press.

BOOK REVIEWS

Speiser, Felix. *Einführung in das Museum für Völkerkunde.* Basel: Museum Press, 1939. (In German: *Introduction to the Museum for Folk Arts.) Cultureel Indie,* 1939, 1.

Federn, Paul, and Meng, Heinrich. *Das Psychoanalytische Volksbuch.* Bern: Huber, 1939, Third Edition. (In German: *The Popular Book on Psychoanalysis.) Cultureel Indie,* 1939, 1:367.

Róheim, Géza. *Psychoanalysis and Anthropology.* New York: International Universities Press, 1950. *The Annual Survey of Psychoanalysis,* 1950, 1:489–492. New York: International Universities Press.

Belo, Jane. *Bali: Rangda and Barong.* Monograph of the American Ethnological Society, XVI. New York: J. J. Augustin, 1949. *Psychoanalytic Quarterly,* 1951, 20:318.

Parsons, Talcott, and Shils, Edward A. (Eds.). *Toward a General Theory of Action.* Cambridge: Harvard University Press, 1951. *Psychoanalytic Quarterly,* 1953, 22:120–122.

Mead, Margaret, and Calas, Nicholas (Eds.). *Primitive Heritage. An Anthropological*

Anthology. New York: Random House, 1953. *Psychoanalytic Quarterly,* 1954, 23:288–289.

Potter, David M. *People of Plenty. Economic Abundance and the American Character.* Chicago: University of Chicago Press. *Psychoanalytic Quarterly,* 1955, 24:456–457.

Bettelheim, Bruno. *Symbolic Wounds. Puberty Rites and the Envious Male.* Glencoe, Ill.: The Free Press, 1954. *Psychoanalytic Quarterly,* 1955, 25:593–595.

Belo, Jane. *Trance in Bali.* New York: Columbia University Press, 1960. *Psychoanalytic Quarterly,* 1961, 30:290–292.

Hendin, Herbert, Gaylin, Willard, and Carr, Arthur. *Psychoanalysis and Social Research. The Psychoanalytic Study of the Nonpatient.* New York: Doubleday & Co., 1965. *Psychoanalytic Quarterly,* 1966, 35:436–437.

Schafer, Roy. *A New Language for Psychoanalysis.* New Haven: Yale University Press, 1976. *Times Literary Supplement,* 1978.

Cole, Herbert M. *Mbari. Art and Life Among the Owerri Igbo.* Bloomington: Indiana University Press, 1982. *The Burlington Magazine,* 1982, 124:779–780.

Lévi-Strauss, Claude. *The Way of the Masks* (1975). English Edition, London: Jonathan Cape, 1983. *The Burlington Magazine,* 1983, 125:773–774.

Tuzin, Donald. *The Voice of the Tambaran.* Cambridge: Harvard University Press, 1980. *The Journal of Psychoanalytic Anthropology,* 1984, 7:421–424.

Freeman, Derek. *Margaret Mead and Samoa: The Making and Unmaking of Anthropological Myth.* Cambridge: Harvard University Press, 1983. *The Psychoanalytic Quarterly,* 1985, 54:101–105.

THE PSYCHOANALYTIC STUDY
OF SOCIETY

Volume 11

1
The Taming of the Deviants and Beyond: An Analysis of *Dybbuk* Possession and Exorcism in Judaism

YORAM BILU

Documented cases of *dybbuk*[1] possession appear in Jewish sources from the 16th century A.D. to the first decades of the 20th century. Since these sources have usually been inaccessible to the general scholar, this uniquely Jewish variant of spirit possession has been largely the subject of literary rather than scientific investigation. Ansky (1926) and Singer (1959) popularized the *dybbuk* phenomenon by emphasizing its colorful and dramatic nature; Ansky's play *The Dybbuk* (subtitled *Between Two Worlds*) was the first to be performed by the Hebrew National Theater, and had widespread success. Recently, a scholar of Judaic studies collected and annotated what appears to be the vast majority of the reported cases of *dybbuk* possession (Nigal, 1980). Most of these reports are to be found in mystically oriented exegeses of the Holy Scriptures and in books of Hasidic tales, usually written to praise and commemorate a renowned rabbi or sage. Some cases are more detailed, and were published in special brochures or booklets, the titles of which attest to their dramatic quality, e.g., "Awful Tales," "Terrible Deeds of the Spirit." These provocative titles had their effect — the brochures were published in numerous editions.

In this paper I shall attempt to clarify the *dybbuk* phenomenon in terms of some of its psychocultural components. My study is based on an analysis of 63 documented cases over the nearly 400-year span in which *dybbuk* possession thrived in various parts of the Jewish world. Most of the cases seem to be authentic, located as they are in known coordinates of time and space. The reports were usually written by eyewitnesses, some of whom actively participated in the expulsion of the *dybbuk;* many of the victims

---

1. In Hebrew, the verb *davok* means "to cleave" or "to stick." The noun *dybbuk* (pl. *dybbukim*) designates an external agent "clinging" to a person.

and exorcists were identified by name, and in some instances the documents were signed by distinguished witnesses testifying to their accuracy. As ethnographic accounts, however, these reports leave much to be desired. Laconic and obscure on some points, overly elaborated and embellished on others, they were written from a definite ideological stance, which imbues them with strong moral overtones. Still, an appreciation of the literary instruction of the documents can contribute to an understanding of the *dybbuk* phenomenon *within its sociocultural context* if the motivation underlying it is correctly deciphered and interpreted.

A *methodological* problem involves the high variability of the sample, composed of cases so far removed in time and place. My analysis will therefore remain on a relatively molar level, concentrating on the commonalities among the various Jewish communities in which the *dybbuk* appeared. One factor which seems to mitigate potentially misleading effects of the variability of the cases is the very stability of the *dybbuk* phenomenon over time and space. The behavioral patterns of the possessed, whether in 16th-century Palestine or 19th-century Poland, bear a remarkable resemblance (although again the literary construction of the cases might have contributed to this resemblance). Throughout its history, *dybbuk* possession was conceived as a disease, and the possessing spirits were negatively evaluated. In contrast to possession phenomena in many other ethnic groups (Bourguignon, 1973; Crapanzano and Gattison, 1977), possession by *dybbuk* did not undergo a transformation into the ceremonial context of a possession cult, wherein possession is not stigmatized but socially approved and the adept seeks to establish a symbiotic relationship with the possessing agent (Bourguignon, 1976a; Bilu, 1980, p. 36).

Dybbuk possession by definition involved spirits of the dead as possessing agents. Although Jews were possessed by demons as long as two millenia ago (as the exorcisms by Jesus demonstrate) and as recently as this century (see Bilu [1980] for demonic possession among Moroccan Jews), cases of demonic possession were never considered to fall within the framework of the *dybbuk* phenomenon. The latter is based on the kabbalistic doctrine of the transmigration of souls (*Gilgul*), which explains why it appeared in mystically oriented Sephardic as well as Ashkenazic circles. The doctrine of transmigration emerged in Jewish mysticism in the 12th century and rapidly became a core concept (Scholem, 1971). The mystics of that era contended that the spirit of a deceased person might transmigrate into a newborn human (and also, although rarely, into animal and inanimate forms) as retribution for certain transgressions the person committed during his lifetime. Although considered a severe punishment, transmigration signified a divine mercy as well, since it was meant to rehabilitate and purify the sinner's spirit by virtue of his re-formed behavior in his new lifetime. In 16th-century kabbala, the idea of the transmigration of souls became a universal law. The doctrine relevant for possession was developed in the second half of the 13th century when the concept was expanded to include the entry of a spirit into a living person after he was born. According to this doctrine, not only wicked spirits but also righteous ones took possession of people (themselves innocent and just) in order to complete their quota of good deeds required for entry into Paradise. But the designation *dybbuk* was reserved for the spirits of the wicked who penetrated humans in order to find refuge from persecution. Since these were spirits of sinners, they were doomed to remain in limbo, wandering between the two worlds, without being allowed to enter Hell. (In Jewish tradition, Hell was not considered a place of eternal torment but of temporary retribution, from which souls would enter Paradise.) In this limbo, the spirits were exposed to ruthless persecution by angelic and demonic beings. Thus, the inhabitation of humans gave these spirits temporary shelter as well as a unique opportunity to be purified, thereby to gain access to the world of the dead, as the description of the exorcistic ritual will later show. It should be noted that the term *dybbuk* was introduced during the 17th century to designate this type of possession and was employed by Ashkenazic Jews only. Sephardic Jews adhered to the terminology of the early kabbalistic literature, in which the possessing agent was named "evil spirit."

The fact that the first cases of *dybbuk* possession appeared in the second half of the 16th century, almost 300 years after the theosophical foundation underlying it had been established, has not yet been explained. It may be that such an interval is required for novel, "disembodied ideas" to be transformed into a set of tangible behaviors; the onset may have been precipitated by specific circumstances within the Jewish milieu (such as the dispersion of the Jews following their traumatic exile from Spain in 1492) or outside it (the witch craze in Europe); or finally, the cases of the 16th century may simply have been the first to have been written down, as part of the general proliferation of Jewish literature in that era.[2] Coordinated interdisciplinary research by Judaica scholars and social scientists should suggest answers to this question.

In any event, the first reports of *dybbuk* possession came from 16th-century Sephardic communities in Safed, Palestine (the cradle of that century's Lurianic kabbala), and in Italy. In the 17th century, cases were reported in Safed, Damascus, and Cairo, and later in Turkey and Italy. Only

---

2. This proliferation was probably related to recently introduced printing devices. Former centuries were relatively mute in contrast.

towards the end of the 17th century did the first eastern-European cases appear, but in the 18th and 19th centuries mystically oriented Hasidic communities, mainly in Poland and Russia but also in Germany, Hungary, and Lithuania, supplied most of the case reports. Throughout this period, cases from the Mideast continued to appear in print. In the 18th century, for example, Jerusalem, Tiberias, Damascus, Beirut, and Baghdad were represented on the *dybbuk* map. The last cases to be documented appeared in the first decades of the 20th century in Lithuania, Palestine (Jaffa and Jerusalem), and Baghdad. Whereas the timing of the onset of *dybbuk* possession has not been fully explained, its disappearance was apparently related to the gradual disintegration of Jewish traditional centers in Europe as a consequence of modernization and emigration, and finally their physical extermination during the Holocaust. The mass emigration of Jews from the Moslem orbit to modern Israel brought an end to possession in those areas as well.

Despite the vast cultural differences between east and west in Judaism, all the communities in which *dybbuk* possession appeared shared a common tradition, with a "complex of commandments which governed the day to day discipline of the Jew, his piety, his morals, his rules for personal life at home, in the synagogue and in the market place" (Bokser, 1981, p. 22). Indeed, it might be argued in somewhat tautological fashion that the very appearance of *dybbuk* possession in these communities points to a certain degree of common mystically oriented understanding. Only a few reported cases emerged from a nonmystical matrix.[3]

In analyzing *dybbuk* possession, I have found it profitable, following Obeyesekere (1970) and Crapanzano (1977a), to conceive of it as an idiom for articulating and structuring certain inchoate experiences and events. An idiom, according to Crapanzano, "provides the basis for those schemata by which reality is interpreted" (1977a, p. 11). An act of articulation separates events from the flow of experience and renders them meaningful. When these events are construed on a phenomenological level within a culturally shared idiom, the entire experience undergoes "symbolization" (Gendlin, 1964): "Chaos [is] fashioned into cosmos" (Schweder, 1980, p. 64). Borrowing Crapanzano's terms, I view the articulatory function of the *dybbuk* spirits as essentially "vectorial." That is, the spirits are a vehicle for articulating unacceptable, conflict-precipitating desires and demands. Since the idiom of possession is culturally constituted, this articu-

---

3. Hasidism, founded by Rabbi Israel Baal Shem-Tov (The Besht) in the first half of the
    17th century, is a movement clearly based on mystical ideas. Unlike mystical trends in
    former centuries, it quickly became a mass movement, the centrality of which has persisted in Judaism up to the present.

lation may result in relief for the actor. He does not suffer "the consequences of his idiom" as a Western paranoid does (even while both are considered sick in their respective cultures).

Although I am concerned in this paper with both individual motivation and societal cultural constraints, my emphasis is on the latter — the collective (or control) level. This is partially due to the fact that I am dealing with written documents rather than with actual cases observed *in vivo*. Starting with the assumption that the desires and demands underlying *dybbuk* possession constituted a threatening challenge to the Jewish traditional way of life, I shall depict the impressive dialectical process by means of which deviance was transformed into a conformity-strengthening vehicle, a process involving three levels of control: (1) The articulation of unacceptable desires within the possession idiom, the tenor of which was set by an externalized, ego-alien agent. (2) The rectification of individual deviance through the exorcism of the *dybbuk*. (3) The strengthening of conformity in the community by way of the moral implications of the *dybbuk* episodes.

In what follows, I shall analyze these three levels of control in detail, drawing on examples from the case reports. I shall then attempt to locate the possessed within a psychiatric diagnostic category, in the light of their social roles in the cultural matrix from which the phenomenon emerged. Finally, some implications for the analysis of culture-specific syndromes will be discussed.

FIRST LEVEL OF CONTROL: OUTWARDLY DIRECTED CULTURAL MOLDING OF ABERRANT IMPULSES

Through the *dybbuk* idiom forbidden wishes were articulated and symbolized in a way that considerably decreased their potential threat both to the individual and his community. From a psychodynamic point of view, this process can be formulated in terms of projection,[4] whereby repressed impulses found expression in an externalized (although internally located) entity — the possessing spirit. What were the cardinal impulses underlying the articulated scheme of the *dybbuk*? One need not be a devoted Freudian to single out sexual wishes as a major motivating force behind this type of

---

4. For an elaborate discussion of culturally constituted projection, see Spiro (1967, p. 77). Crapanzano (1977a), in contrast, contends that the Western metaphor of projection involves dimensions different from those associated with the articulated idiom of spirit possession. In the latter, "the tenor [of the metaphor] is located outside the individual from the start" (p. 12).

possession. Open expressions of sexuality were strictly regulated and cur-
tailed in Jewish traditional communities of former centuries (Zborowski
and Herzog, 1962, pp. 134–138), leaving few nondeviant forms of expression (without resulting, however, in an overall devaluation of sexuality).
Since a discussion of these regulations and prohibitions, relevant as it may
be to an understanding of the cultural matrix from which the *dybbuk* phenomenon emerged, is beyond the scope of this paper, I shall focus here instead on the textual evidence of sexual themes in the documented cases.

Dybbuk *Possession as an Articulation of Sexual Urges*

According to Crapanzano (1977a, p. 18) and Spiro (1967, p. 72), the elements in the idiom of spirit possession must constitute appropriate metaphorical representations of the impulses putatively underlying them —
there must be some degree of congruence between symbol and referent.
Such congruence is pronounced in the phenomenon under discussion, in
that an act of penetration is essential both to *dybbuk* possession (and spirit
possession in general) and sexual intercourse. So compelling is this congruence that the scholars who elaborated the theosophical doctrine underlying the *dybbuk* could not disregard it. The first kabbalists linked transmigration specifically with sexual transgressions (Scholem, 1971), and in
Jewish mystical texts the residence of a spirit in a human being was designated "impregnation" (*ibbur*).

The sexual meaning of penetration in spirit possession is even more accurately (and therefore more convincingly) conveyed when the genders of
the *dramatis personae,* penetrator and penetrated, correspond with those
in the standard heterosexual act. Hypothetically, since spirits and victims
alike are unequivocally sex-typed, four gender combinations are possible.
What is their distribution in the cases under discussion? The sample
consists of 41 female victims and 22 male victims. The ratio of almost two
to one is consistent with massive evidence for the preponderance of
women among the possessed in a great variety of culturally unrelated social groups (Bilu, 1980; Bourguignon, 1973; Lewis, 1971; Oesterreich,
1930; Prince, 1977; Walker, 1972). Explanations of this recurrent finding
usually emphasize the culturally defined inequality of the female role in
male-oriented societies (see, especially, Lewis, 1966, 1971), which is also
consistent with Jewish mystical traditions concerning spirit possession.
The author of *Emek Hamelech* ("The Valley of the King"), a kabbalistic
text, argues that women are excessively vulnerable to possession because
"the impurity stemming from the serpent still abounds in them." Here an
allusion is made to Eve's primordial sin of succumbing to the temptation
of the snake, the nature of which temptation was blatantly sexual, accord-

ing to mystically oriented sources (Rubenstein, 1968, p. 54). In another text, *Minkhat Eliahu* ("The Gift of Elijah"), the relative immunity of men to possession is attributed to the fact that "a man cannot refrain from the sin of nocturnal pollution, out of which demons are engendered; these creatures always encircle him, so how can [the possessing spirit] enter him?" Male sexuality procreates demons that haunt wandering human spirits and dispel them. This cosmological proposition, which is verified by many *dybbukim* in the recitations of their ordeals, is based on a conception of male sexuality as outer-oriented, rendering men relatively immune to penetration, in contrast to women, who are relatively accessible to penetration because their sexuality is inner-oriented, a point to which I shall return below.

The gender distribution of the spirits is even more one-sided. Fifty-eight of the spirits (92 percent) were male, only five female. As a result, the most prevalent gender combination in the sample is that of a male spirit with a female human (36 cases). This too is a recurrent finding cross-culturally (Oesterreich, 1930, p. 21). Second in frequency is the male-male combination (22 cases). Significantly, all five female spirits penetrated women. Hence, most of the *dybbukim* comply with the heterosexual or, less frequently, the male homosexual metaphors; female spirits rarely assume the role of a possessing agent, but when they do, the idiom is exclusively female homosexuality. The penetration of a male human by a female spirit, which is the least plausible alternative as long as sexuality is the guiding metaphor, is left an empty category, even though it is hypothetically feasible. It should be noted that female-in-male possession is not *universally* an empty category. In various forms of socially approved ceremonial (institutionalized) possession, as in Afro-American religions (Pressel, 1973) and North African Muslim cults (Crapanzano, 1973, 1977b), the pattern is quite common. The difference apparently lies in the moral dimension, as to whether the possessing entity is positively or negatively evaluated. When the possession is positively or ambivalently valued, female-in-male possession can occur because the possessed-to-be is alleged to "open" himself up to it. The prevailing images in these cases are of sexual seduction and willing consent, tending sometimes to lasting romantic alliances and marriage. When the possessing agent is negatively evaluated, so that possession is considered an illness rather than a sought-for religious accomplishment, the implicit sexual image is of rape rather than consensual indulgence. And whereas males can rape females or other males, females cannot rape males. Indeed, the self-reports of some female victims in the sample include descriptions of experiences that closely resemble rape. An 11-year-old girl from 19th-century Jerusalem described a violent struggle in which "I stumbled, I was pushed, then I had to lie down and was turned over." A 17-year-old adolescent girl in Baghdad at the turn of the century experienced "something like a big cat [that] fell on my hips, in between the shoulders, stretching me in order to force his way into me." Both victims were virgins, for whom the metaphor of possession-as-rape seems particularly applicable, since penetration is difficult both physically and, given the pre-marriage moral purity accorded to females, mentally (see Beit-Hallahmi, 1976; Dwyer, 1978, p. 73).

Unlike the organ of departure, which towards the climax of the exorcistic ritual is stereotypically located by the exorcist in one of the toes, the penetrated organ is seldom described. When it is mentioned, it is most frequently the vagina (four cases, each of the victims married women). The evasive, reluctant language used in these cases (e.g., "it is disgraceful to say") suggests that other such penetrations were left unreported. The only case that involved penetration through the anus was of a male spirit taking possession of a male adolescent. The selection of these erogeneous zones further implicates the sexual meaning of *dybbuk* possession.

Generally speaking, *dybbuk* possession is a drama of the young. When the victim's age is explicitly indicated (in about 20 percent of the cases), it does not exceed 35. When age is not specified, age-linked status categories of the victims, which appear in most of the case reports, included "babies,"[5] "children," "girls," "virgins," "young men," and "women." No mention is made of older adults. Female victims in the sample were predominantly newly married young women. In sum, the sample reveals the victims' ages to be those at which sexuality emerges as a potent drive. The spirits, although older than their victims in most of the cases, were originally those of people who died quite young. The few cases of possession by an elderly man's spirit clearly represent a different, more positively valued type of possession. These spirits belonged to righteous people who required only minor rehabilitation. They utilized the possession episode to deliver reproachful messages to the community and were willing to depart peacefully once their mission was completed.

The sample also reveals that male victims were generally younger than female victims. About 75 percent of the former were less than 20 years old, as opposed to 49 percent of the latter. Among the female victims the largest subcategory was of "women," a term usually used for married women, whereas only two male victims were explicitly described as married. Of these, one was a young religious scholar from Mogalnitsa, Poland, who was possessed eight weeks after marriage, the other — a borderline case of *dybbuk* possession — also a religious scholar, from 19th-

---

5.   In traditional Jewish terms, children up to the age of ten might have been so designated.

century Jerusalem, obsessively haunted by the spirit of a Christian minister without being uequivocally possessed by it. Thus, women were liable to possession over a relatively wide age range, particularly after being married. Indeed, in those cases where the penetrated organ of the female victim was mentioned, the site of entry was further specified as the "opening" in the vagina, normally formed during the wedding night and symbolic of the consummation of sexuality. In a case report from 19th-century Stolovitsch, Poland, entitled "A Terrible Happening" ("Maaseh Noraah"),[6] the spirit explicitly states that "as long as she [the victim] is a virgin, we are forbidden to approach her, but when she is married, then we shall have our share too." In contrast, the marriage of a man afforded him a kind of prophylaxis, a relative immunity to *dybbukim*. Thus, the emergence of sexuality and the consummation of the sexual act have different meanings for the sexes vis-á-vis the *dybbuk* phenomenon: Whereas consummation for the male turns him into a penetrator, thereby rendering him almost impenetrable, the female, by having been sexually "opened" and penetrated, becomes all the more accessible to penetration. These meanings correspond, of course, with transcultural images of male and female sexuality (Dwyer, 1978, pp. 165–184), and are implicit in the kabbalistic texts I cited above.

The sexual implications of the *dybbuk* phenomenon, as "emically" reflected in the motivations of the possessing spirits, are represented throughout the case reports. A gentle spirit from 17th-century Cairo "entered a woman for his passion." Other spirits described the possession by using the verbs "to come to" and "to know," which in biblical Hebrew were euphemisms for sexual relations. One of the aforementioned Stolovitsch spirits testified that "he never touched [the girl] as a husband does." The most lucid and elaborated example is a turn-of-the-century Baghdadi mystical text. The author gives instructions for identifying male-in-female possession with reference to the following conditions: "If she sees in her dream a man standing against her, or lying with her; or inflaming her heart with the passion of intercourse; or rubbing her genitalia or anus ... or preventing her from having sex with her husband in order not to be sexually penetrated by him." It is hard to imagine a more straightforward exposition of the sexual wishes attributed to the spirit. Assuming that those sexual proclivities represented the repressed sexual fantasies of the possessed, the thin, almost nonexistent cover of the disguise is surprising. In all likelihood, the motivations expressed did not have to undergo desexualization because the externally located idiom of the *dybbuk* rendered their man-

---

6. This episode was apparently a major source for Ansky's play.

ifestation safe. In other words, the centrifugal (inner to outer) trans-
formational disguise, rooted as it was in a sociocultural construction of reality, was so effective as to make any *content* transformation superfluous.

The sexual motivations underlying *dybbuk* possession can be examined
more specifically as reflected in the *sins* of both participants in the possession episode. That the victims' wrongdoings, considered the precipitating
factor for possession, were nevertheless laconically portrayed is not surprising, in that these were the only behavioral aspects of the case for which
the possessed was deemed responsible — the only ones which did not fall
under the idiomatic cover of the *dybbuk*. The sexual transgressions of the
victims, if mentioned at all, seem mild, even negligible, when compared to
those of the possessing spirits. Against a background of expressions of libidinal desires by the victims rarely going beyond a caress, a kiss, or obscene utterances, the accounts of the scandalous misconduct of the spirits
during their human lifetimes represent, from a psychodynamic point of
view, acting out in fantasy of the most forbidden repressed (or suppressed)
sexual urges. To illustrate the spirits' uninhibited sexual profligacy, I
should like to return to the Baghdadi corpus of cases, which provide the
most detailed and colorful descriptions of Jewish possession. The misconduct of a spirit possessing his own sister is described as follows: "He was
tender of age but a veteran in vices and wickedness as a hundred-year-old.
Very handsome was he, and the generals loved him, because he was ready
to satisfy their desires, as well as those of their wives, and he took his hire
from both sides. Some prostitutes would solicit him to do with them whatever he craved, from whichever side he preferred, any time he wanted,
even during their menstruation period." It was no wonder, then, that
"since he is long experienced in adultery and prostitution, he cannot calm
down even now [after death, being a spirit] and he lies with his sister whenever he desires." In an other Baghdadi case, a person was possessed by
Shabtai Zvi, the notorious false Messiah of the 16th century. It is significant that the major sins for which he became a wandering spirit involved
promiscuous sexual misconduct. He admitted that he had sinned with
Gentile and menstruous women as well as with prostitutes, that he had
committed adultery, that he had encouraged a young disciple of his to
have sex with his wife, and that he had practiced sodomy wrapped in his
prayer shawl and phylacteries. These cases were, indeed, the most extreme
examples of sexual misconduct, but many other spirits, particularly in the
first documented cases of the 16th century, were characterized as lecher-
ous profligates. Some of them were specifically identified as pimps and
rapists. It seems that the most dark, unutterable desires were projected
onto the spirit, thereby gaining cathartic outlet.

Another socially accepted channel supplied by the *dybbuk* idiom for the verbal expression of sexual wishes derived from the special ontological status of the spirits, which afforded them extraordinary skills of divination. These skills were employed to unravel cosmological aspects of the afterlife, foretell future events, and expose and denounce hidden sinners in the community. The spirits' revelations, particularly in the last regard, were saturated with sexual content. From the 16th century on, possessing spirits identified adulterers and homosexuals among the observers and generally criticized the growing sexual permissiveness of the community: "In our time, half of the women are disloyal to their husbands," complained a Baghdadi spirit. This preoccupation with sexual matters, presented as virtuous reproach, constituted another socially acceptable outlet for forbidden wishes.

The acting out of sexual urges within the *dybbuk* idiom was not limited to the fantasy level. As in other cultural variants of possession, uncontrollable ecstatic behaviors, sometimes mimicking the violent convulsions of epileptic seizures, were prevalent in *dybbuk* cases. These rhythmical fits resembled the grand paroxysms of *hysteria major* of the 19th century, so minutely described by Charcot and others (Smith Rosenberg, 1972). Whereas in ceremonial possession "ecstatic possession seizures were sometimes explicitly interpreted as acts of mystical sexual intercourse between the subject and his ... possessing spirits" (Lewis, 1971, p. 58), this interpretation was never made in *dybbuk* reports. In some early, prototypical cases, however, the sexual connotations of paroxysmic behavior are implied in the texts. For example, a spirit in a woman from Safed in the 16th century indicated his readiness to depart through the big toe "by bringing her [the victim's] feet up and down in successive movements, time after time, and with these violent movements her gown fell from her feet and thighs so that she was contemptibly exposed." By itself, this description might seem an insufficient basis for interpreting the seizures as a simulation of intercourse, but in this case the spirit had penetrated through the victim's vagina, and when asked by the rabbis if he did not fear her husband's wrath, insolently replied: "Not at all! Since her husband is not here but in Saloniki." Psychodynamically, then, this might have been a well-organized sexual fantasy, of which the fits were an integral part. Another early case involved the spirit of an Italian shepherd, a gentile, who took possession of a 25-year-old woman "when her husband ... had to go." Here also the woman was penetrated through the vagina, at night. She was depicted as lying breathless, open-mouthed in her bed, "all her organs ... in agony and ... shaking forcefully and jerking as if fever-stricken."

The heterosexual aspects of *dybbuk* possesion were thus revealed through the constructed idiom of a male spirit penetrating a female human, providing various paths for the expression of sexually loaded content on the verbal and psychomotor levels. The victim's overt prepossession behavior — his moral transgressions, left uncovered by the idiomatic shield — gave only a scant indication of the contained sexuality.

Showing the same correspondence of sexual patterns and gender combination, descriptions of male-in-male possession — which constitute about a third of the sample — disclose homosexual themes with varying degrees of explicitness. (The penetration of the spirit itself can of course be viewed as homosexually motivated.) The town of Nikolsburg, in Moravia, provided two classic *dybbuk* cases in the 17th and 18th centuries. In one case, after the spirit had been exorcized, he presented himself to his victim and "held his small finger, through which [he] had been expelled, and embraced him like a man fondling his friend's hand with affection and desire." In the other, according to a story in *Maiseh Buch* (in Yiddish "The Book of Tales"), considered by some the first documented *dybbuk* case, the spirit that took possession of a young adult accused two of his friends of practicing homosexuality. To the astonishment of the crowd gathered around, both immediately admitted their sin. The aforementioned spirit of Shabtai Zvi, whose most shocking transgression was self-portrayed as pederasty, took possession of a young Baghdadi male in the beginning of this century. In another Baghdadi male-in-male possession, the spirit confessed that "on the Holy Sabbath, he committed pederasty in the orchard of village B." The spirit was allowed to take possession of his victim because the latter, "went he was still a child, with his father to village B and entered the same orchard in which I committed my sin. There, on Sabbath, he had picked [a fruit] from the same tree under which I committed pederasty." When viewed psychodynamically, the sins of the spirit and his victim — picking a fruit on Saturday is a transgression of the Sabbath rest laws — fit neatly together to produce a coherent fantasy. Given the identical coordinates of time and space, the metaphor of plucking a forbidden fruit can be considered a very cogent symbolic substitute for the homosexual event. This correspondence might hint at a childhood recollection of an actual homosexual experience (under the same tree in the orchard of village B ...), barred from consciousness by attributing it projectively to the spirit and by translating it metaphorically into a desexualized equivalent.

An explicit association between male-in-male possession and homosexuality is revealed in the case from 19th-century Mogalnitsa already cited. A few weeks after his marriage, a religious student fell into a severe depression following his harassment (but not yet possession) by a spirit. As later revealed by the young man, this was the spirit of a man who had attempted during his lifetime to molest him sexually. The sick student said he had not succumbed to the seduction, which he had promised to keep secret. Despite his promise, he revealed this intimate information to his rabbis during his illness whereupon the spirit took possession of him. Assuming that the spirit possession represented the acting out in fantasy of a homosexual impulse, the timing of the episode is singularly significant. It might be speculated that the young groom was flooded with "homosexual panic" when he had to display sexual behavior incompatible with his homosexual proclivities. Wedding time was also a critical period—but now for a spirit's *departure*—in one of the rare cases of female-in-female possession from the Baghdadi corpus. The victim was a 17-year-old fatherless girl brought up and surrounded by female figures. The possessing spirit, which had tenaciously endured the healer's persecution, eventually gave its promise to depart from the victim once she married, during the time of defloration. The idea, already cited above, that the spirit's entry and the husband's sexual penetration are mutually exclusive, is presented here quite explicitly. (It is worth noting that in classical Greece marriage was a recommended cure for hysteria, which was allegedly caused by disordered sexuality—the product of a "wandering womb". [Ullman and Krasner, 1969, p. 110].)

A discussion of the sexual urges implicit in *dybbuk* cases would be incomplete without a consideration of oedipal themes, which, according to Freud's (1923) classical analysis of a case of demonic possession in the 17th century, may play a major role in the phenomenon. If one considers the possessing agent to be a father image or representation, then the male-in-female form of *dybbuk* possession might reflect a symbolic realization of female oedipal desires toward the father. Since most of the case descriptions contain only skimpy and fragmented background information as to the spirit's characteristics, it is impossible to examine the father-as-spirit hypothesis except in its direct, undisguised manifestation—that in which the possessing agent was the spirit of the victim's father. Two of the 36 victims of male-in-female possession were possessed by their fathers, whereas none of the 22 male victims was thus possessed.

The first case, which I have already discussed in another context, involved a multiple possession of incestuous nature. First the spirit of the brother, whose sexual licentiousness in his lifetime was boundless, penetrated his sister, who explicitly experienced possession as a sexual assault or rape. The second possessing spirit was the father's, whose posthumous persecution was related to the fact that he had been tempted by a married woman to commit adultery. This sin, which caused his spirit to wander and seek refuge in his daughter's body, might very well have represented the girl's fantasy of tempting her father. The unexpected epilogue of this case report converges in an intriguing way with the ending of the original Oedipus myth: Of the transmigration of the brother's spirit into the body of a newborn baby, it is said, "and who is as wise as the Blessed One to understand the meaning of things. For He plagued the boy with smallpox that maimed his face and blinded his two beautiful eyes ... so that he would never be involved in pederasty nor in adultery." Nor in incest, one is tempted to add.

The second case, which involved a famous Hasidic rabbi and his beloved daughter in 19th-century Russia, is too complex to be presented in detail here.[7] The core of this tragic drama involved the rabbi's boundless love for his daughter Eidel, whom he preferred over his other children (boys included!), and his pathetic attempts to disregard or repair "Satan's mischievous interference that prevented her from being born a male." That he considered Eidel a boy was reflected in such extraordinary gestures as adorning her with male religious artifacts — specifically, his phylacteries.[8] In the light of this intimate relationship, colored moreover by the rabbi's loving but tragically short-lived relationship with his own mother, it is no wonder that Eidel could not accept the accession by inheritance of one of her brothers to the throne of the Hasidic court when their father passed away. The climax of the bitter struggle between the two siblings came in an exorcistic ritual in which Eidel, possessed by a spirit who claimed to be her father (but considered an impostor by her adversaries), confronted the rabbi-exorcist, her brother. Under the shield of the *dybbuk,* she desperately fought to discredit her brother's moral authority. Eventually, however, her father's strong voice faded away and she was defeated. Following the exorcism, she lived in complete apathy, dissociated from her surroundings. Eidel's son, a famous rabbi in his own sake, was born blind! The oedipal theme, interwoven with such related themes as sibling rivalry and sex-role conflict, appears as a leitmotif of the plot, which is no less dramatic or bizarre than any by Singer.

Nonsexual Aberrant Impulses Articulated within the
Dybbuk *Idiom*

The *dybbuk* idiom also served as a culturally molded outlet for nonsexual urges and desires whose expression was forbidden in Jewish communities. In fact, the emergence of such desires can partially be un-

---

7. I shall present it in full length in another paper.
8. Phylacteries (*tefillin*) are sacred ornaments which all male Jews from their 13th birthday on are commanded to wear during morning prayers.

derstood as a reaction to the strict, instinct-suppressing regulations governing all spheres of communal life, based as these were on rigid religious codes and prohibitions. Overt expression of such desires would have undermined the very foundations of the Jewish way of life. As with sexuality, these urges received only minimal expression on the nonidiomatic (therefore undisguised) level of the victims' prepossession misconduct. The majority of their misdeeds were associated with such religious transgressions as not fulfilling one of the Sabbath duties, disregarding a prayer, or misusing a ritual artifact. Other more serious transgressions, usually committed by women, included doubting the validity of episodes of Jewish history (Exodus, for example) or diverting a spouse from religious studies to mundane affairs. But these appear negligible in comparison with the spirits' (nonsexual) sinfulness during their lifetimes. *Dybbukim* of this type make an impressive gallery of infamous characters — apostates who converted to Christianity, informers who handed Jews and their property over to Gentile authorities, robbers and thieves. Four of the *dybbukim*-to-be committed suicide — an inexpiable sin according to Jewish law — and five were notorious criminals and murderers of fellow Jews. Thus, a *dybbuk* from 18th-century Detmold, Germany, admitted that he had killed two Jews with his own hands, and caused the death of three others. A female spirit who took possession of a girl in Radin, Lithuania, at the beginning of this century confessed that she had strangled two Jewish children. The first *dybbuk* from Nikolsburg, who was the head of the Jewish community in his home town, coldbloodedly murdered two rabbis who reproached him for his bad manners. There was even a biblical murderer: A *dybbuk* from the shtetl of Koznitz identified himself as the man who had initiated the stoning of the prophet Zechariah.

The merging of these exemplars of uninhibited licentiousness (some of whom boasted that none of the 613 commandments regulating Jewish life was observed by them) with their victims, modest sinners at worst, can be explicated within two frames of reference. From the perspective of *control* — essentially the perspective of the participants' conscious minds — the fact that a person who drank without a blessing was possessed by the spirit of an apostate constituted a warning signal indicating where ostensibly innocent negligence of commands might lead. The view that "one transgression brings on another" and "of one ill come many" was soberly acknowledged and gloomily repeated by the Jewish rabbis. From a *psychodynamic* perspective on deviance, it might again be argued that the victim's humble sins were the visible part of a mental iceberg of darker, unutterable desires, which found idiomatic expression and metaphorical outlet in the profligate *dybbuk*. Apart from the reported sinfulness of the spirits, the behaviors of the victims while possessed — while presumably controlled by the spirits — cogently reflect the nature of these hidden subversive wishes. Not only did many of the victims actively avoid basic ritual duties, they made violent attempts to desecrate the most sacred symbols of the Jewish religion. When taken to the synagogue, for example, where many of these symbols were located, the possessed would jerk and contort violently, spit on holy books and artifacts, insult and physically attack the shocked worshippers. Obversely, they were irresistibly attracted to Christian sacred paraphernalia. Kissing the New Testament, "eating and praying as the Gentiles do," and compulsively making the sign of the cross were repeated symptoms. It should be pointed out that most of these extreme anti-religious behaviors were enacted by males, on whom rested the lion's share of the burden of Jewish commandments.

Whether or not these behaviors and underlying subversive wishes were specifically expressions of a yearning to be released from the cumbersome yoke of religious law, they would certainly have constituted a threatening challenge to the essence of the Jewish way of life had they not been attributed to an external agent. The fact that they, like aberrant sexual impulses and their associated behaviors, were culturally molded into the *dybbuk* idiom, substantially mitigating the harm done to the community, is what I mean by the "first level of control" in the process by which deviance was combated.

Second Level Of Control: Rectification Of Deviance By Exorcism

By enabling individuals to articulate forbidden inner urges through an externalized, ego-alien agent, the *dybbuk* idiom significantly decreased their destructive potential. As to the behavioral *manifestation* of deviance, however, the contrary was true. The fact that the evil spirit of an outstanding sinner was considered the motivating agent underlying the victim's behavior, served to accentuate and dramatize the deviant nature of the possession episode: The possessed publicly engaged in behavior that was considered blasphemous even to think about. The danger therefore existed that these behaviors might be added to the observers' repertoire. Through the *dybbuk,* the inexpressible became possible and real. In order to assure that the potential for such behavior was actualized, the *dybbuk* had to be exorcized. Deviance had to be rectified. That this was, indeed, the ordinary consequence of the exorcistic ritual suggests that exorcism was a traditional and effective equivalent of individual psychotherapy.

As in other cultural variants of spirit possession wherein the invading agent was considered evil, and the alliance with it forced and undesirable (Oesterreich, 1930, p. 103), the exorcism of the *dybbuk* was understood to require the strict observance of a set sequence of steps, which perforce culminated in its expulsion (Bilu, 1980; Patai, 1978). Its uniquely Jewish, culture-bound aspects were prominently expressed in the therapeutic phase. The exorcist was a mystically oriented rabbi, whether a kabbalist or a Hasidic *tsadik* (a pious, holy man). Often the exorcism was performed in the synagogue with the active participation of a *minyan* (a kind of religious quorum — a group of ten male adults without which public prayer could not take place). Jewish sacred paraphernalia were generally employed during the critical stages of the exorcism in order to facilitate the expulsion of the spirit.

Even though successful exorcism was the rule in cases of *dybbuk* possession, the rabbi-*dybbuk* encounter was usually depicted as a long, bitter, emotionally charged, and exhausting struggle. The healer had to mobilize all the stamina, sagacity, and resourcefulness at his disposal to overpower his insidious adversary, for whom, it should be recalled, the victim's body constituted a longed-for refuge from the incessant and merciless persecution of the vindictive angels of destruction.

The exorcistic ritual was performed in a fixed, graded order, with milder measures of verbal coaxing of the spirit giving way to adjurations and decrees of excommunication against it. Coercive methods of fumigating or beating the *dybbuk* were resorted to only after the aforementioned verbal alternatives had been exhausted. When a synagogue was the arena for the exorcistic ritual, its dramatic nature was particularly enhanced. In this public setting, the rabbi's performance was accompanied by an orchestrated set of activities performed by the audience. These included the taking out of Torah scrolls from the ark, the blowing of ritual ram's horns, and the successive lighting and extinguishing of black candles. The quorum participated in special prayers and incantations. Sometimes the victim was tied and laid down in front of the ark. The tension in the crowded synagogue (even non-Jews occasionally came to observe the extraordinary scene) mounted gradually with each step or "round" in the rabbi-*dybbuk* struggle until it exploded ecstatically with the spirit's forced exit.

The first step of the exorcistic ritual was aimed at ascertaining the authenticity of the case as one of *dybbuk* possession. This was particularly necessary when the spirit deliberately concealed his presence. In questionable cases, various indications were used as diagnostic criteria, such as speaking without moving the lips, the swelling of peripheral organs (e.g., the neck or breasts), and bodily sensations of extra-heaviness. Sometimes, more sophisticated, quasi-medical examinations were made. For example, the exorcist might look for a particular pattern of pulse in the victim's forearm, indicative of the spirit. Once the differential diagnosis was completed, the healer turned to the second step, in which the spirit was identified and compelled to disclose background information concerning his transgressions, the circumstances of his death, and his vicissitudes between that event and the onset of possession. It was assumed that without communicating with the spirit, and retrieving these identifying details, successful exorcism was not possible (Bilu, 1980, p. 6). The *dybbuk's* recitations concerning his experiences as a wandering spirit were overwhelmingly impressive in their disclosure and detailed description of various aspects of Jewish cosmology. For the participants in the exorcistic ritual, this was a unique opportunity to witness "directly" an entity with special ontological status, reporting from the "other world" and specifying its nature.

Following the inquiry, a lengthy negotiation took place between the parties. The exorcist tried to gain the spirit's consent to free his victim, or at least, discuss the conditions for its departure. This was the most crucial phase in the ritual, the one that determined its consequences. Against the rabbi's resourceful application of exorcistic devices, the *dybbuk* assumed an obstinate position from the outset, disobeying the exorcist's commands, deriding and depreciating his authority, and occasionally attacking him physically. (More often the spirit directed his violence at the victim.) The spirit's insidiousness was particularly revealed in those instances where its readiness to depart was followed by a stubborn refusal. To counteract his adversary's deceitfulness, the rabbi would compel the spirit to pledge its readiness to leave with a public oath, sworn over a handkerchief or phylacteries. Sometimes a bond would be signed by the two parties to guarantee the departure.

For the *dybbuk* to be expelled, certain conditions had to be fulfilled. These usually involved activities aimed at redeeming the spirit from his liminal position. Whether they were requested by the spirit or initiated by the rabbi, these post-exorcistic obligations were to be performed mainly by the possessed. They included the observance of certain mourning rituals for the *dybbuk,* the donation of a meal for poor religious students, sacrificial slaughter, and the lighting of memorial candles. Sometimes the rabbi himself and other participants in the exorcistic ritual would promise to recite prayers for the *dybbuk's* spiritual redemption. These activities were performed from one to twelve months after the exorcism. Their omission would render the formerly possessed victim liable to further assaults by the spirit.

A hot debate over the body site of the spirit's departure often terminated the negotiation phase. The *dybbuk* would try to transform his coming defeat into a partial victory by causing major damage to the organ through which he departed. Stereotypically, his preferences, strongly opposed by the exorcist, were an eye, ear, mouth, or limbs. Departure through one of these might have rendered the victim blind, deaf, mute, lame, or paralyzed. Under the healer's pressure, the spirit agreed to leave through one of the fingers or, most often, one of the big toes, where its exit was not deemed hazardous.

The tension that accumulated during the various stages of the exorcistic ritual was climatically discharged with the *dybbuk's* departure. Even though successful exorcism was immediately reflected in the victim's regaining ordinary consciousness, additional signs were sought to validate the spirit's expulsion. Without them, no one could guarantee that the insidious *dybbuk* would not reenter its victim. A small scar on the big toe, or a sharp pain in the toe, an exploding sound in the air, or, most impressively, a broken window were frequent manifestations of the departure. In the case reports, this final stage of the exorcism was particularly overdramatized. For example, a *dybbuk* exorcized from a child in 17th-century Constantinople "shaked the house, and forced his way into a dish which he moved to and fro, downward and upward several times ... [then the spirit] violently rolled the dish away from the house and it fell upon a pitcher which was broken into pieces."

Following the exorcism, the formerly possessed, weak and exhausted, was carefully guarded against further assaults by the spirit. He was arrayed with amulets and encircled by religious students who recited prayers around him until he was altogether recovered from the possession episode.

Judging from the sample of reported cases, exorcism was a highly efficacious psychotherapy. More than 90 percent of the possessed were completely, irreversibly cured. (The success rate in the general population might have been lower, of course, if failures were underrepresented in the written reports.) When failure was admitted, it was usually associated with the exorcist's shortcomings rather than with the incurable nature of the disease. Thus, after two futile attempts to exorcise a *dybbuk,* a Hasidic rabbi from Lithuania candidly admitted that "I learnt that it is not my mission to exorcize spirits, therefore I stopped." It was probably his lack of assertiveness which underlay his failure, as implied in the *dybbuk's* remark: "At first I feared him, but later on the situation was reversed, and he was afraid of me." Three cases of death following exorcism were attributed to the spirit's rancorous, ruthless revenge for having been expelled. The fact that all three were early 16th-century cases might be taken as an indication of the novelty of the phenomenon as evidenced by the difficulties in coping with it. The delicate relations between the *dramatis personae* in their complementary roles had yet to be settled and regulated.[9] Since it was mentioned more than once that a spirit would try to strangle its host, the possibility that asphyxiation by "overfumigation" was the cause of death seems reasonable.

The therapeutic effectiveness of *dybbuk* exorcism was revealed most strikingly in terms of the *contrasting effect* it produced. Typically, the symptom-free former victim displayed new, positively valued behaviors which had not been in his repertoire before the possession episode. This was particularly true in cases of extreme anti-religious sentiments voiced by male victims, but it also held for profligate women tamed into penitence and strict observance of commands. Through the idiom of *dybbuk* exorcism, change could be formulated as an abrupt transformation whereby deviant identity was expunged, and replaced by a positive conformist one. In the first case from Nikolsburg, for example, a male adolescent who could not pray for six years became, shortly after exorcism, "a new creature, a faithful observer of the commandments, blessed with good health, and erudite in the Torah." A child from 19th-century Pressburg who, during possession, used to tear Jewish sacred artifacts and kiss Christian holy books, became "a disciplined person who followed the right way all his life."

Thus, the exorcism of the *dybbuk* caused deviant behavior to be replaced by exemplary behavior. The rectification of individual deviance through exorcism, depicted here as a traditional (and more effective) equivalent of individual psychotherapy, represents the "second level of control" in the process I am describing.

THIRD LEVEL OF CONTROL: STRENGTHENING OF
CONFORMITY IN THE COMMUNITY THROUGH THE *DYBBUK*
EPISODE

The implications of *dybbuk* possession and exorcism were too far-reaching to be exhausted by the aspect of individual control. A major difference between curing rituals in traditional societies and modern psychotherapies lies in the fact that the rectification of deviance in the former did not take place in a social vacuum (Crapanzano, 1973, p. 215, 1977a, p. 33; Kennedy, 1967; Landy, 1977; Torrey, 1972): It often had profound reverberations in the social world and contributed to its reorganization. In this

---

9. On the other hand, *all* the first cases were written in a matter-of-fact style, with no evidence of wonder at the bizarre, unprecedented occurrence. As was stated earlier, the question of the onset of the *dybbuk* phenomenon is still unsettled.

manner, deviance was harnessed to enhance social control and conformity in the community.

The elaborate cultural processing of the *dybbuk* made it a powerful vehicle for enhancing obedience and discouraging deviance, largely by virtue of the multifaceted manifestation of the idea of *reward and punishment* expressed within the idiom. As an ideological doctrine, the principle of the transmigration of souls provided a solution to the question of the "ill-fated righteous," a problem of great significance in Jewish history, both to the individual and society. A present-day Hasidic book (*Shomer-Emunim*), for example, contends that the victims of the Inquisition of Spain and Portugal were inhabited by the transmigrated souls of the First Temple Israelites, who had engaged in idolatry. By the same token, the persecution of Jews in Czarist Russia was meant to rectify the evildoing that had precipitated the destruction of the Second Temple. Finally, the Holocaust is alluded to as the ultimate rectification!

The *dybbuk* idiom contained within it two levels of retribution. By attributing the penetration of the spirit to the host's past transgressions, moderate though they might have been, a clear principle of retribution was established, which contributed to social control. The second, more severe form of retribution was of course reserved for the *dybbuk* itself, brutally and multifariously punished for its sins, its sufferings minutely described before the audience of the exorcistic ritual. These included both the quality of their deaths in this world and their sufferings in the hereafter. Thus, the majority of possessing spirits were originally persons who had died young, very often of unnatural causes. A few had committed suicide (in a case from 17th-century Constantinople, the spirit was identified as "a vicious apostate, involved in ugly affairs, who killed himself because he could not find rest from his wrongdoings"); others were hung, drowned, or massacred by gentiles (the aforementioned *dybbuk* of Koznitz was the first to be killed by the invading Babylonians). Some of the spirits reported particularly agonizing deaths. A vicious sorcerer whose spirit took possession of the girl in Stolovitsch died after he had fallen into the wheel of a grinding mill. His arms were mutilated and his back broken. The young Baghdadi whose spirit possessed his sister lost his foot while serving in the Turkish army during World War I: "So intense was his suffering that he was rolling on the ground forward and backward.[10] No remedy could cure him until gangrene inflicted upon him a bizarre death."

But it was the reported vicissitudes of the spirits in the hereafter that provided the most comprehensive and impressive accounts of retribution.

---

10. Here an interesting correspondence is implied between his death and sexual behaviors. See p. 10 above.

It bears repeating, in this context, that these episodes offered a unique encounter between the living and the dead, until then almost nonexistent in Judaism. The spirit's recitation was one of the high points in the exorcistic ritual precisely because it constituted dramatic and emotionally charged *evidential confirmation* (Spiro, 1967) of metaphysical beliefs concerning the nature of the "other world." Jewish traditional cosmology was confronted, as it were, with empirical reality and translated into everyday language.

The spirits described their persecutions by angels of destruction and demons in such realistic detail as to make the mere thought of committing a sin frightening. In the early cases from the Mediterranean area, for example, they were reported to be hit with sticks of fire, "each blow caus[ing] them unparalleled agony, just like that of a living person whose flesh is cut, little by little, with a knife until he passes away." A spirit from the shtetl of Korits was torn from its body by the angels of destruction, to be successively swallowed and spit out by demons; then it was ground in a mill and had to transmigrate into a pig and other animals. The Baghdadi cases from the turn of the century again supply the most detailed descriptions. The spirit of Shabtai Zvi, for example, was beaten in his tomb for twelve years. Afterward he was transmigrated into a wild animal, "and every Friday, from two o'clock to half past four in the afternoon, he was condemned to a cell of boiling excrement...." Another spirit was flogged by 35 angels of destruction 15 hours a day, "and the remaining nine hours I had to spend in a desolate desert full of snakes and scorpions that bit and ate my flesh for four years." The spirit of an adulterous woman from Baghdad gave the most detailed account of her post-mortem punishments. At first she was beaten incessantly with sticks of fire for three days. Then she had to stand trial before the grand jury in Heaven. Upon refusing to answer the charges, she was beaten until she was dissolved into ashes. Her sentence was to be handed over to the vindictive angels for 100 years, in punishment for 100 incidents of adultery. The latter flogged her 27 times a day and 17 times each night, the sum, 44, equalling the numerical value of the Hebrew word for blood, (*dam*), to remind her that she did not cease her sexual misconduct even during her menstrual period. In addition, she had to chop trees each night to fuel a furnace on which she was burnt for three hours in front of the celestial jury. Only on Saturdays could she rest, though chained and imprisoned; spirits who had desecrated the Sabbath were persecuted on Saturdays as well.

The credibility of the accounts was enhanced by the realistic quality of the spirits' descriptions of the "other world." The garments of its inhabitants, the structure of the Heavenly Court (including exact measurements of the rooms in which it was located), even the form of certain sections of

Hell, into which some spirits were allowed temporary entrance, were portrayed in detail. All this information supplied a convincing context for conveying the idea that in the coming world, regulated by principles of reward and punishment, the righteous were prosperous and the wicked doomed. It is hardly surprising, indeed, that some exorcists could not let this rare opportunity pass without seeking to elicit information concerning matters unrelated to the exorcism itself. In some reports, intellectually curious rabbis sought from the *dybbuk* an elucidation of the laws of the universe. In one of the Baghdadi cases, for example, the exorcist asked the spirit: "Tell me whether the sun rolls upon heaven like a ball, or does it break its way through it, or does it pass underneath, in the air of this world." Sometimes the spirits were employed to solve such unsettled cosmological issues as this: "Since it is known that in heaven night is no less bright than day, is there any difference between the two and how can the sunrise be recognized?"

The impact of the spirits' recitations was all the greater when the setting of the exorcism was public. Aware of the effect of the formidable spectacle, some of the exorcists spared no effort to increase the size of their audiences. Thus, a 19th-century Hasidic rabbi, who originally thought to exorcize the *dybbuk* with only the participation of a quorum, changed his mind and decided to make the exorcism public "so that many people would observe and repent." The same reason underlay another exorcist's command that the *dybbuk* confess in front of an audience, even though his sins had already been recited privately. It seems evident that a major motivation for writing and publishing *dybbuk* episodes was the need to promulgate their moral lessons. Although the proliferation of brochures and pamphlets dealing with *dybbukim* was partially due to their dramatic plots, in which dreadful adventures, suffering and agony, sex and violence, relief and salvation, on both real and celestial levels, all played a part, the published accounts also served as an important means of indoctrination and strengthening community conformity. In most of the publications, the latter tendency was clearly indicated, as, for example, in one of the first documented cases from Safed: "It is important for them [the audience] to subdue their hearts before heaven, and to fear doomsday, since everything is taken into account, and there is no refuge in Sheol [the underworld]."

Apart from testifying to their tantalizing sufferings, the *dybbukim* also served as direct agents of social control by exposing sinners in the audience and by demanding stricter observance of the commandments. All these activities, embedded within the dramatic, sometimes shocking spectacle of the exorcism, electrified the observers and produced immediate effects. An early report from Safed ends: "Many people were present, all of them weeping, as the fear of doomsday fell upon them; and the whole country

was strongly moved." In an Italian case from the 17th century, the spirit
exposed the sins of people in the community, whereupon "all of them
whole-heartedly repented, having learned that the spirit revealed their
most profound secrets." A hundred years later, in Nikolsburg, an eyewit-
ness reported that "the extent of penitence, experienced by the large
crowd, was inconceivable." In fact, deep sentiments of compunction and
repentence as aftereffects of exorcism were reported in most of the cases.
In some of the accounts, even non-Jews were moved to repent.

In this way, the circle was closed. Symptoms representing aberrant
wishes, which, if directly expressed, would have damaged the foundations
of Jewish life, were transformed into a conformity-enhancing device. This
dialectical transformation could only have happened, moreover, in close-
knit, traditional communities, which monitored and governed the entire
living environment of each of their members. In my concluding remarks, I
shall elaborate on this functionalist argument at some length.

In addition to expressing the principle of reward and punishment, the
dybbuk idiom served as a means of validating the status and enhancing the
sociopolitical prestige of certain individuals. The moral authority of the
rabbi-exorcists, in particular, was indisputably confirmed by the fact that
the spirits eventually acknowledged their authority and submitted to it.
Sometimes it was hinted that this acknowledgment was based on information that the spirit had gathered in Heaven. The spiritual ascendency of
well-known Hasidic rabbis was convincingly confirmed by spirits even
when those rabbis were not involved in their exorcism. Thus, a *dybbuk*
from Peelts in Poland complained that ever since a certain Hasidic rabbi
had passed away *dybbuk* cases had multiplied, implying that only the late
rabbi could redeem the spirits. A temporary exit from the girl he had possessed was explained by this spirit as a desperate attempt to gain salvation
on the rabbi's tomb. This attempt failed when thousands of souls assem-
bled in the cemetery for the same purpose, and he could not get through.
The manipulative use of *dybbuk* cases to enhance status was particularly
evident in the context of power struggles between individuals, groups, or
sects. Rabbi Haim Vital, a renowned student of Rabbi Isaac Luria
Ashkenasi (the founder of a major tradition of kabbala in 16th-century
Safed), was assisted by a *dybbuk* in Damascus in his bitter struggles with
other mystically oriented rabbis, the spirit denouncing his foes while
praising and exalting Rabbi Haim. Delicate status ratings were construed
out of the differential skillfulness of rabbi-exorcists. In one Hasidic
source, for example, it was contended that the Belze rabbi could exorcize
spirits only in the vicinity of his hometown, and that his exorcistic inter-
ventions took several weeks. The rabbi from Rozin, in contrast, had no geographical limits to his exorcistic skill, nor had he to spend more than a

few hours to expel a spirit. The superiority of the latter was thus displayed. The bitter conflicts between Hasidim and their opponents (Mitnagdim) found expression in *dybbuk* cases when spirits of persons who had insulted Hasidic rabbis described their consequential sufferings and repented their sins.[11] In the struggles over control within Hasidic courts, *dybbuk* cases were again manipulatively exploited, as reflected in the aforementioned case of Eidel, who roundly criticized her brother, the leader of a Hasidic sect, under the cover of *dybbuk* possession.

Ultimately, the validation of the moral ascendancy of religious leaders through the *dybbuk* idiom contributed to social control: The rabbi, more than any other figure, served to maintain the Jewish identity of his community. Moreover, the exorcistic ritual reinforced traditional status rankings based on age and sex variables. The rabbi-exorcists, males by definition, were typically middle-aged or old. The possessed, mostly females, were usually quite young. The exorcistic ritual constituted a conservative mechanism that facilitated the perpetuation of the traditional status hierarchy in the community.

CONCLUSIONS: *DYBBUK* POSSESSION AS A CULTURE-
SPECIFIC SYNDROME

My analysis of *dybbuk* possession and exorcism, with its heavy functionalistic, control-oriented emphasis, obviously needs to be qualified. The conditions must be specified under which deviance may undergo a transformation such that it enhances conformity. By elucidating and circumscribing these conditions, moreover, in the dialectical process by means of which personally and socially disruptive experiences were harnessed to contribute to the maintenance of the social order, some insight may be gained into the nature and limits of "culture-specific syndromes." Since the process necessarily involves an elaborate, coordinated interplay between individuals and societal institutions, the analysis should encompass both levels. Specifically, the recruitment into the *social role* of the possessed, with its culturally prescribed role definitions and script, should be explicated.

With regard to the societal level, I have already emphasized that the *dybbuk* phenomenon appeared in close-knit, traditional communities, which exerted extensive control over their members. This would appear to be a necessary condition for the success of a deviance-transforming idiom.

---

11.   On the same use of possession in the struggle between Catholics and Protestants, see Oesterreich, 1930, p. 30.

The fact that deviants could be so smoothly tamed reflects a major dimension of this control. With regard to the individual level, I have argued, in line with general psychodynamic reasoning, that the enactment of the role of the possessed served to express and partially gratify urges otherwise unfulfilled. Even beyond the articulation of forbidden impulses within a culturally constituted and socially accepted idiom, however, the possessed — precisely because of their sufferings — enjoyed considerable secondary gain. Some of the *dybbuk* victims shrewdly exploited their conditions to become the focus of general attention, to elicit sentiments of respect, pity, and awe, and to be pampered and cared for. So conspicuous was this secondary gain that in some cases people were reported consciously simulating *dybbuk* possession in order to gain material rewards and sympathy from onlookers.

So much for the *motivation* of individuals to enter the role of the possessed. But a crucial selection factor in the enactment of any social role concerns the *ability* or *skill* to generate the socially prescribed behaviors involved in that role (Ullman and Krasner, 1969, p. 71). Since the *dybbuk* role embodied a complicated set of behaviors, culturally defined and constrained (and compellingly conditioned by the complementary role of the exorcist), its enactment called for certain assets that only a select group of "deviants" possessed. Thus, it is highly unlikely that the severely disturbed (i.e., psychotics) could comply with the elaborate behavioral specifications and constraints of the *dybbuk* role. (Recall the highly structured stages of the exorcism.) In the Hobbesian (or Freudian) sense of a constant battle between individual impulses and societal control, the *dybbuk* epoch clearly represented the triumph of society. But the triumphant endeavor itself was limited to those individuals who were willing and able to articulate their aberrant wishes and inner conflicts within the *dybbuk* idiom. Even in Jewish traditional communities, where conformity to sociocultural dicta was powerfully enforced, only *some* deviants could be tamed so effectively.

Who were those willing and able individuals? According to contemporary psychiatric diagnostic systems, most of them would probably be labeled "hysterics." But hysteria, as Krohn (1978) puts it, is an "elusive category," given the multitude of contexts in which it has been applied, and of meanings ascribed to it. In his insightful effort to elucidate and decipher the core dynamics underlying hysterical variants across times and cultures, Krohn analyzes hysteria using formulations that seem tailor-made for an explication of *dybbuk* cases. He begins with the thesis that "hysteria can be viably defined as a disorder which plays out *dominant current cultural identities, often to a marginal but never to a socially alienating extreme,* in an attempt to promote the myth of passivity" (p. 153; my italics). He defines the "myth of passivity" as "an attempt to disown, both internally and interpersonally, responsibility in the broadest sense for thoughts, acts and impulses" (p. 153). In Jewish traditional communities, *dybbuk* possession was just such a myth. The ability of the hysteric to resolve individual conflicts by astutely using the dominant forms of the culture attests, according to Krohn, to "his capacity for góod reality testing, impulse control and interpersonal sensitivity ... the capacity to regress and to be flamboyant within the bounds of convention ... [and] the resiliency and advanced development and differentiation definitional of the hysterical ego" (p. 162). It is not surprising, therefore, that hysterics were rarely considered substantially deviant. Moreover, "in living on the myths treasured by his reference group, the hysteric becomes a *living advocate of the moral and stylistic positions of the culture, a "yes" man for the social axioms of his milieu....* In remaining for psychological reasons within the limits of convention, they are a *natural conservative force*" (p. 208; my italics). This seems a very appropriate summary of the analysis of *dybbuk* possession and exorcism I have presented.

The intimate liaison between "emically" deviant individuals and sociocultural dicta as formulated by Krohn and as exemplified by *dybbuk* possession may constitute a basis for delineating a distinct subgroup within the broad category of culture-specific syndromes.[12] That individuals in this subgroup may be considered hysterical from a Western psychiatric perspective does not invalidate, in my opinion, their inclusion in this category. Hysteria in the above formulation is defined in terms of *dynamics* and *psychological mechanisms* rather than in terms of symptomatic content. The fact that most culture-specific syndromes are reducible to psychiatric diagnoses insofar as processes are examined is widely acknowledged (Kiev, 1973). "Most such 'ethnic psychoses,'" contends Wallace (1970), "which reflect in their behavior the specific cultural content of the victim's society are simply local varieties of a common disease process to which human beings are vulnerable" (pp. 218–219). Not only is it justified to consider *dybbuk* possession an example of culture-specific syndromes, but, in some respects, it might serve as the prototype of "pure cases" in this category. To be considered culture-specific in the precise, restrictive sense exemplified by *dybbuk* possession, then, a syndrome should meet the following criteria, of which not a few of the disorders so designated fall short.

It should be considered a disease (or a social deviance) on the "emic," native level. This apparently trivial requirement eliminates some of Krohn's cultural variants of hysteria, such as shamanism and overlapping

---

12. Also called "culture bound syndromes" (Lebra, 1976; Yap, 1969), "exotic psychotic syndromes" (Arieti, 1959, p. 546), and "hysterical psychoses" (Langness, 1967, 1976), to mention but a few such designations.

cases of ceremonial possession (see Langness's [1976] suggested distinction between "hysterical psychoses" and "possession").

The cultural processing of the syndrome should be manifested in the form of specific, meticulously followed role behaviors, through which a dominant set of beliefs is personified and "empirically validated." To what extent culture participates in the formation of symptoms is crucial, since *some* cultural coloring is typical of many recognized psychiatric disturbances as manifested in ethnically distinct groups (Kiev, 1964, 1973; Opler, 1959). Even though classical culture-specific syndromes such as *amok, latah, koro,* and *negi negi* "are learned, patterned, recurrent and culturally transmitted" (Langness, 1976, p. 60), their enactment does not necessitate the same extent of structuring as is required in the case of *dybbuk* possession. In particular, indigenous *etiologies,* esoteric and culturally unique as they may appear to the Westerner, cannot constitute a basis for designating a disease entity culture-specific in the restrictive sense suggested here, insofar as they are not *fully* expressed on the visible, "participational" level (Bilu, 1980, p. 31). *Susto,* another classical culture-specific syndrome, derives its cultural distinctiveness primarily from its peculiar etiology — soul loss — rather than from its symptoms, which include "listlessness, loss of appetite, and withdrawal from social interaction" (Uzzell, 1974, p. 369; see also Gillin, 1961; Rubel, 1964). What appears to Uzzell to be "the most important characteristic of *susto* as an illness role ... [,] its flexibility" (p. 372) removes it from the *dybbuk*-type subgroup of culture-specific syndromes. In contrast to the *dybbuk, susto,* "in terms of performance ... is a very loose script indeed" (p. 372). I am well aware of the fact that the *dybbuk* would probably appear more flexible *in vivo* than it does in the written texts. Still, especially during the elaborate exorcistic ritual, but also before it, the acting out and personification of an entity deeply rooted in a complicated cosmological belief system must necessarily have called for a high level of structuring. This also seems to hold true for other forms of possession-as-illness (Bilu, 1980; Obeyesekere, 1977).

The syndrome should be utterly curable. Culture-specific syndromes such as the *dybbuk* are syndromes with which a culture is able to cope. Since they emerge from a cultural idiom, accepted as part of the prevailing belief system, the elements in the idiom can be manipulated to regain conformity. The symptoms are not idiosyncratically construed, but rather derive their form and significance from a set of public symbols shared by all members of the community. From onset to cure, the script of a *dybbuk*-type culture-specific syndrome takes a predetermined course, well known to the participants. As I have already stated, only a small subgroup of potential deviants (one may call them "the truly cultural deviants") are able to resolve their inner conflicts by personifying cosmological identities and themes. This personification requires, on the one hand, that there exist in the community a potent, widely accepted cosmology, and on the other hand, that these individuals possess personal attributes (e.g., good reality testing) that seriously disturbed people do not possess. Consequently, I would exclude any psychotic disorder from the subgroup suggested here, even though benign forms of psychosis are represented among culture-specific syndromes (Arieti, 1959; Langness, 1976). (That malign psychosis is not liable to *heavy* cultural processing was demonstrated in various anthropological studies; see, for example, Edgerton, 1966; Murphy, 1976.) Whether basically hysteric or not, those individuals who are capable of molding their inner conflicts in the service of society are only moderately disturbed.

The syndrome should not persist following substantial sociocultural changes. By definition, any culture-specific syndrome is vulnerable to more than superficial modifications in the sociocultural constellation of factors from which it emerged. This is all the more true for "pure cases," modeled on *dybbuk* possession, as they epitomize core elements of a traditional cosmology. When the cosmology decays — when society uses other, incompatible idioms — the syndrome is doomed to disappear.

In addition to these conditions, it appears that a state of *dissociation,* or more broadly, *altered consciousness,* plays a major role in "pure-case" culture-specific syndromes, constituting a psychic matrix conducive to the display of cultural identities markedly at odds with the "regular" self. Indeed, dissociation is amenable to a multitude of cultural interpretations and elaborations, according to Bourguignon (1973; 1976b, pp. 47–48). Her illuminating distinction between "trance" and "possession" is frequently represented in various classifications of culture-bound syndromes (Kiev, 1964; Yap, 1969) in which possession syndromes explicitly appear.

In all of this, I do not mean to suggest that the traditional classification of culture-specific syndromes should be narrowed. Rather, I mean to call attention to "pure forms" of cultural disorders which comply with the above criteria and which may be designated "culture-dictated syndromes." This subdivision of culture-specific syndromes may be viewed as located at the extreme end of a continuum representing the extent to which culture intervenes with symptomatic content, the other pole of which involves minimal cultural coloring of the disorder.

In sum, I have argued that *dybbuk* possession is an example of a subgroup within culture-specific syndromes that involves a kind of working alliance between society and a selected group of deviants. In the process through which deviance was transformed into enhanced conformity, the possessed played a conservative role, endorsing cultural dicta and contributing to social stability. I think it reasonable to assume that culture-specific syndromes such as the *dybbuk* were prevalent in times of crisis precipitated by rapid sociocultural changes; in line with this thesis, their enactment would have constituted a valuable resource of society in protecting and revalidating its endangered myths. (This assumption might be a promising lead in understanding the enigmatic onset of *dybbuk* possession.) Beyond a crucial amount of cultural change, however, this societal mechanism of defense would fail. Indeed, the disappearance of cases of *dybbuk* possession attests to the profound attenuation of the Jewish traditional way of life in our century. With the exception of secluded ultraorthodox communities (where, indeed, the possibility that rare, unreported cases of *dybbuk* possession still appear cannot be ruled out), no more does Jewish traditional culture pervasively control and monitor the lives of Jews, nor does it offer potent, acceptable idioms for articulating inner experiences and conflicts. As a result, it has lost its capacity to mold and rectify deviance with the vitality and vigor exhibited in *dybbuk* possession and exorcism.

BIBLIOGRAPHY

ANSKY, S. (1926). *The Dybbuk*. New York: Liveright.
ARIETI, S., ed. (1959). *American Handbook of Psychiatry*. New York: Basic Books.
BEIT-HALLAHMI, B. (1976). *The Turn of the Screw* and *The Exorcist:* Demoniacal Possession and Childhood Purity. *Amer. Imago, 33*:296–303.
BILU, Y. (1980). The Moroccan Demon in Israel: The Case of "Evil Spirit Disease." *Ethos,* 8:24–39.
BOKSER, B. Z. (1981). *The Jewish Mystical Tradition*. New York: Pilgrim.
BOURGUIGNON, E., ed. (1973). *Religion, Altered States of Consciousness and Social Change*. Columbus: Ohio State University Press.
_____ (1976a). *Possession*. Corta Madera, Ca: Chandler and Sharp.
_____ (1976b). Possession and Trance in Cross Cultural Study of Mental Health. In *Culture Bound Syndromes, Ethnopsychiatry and Alternative Therapies,* ed. W. P. Lebra. Honolulu: University Press of Hawaii.
CRAPANZANO, V. (1973). *The Hamadsha: A Study in Moroccan Ethnopsychiatry*. Berkeley: University of California Press.
_____ (1977a). Introduction. In *Case Studies in Spirit Possession,* ed. V. Crapanzano & V. Gattison. New York: John Wiley & Sons.
_____ (1977b). Mohammed and Dawia: Possession in Morocco. In *Case Studies in Spirit Possession,* ed. V. Crapanzano & V. Gattison. New York: John Wiley & Sons.
_____ GATTISON, V., eds. (1977). *Case Studies in Spirit Possession*. New York: John Wiley & Sons.
DWYER, D. H. (1978). *Images and Self-Images: Males and Females in Morocco*. New York: Columbia University Press.
EDGERTON, R. B. (1966). Conceptions of Psychosis in Four East-African Societies. *Amer. Anthropologist,* 68:408–425.

FREUD, S. (1923). A Seventeenth Century Demonological Neurosis. *S.E.*, 19:72-105. London: Hogarth Press, 1961.

GENDLIN, E. T. (1964). A Theory of Personality Change. In *Personality Change*, ed. P. Worchel & D. Byrne. New York: John Wiley & Sons.

GILLIN, J. P. (1961). Magical Fright. In *Social Studies and Personality: A Case Book*, ed. Y. A. Cohen. New York: Holt, Rinehart & Winston.

KENNEDY, J. G. (1967). Nubian Zar Ceremonies as Psychotherapy. *Human Organization*, 4:185-194.

KIEV, A., ed. (1964). *Magic, Faith and Healing: Primitive Psychiatry Today*. New York: Free Press.

_____ (1973). *Transcultural Psychiatry*. New York: Free Press.

KROHN, A. (1978). *Hysteria: The Elusive Neurosis*. [*Psychological Issues*, Monogr. 45/46.] New York: International Universities Press.

LANDY, D. ed. (1977). *Culture, Disease and Healing: Studies in Medical Anthropology*. New York: Macmillan.

LANGNESS, L. L. (1967). Hysterical Psychosis: The Cross Cultural Evidence. *Amer. J. Psychiat.*, 124:47-56.

_____ (1976). Hysterical Psychoses and Possession. In *Culture Bound Syndromes, Ethnopsychiatry and Alternative Therapies*, ed. W. P. Lebra. Honolulu: University of Hawaii Press.

LEBRA, W. P., ed. (1976). *Culture Bound Syndromes, Ethnopsychiatry and Alternative Therapies*. Honolulu: University of Hawaii Press.

LEWIS, I. M. (1966). Spirit Possession and Deprivation Cults. *Man*, 1:307-329.

_____ (1971). *Ecstatic Religions: An Anthropological Study of Spirit Possession and Shamanism*. Baltimore, Md: Penguin.

MURPHY, J. (1976). Psychiatric Labeling in Cross-Cultural Perspectives. *Science*, 191:1019-1028.

NIGAL, G. (1980). The *Dybbuk* in Jewish Mysticism. *Daat*, 4:75-100 (Hebrew).

OBEYESEKERE, G. (1970). The Idiom of Demonic Possession: A case study. *Soc. Sci. & Med.* 4:97-111.

_____ (1977). Psychocultural Exegesis of a Case of Spirit Possession in Sri Lanka. In *Case Studies in Spirit Possession*, ed. V. Crapanzano & V. Gattison. New York: John Wiley & Sons.

OESTERREICH, T. K. (1930). *Possession, Demoniacal and Other*. New York: Richard R. Smith.

OPLER, M. K. (1959). *Culture and Mental Health*. New York: Macmillan.

PATAI, R. (1978). Exorcism and Xenoglossia among the Safed Kabbalists. *J. Amer. Folklore*, 91:823-835.

_____ (1977). Negative Spirit Possession in Experienced Brazilian Umbanda Spirit Mediums. In *Case Studies in Spirit Possession*, ed. V. Crapanzano & V. Gattison. New York: John Wiley & Sons.

PRINCE, R. H. (1977). Foreword. In *Case Studies in Spirit Possession*, ed. V. Crapanzano & V. Gattison. New York: John Wiley & Sons.

RUBEL, A. J. (1964). The Epidemiology of a Folk-Illness: Susto in Hispanic America. *Ethnology*, 3:268-283.

RUBENSTEIN, R. L. (1968). *The Religious Imagination: A Study in Psychoanalysis and Jewish Theology*. Boston: Beacon.

SCHOLEM, G. (1971). Gilgul. In *Encyclopedia Judaica*, 7:573-577. Jerusalem: Keter.

SHWEDER, R. A. (1980). Rethinking culture and personality, Part III. *Ethos*, 2:60-94.

SINGER, I. B. (1959). *Satan in Goray*. New York: Noonday.

SMITH ROSENBERG, C. (1972). The Hysterical Woman: Sex roles and role conflict in 19th century America. *Soc. Res.,* 39:652–677.

SPIRO, M. E. (1967). *Burmese Supernaturalism.* Englewood Cliffs, N.J.: Prentice-Hall.

TORREY, F. E. (1972). *The Mind Game: Witchdoctors and Psychiatrists.* New York: Emerson Hall.

ULLMAN, L. P., & KRASNER, L. (1969). *A Psychological Approach to Abnormal Behavior.* Englewood Cliffs, N.J.: Prentice-Hall.

UZZELL, D. (1974). Susto Revisited: Illness as a strategic role. *Amer. Ethnologist,* 1:369–378.

WALKER, S. S. (1972). *Ceremonial Spirit Possession in Africa and Afro-America.* Leiden: Brill.

WALLACE, A. (1970). *Culture and Personality,* 2nd ed. New York: Random House.

YAP, P. M. (1969). The Culture Bound Reactive Syndromes. In *Mental Health Research in Asia and the Pacific,* ed. W. Caudill & T. Y. Lin. Honolulu: East-West Center Press.

ZBOROWSKY, M., & HERZOG, E. (1962). *Life Is with People: The Culture of the Shtetl.* New York: Schocken.

2

After the Death of The Primal Father

GÉZA RÓHEIM, Ph.D.

Osiris, the son of the goddess of the heavens, Nut, and the earth god, Sebk, cohabited with his sister Isis, while still in their mother's womb. He became ruler over Egypt and traveled through the country, mitigating wild customs and introducing agriculture and civilization. During his absence his brother Set ruled in his place. Yet upon Osiris' return, Set cunningly plotted against him, with 72 accomplices and the assistance of an Ethiopian queen named Aso. At a sumptuous banquet he lured Osiris by trickery to lie down in a chest. The conspirators slammed the lid on him, sealed the chest with nails, and lowered it into the sea. The chest was found by Isis, but she put it aside in order to travel to her son, Horus, in the marshes of Buto. While hunting a bear by moonlight, Set found instead the chest and the body of Osiris and tore it into 14 pieces and scattered them about. Later, Isis sought and found most of the individual pieces, but of all the parts of Osiris, she could not find his genitals, for these had been cast into the river and devoured by the detested fish Lepidotos, Phagros, and Oxyrhynchos. In place of the genitals Isis made an artificial phallus and sanctified it as the sacred object which the Egyptians venerate to this day. From the dead Osiris Isis conceived Horus who went forth as his father's avenger and conquered Set and his accomplices. In the fight Set took the part of a black boar and robbed Horus of his eyesight by throwing feces in his eyes, while Horus cut off Set's genitals. After his victory, Horus became the ruler of Egypt (Erman, 1909, pp. 38–41; Frazer, 1906, pp. 269–276; Plutarch, 1936, pp. 31–55; Roeder, 1915, pp. 196, 242, 271).

Originally published as "Nach dem Tode des Urvaters," *Imago,* 1923, 9:83–121; translated by Werner Muensterberger and edited by Muensterberger and L. Bryce Boyer. This article represents "simply" a historically significant publication in response to both *Totem and Taboo* (Freud, 1913) and the first influence of psychological considerations. It appears here for the first time in English; at the time of its original publication, it was widely discussed. The editors are grateful to Mrs. Lois Danton for librarian assistance.

In interpreting this legend, we will have to be brief, since an extensive analysis of this basic Egyptian myth[1] would easily expand into a book. As is well known, one problem standing in our way is the fact that all myths develop over time such that individual characters are split into doubles and the original *dramatis personae* end up appearing in several guises. It is very likely that the Osiris legend also follows this typical pattern and that the originally simple characters are represented by several, sometimes even contradictory, components. A study of pyramid texts, for example, discloses no reference to an enmity between Horus and Set, and portrays the two as twin gods, or possibly as the same deity with a twin head (Budge, 1904, Vol. 1, p. 194, Vol. 2, pp. 241, 242).

If we then eliminate Horus the Avenger, for a moment, we would arrive at the following story (Plutarch, 1936, pp. 77–81; Roeder, 1909–1915, p. 63; fasc., 1910, p. 779): Horus (or Set) the son of Osiris, the wild boar, with his associates and with the aid of Queen Isis, kills his father, and then cuts him to pieces, castrates, and eats him. There is no doubt that we are dealing here with a primal horde fight, for the animal sacred to Set is the rhinoceros of which Plutarch remarks that it is the most shameless of all animals, since it kills its father and forces its mother to sleep with it. Yet what happened to Osiris was only to be expected after his own like deed. For according to one recorded tradition among the many existent versions, he is supposed to have slept with his sister Isis (a split-off figure from his mother, Nut) in their mother's womb, and also to have castrated his father, Sebk (Brugsch, 1891, p. 581; Budge, 1904, Vol. 2, p. 99). Now the same thing happens to him, for he can only be interpreted as a condensation of innumerable primal fathers who all in turn had ruled the horde and were killed by their sons, fighting each other for succession. Against him Horus and Set, with their associates from the brother clan, formed one unit, but after his death that unity fell apart. Horus, the avenger of his father and the principle of Good, and Set the spirit of Evil, the murderer, fought each other until Horus emerged triumphant and, like his father, became ruler of Egypt. This whole legend is actually continuously repeated in the death ritual, for according to Egyptian tradition the slain god Osiris is the prototype of all dead, and after death everyone becomes an Osiris (Erman, 1909, p. 110). The prototype of the death rite is thus the violent death of the father in the primal horde.

Let us now try to take the opposite point of view and draw some conclusions from the death rites of today's primitive peoples about conditions after the death of the primal father. As we know, some primitives inflict

---

1. As early as the year 4241 B.C. we find the legend cycle of Osiris in the center of Egyptian ideas of religion.

cruel wounds upon themselves after the death of a relative. Preuss (1896) is already on the right track in his explanation of these rites. He says that because the conscience of the primitive is not easy, self-punishment follows after every death (p. 223).

It is as if the primitive wanted to say: It is not ourselves, the survivors, who delight in the loss of the dead; rather, we are saddened and mourn; yet strangely, the departed has now changed into an evil spirit who gets pleasure from seeing us suffer, and who is out for our blood (Freud, 1913, pp. 62–63). This explains, on the one hand, Furies, who torture those who have sinned against the moral commandments of filial duty (Rapp, 1884–1886, p. 1321), and also the general origin of the fear of the spirits of the dead. In many rites the original aggressiveness toward the dead becomes manifest: The corpse is beaten up, pierced with an impaling pole, mutilated or tied up, and the spirit exorcised by warlike remonstrations (Lippert, 1886–1887; Spencer, 1879–1896; Tylor, 1870). From this, we can easily understand the meaning of the wounds which the mourners inflict upon themselves as a turning against the self; just as no neurotic feels any suicidal impulses without previously wanting to kill someone else, so we can also say: After another's death the primitive commits suicide due to his unconscious guilt. The correct interpretation has been given by Lambert (1921, p. 28) who sees in these rites symbolic attempts at suicide (Elhorst, 1921, p. 98). Just as a child who has really had no opportunity of witnessing his parents' coitus is phylogenetically prepared for the knowledge of cohabitation, in the case of the primitive, we need not have recently repressed death wishes for the deceased in order to account for the evolution of the rites we are discussing.

Even if primitive man never had such wishes at all, he would abreact an inherited feeling of guilt in the death rite:[2] He is tormented by the bloodthirsty ghosts of innumerable slain fathers, whose deaths he had caused, and he now atones for this repeatedly by punishing his own body. But how does aggression turn back upon the self in this way? Indeed this problem can be differently formulated today than would have been possible before the publication of "Beyond the Pleasure Principle" (Freud, 1920). From the assumption of a death wish, which is only later projected outward as a destructive urge (sadism), it is evident that we are speaking of aggression turning against the self. Yet from this it does not follow that we have been absolved of the duty of discovering in every individual case the circumstances leading to that turning point. We assume that these are to be looked for outside the individual, in the first instance, namely in the obstacles which the outside world holds up to block his aggressiveness. Ex-

---

2.   Editors' note: Róheim's (1950) later "ontogenetic" theory refutes this earlier hypothesis.

ternal inhibitions will be determinant as soon as the destructive urge turns on the ego as a primal goal, when it regresses to that "autistic" phase of development.

The question of what kind those external inhibitions might be is identical with another question: What occurred in the primal clan after the brothers had succeeded in removing the primal father? We must never forget that we are dealing here not with individual events, but with a long period of human evolutional history about which we are used to writing in a form of dramatic condensation (Freud, 1913, pp. 141–146n.). In other words, the organization of the primal clan must have continued for some length of time, passing from one primal ruler of the clan to the next. But what happened between the murder of the king and the time the new ruler took over?

The father who had forced the brothers to be members of the group was dead now so that its solidarity no longer held. The associates of yesterday now became deadly enemies, each wanting to become father by driving out the competing brothers. After the father's death a state of *bellum omnium contra omnes* followed, which would last just as long as it took for the emergence of a new leader who had succeeded either in killing off the other brothers in the clan or in forcing them back into the group. Atkinson (1903) has himself observed these conditions among wild hoofed animals, noting that the young males unite in a group and then continue to fight one another until the old order – a horde of wives with one male, and the separate clan of brothers – is restored (pp. 222, 223, 228). After the father's death follows the war of brothers. In the Maori myth that corresponds to the Greek saga of Chronos, Uranos, and Gaia, the separation of sky and earth is followed by conflict and war among the brothers previously united in their fight against the father. So also in the Bible: After the fall from grace, the one brother kills the other. Moreover, in many primitive tribes we find, as indeed we do in many semi-civilized peoples, that fighting invariably breaks out at the grave; soon this takes on more ceremonial forms – e.g., in Olympic contests in honor of the dead or, in Southeast Australia, with more hate and rage and with mutual accusations of having caused the death. In other words, each individual suffers on his own body punishment for the murder committed, and wounds himself with weapons or the teeth and claws of his former associates. By inflicting this punishment upon himself after a bereavement, the primitive repeats, by playing all of the parts himself, the happenings of primal history, albeit in an abridged form.

We now suspect that in the period of fratricidal war and psychological upset that was bound to occur after the death of the father, lie the keys to conflicts of the ego. The war was once a war with real enemies, and from the engrams of past fights in the clan emerged the readiness for conflict in the individual. After the death of an Unmatjera or Kaitish man one of his sons-in-law is given the dead man's hair. With this gift is linked a duty: He has to head an expeditionary army and challenge some other "son-in-law" of the deceased to a duel. After they have inflicted sufficient wounding cuts on each other, they embrace and the first passes the hair of the deceased to the second, who is now likewise under an obligation to find a third "son-in-law" (in the classificatory sense) to repeat the scene, until the hair has made the round through the whole range of "sons-in-law" (Spencer and Gillen, 1904, pp. 510, 511). If we project these happenings back into the primal clan, we soon get an insight into the conditions that were bound to follow on the death of a leader animal, and moreover, an explanation of customs among today's primitives.

The class of the *Gammona* consists of the "sons-in-law" – the husbands or future husbands of the deceased man's daughters. These men were, however, the brothers in the primal clan; once they had succeeded in their deed, their organization fell apart and the former friends became enemies. The sudden change of their situation necessarily had to lead to the first split in the ego. Now men fought against their brothers with whom they had united to conquer their father, and each one of them acted just as their father had earlier on, each one turning unwittingly, as it were, into his father's avenger. Emancipated and stepping forward from the group, each one was a single unit of the clan, an individual on his own, a person standing, as his father before him, against his tribal group. In addition, a physical basis of identification had been provided, in that they had killed their father, devoured him, wrapped themselves in his skin, kept his shinbones, hair, or head as a trophy. Yet the identification was still not a complete one. A residue of the personality remained within the brothers, in their revolutionary attitude; for the fights that followed after the father's death, and the aspects of the ego involved, were merely innumerable new editions of that first great battle. If among the Baputi the chieftain of the Duik clan has died, the men organize a great hunt for their totemic animal. The latter is killed, the skin is drawn, and the dead chieftain is wrapped in it before being buried (Stow, 1905, p. 415). Here we see quite clearly: The sacrifices at death were repetitions of the unconsciously committed murder. The slaves slaughtered at the chieftain's grave, the animals killed in his honor (mainly chickens or birds that take his spirit along into the other world [Freud, 1921]), are the brothers who had to be slain at the very grave of the father, and at the same time they are doubles of the primal father. Thus on the one hand the individual repeats his rebellious sin, and on the other he repeats it in a form which at the same time appears as a punishment for that sin. Of course, he also has the idea of having gained new strength by devouring his father; "ideal" comes from *eidolon,* the memory image, soul of the dead (Crawley, 1909, p. 186); that is to say, the brothers created for themselves an ego ideal by identifying themselves with the dead father. They had eaten him, introjected him, and he had become part of their egos, and "what before he had prevented by his existence, they would now themselves forbid one another in the psychological situation of the 'deferred obedience' " (Freud, 1913, p. 143) so well known from psychoanalytic practice. Another part of their egos had still remained identical with the group ego of the fraternal clan, i.e., the other brothers, crystallized around the two points in the ego which we usually distinguish as "ego ideal" and "actual ego." Man will forever resist the multitude, striving for an ideal which he can attain just as little as children can emulate their father, and yet, man remains the man he really is: one of many. Only by killing his father and identifying himself with him can he gain for himself an "ego ideal" (Freud, 1923), and the supernatural strength so gained stems from the second person who has now become immanent within him. Some primitive peoples believe that the murderer, especially when he has eaten his victim or kept part of his body as an amulet, is accompanied by the dead man's spirit as his protector. In North America the youngster withdraws into the solitude of the forest in the years of puberty. There he chastises himself, fasting and incessantly weeping. He entreats the Manitou to have pity on him and grant him a vision. If then, in a waking vision or in a dream, an animal appears — frequently it is the same animal that had appeared to his father — it will be his duty to hunt until he has killed such an animal, and from its skin he makes a medicine bag.[3] His attitude toward this "personal totem," as some anthropologists rightly call it, is entirely analogous to the ambivalent attitude of primitive tribes toward their totem animals. Although he has slain the animal, he must never repeat this kill, nor eat of the flesh of the beast. The animal protects him in all dangerous situations throughout his life; in return, he has to hold special feasts and sacrifices in honor of his protector spirit. Yet the totem also determines the personal qualities of the individual and specifies his character development — the protective spirits of warriors are wild beasts, those of the shaman snakes and supernatural creatures, whereas cowardly people have cowardly animals for protection. Man is like the spirit he worships; his protector spirit is as he would like to be, his ego ideal. He will acquire such an ideal by killing an animal in the years of puberty, which frequently

---

3.   The material is Frazer's (1910, Vol. 3, pp. 370–456) and compiled after him. Freud (1900, 1921) believed that small animals in dreams and fairy tales have siblings as one of their meanings.

is his father's totem animal, such as once the brothers in the primal clan had killed the father, and he keeps the skin of the beast in a medicine bag as a source of its supernatural strength. We thus gain the important insight that the splitting off of a part from the actual ego in the primal clan followed after the father's death due to the brothers' identification with their father. In the external conflict of the fraternal war, cause was given for an internal split, the war of the brothers was introjected, and lives on within us in the conflicts between the ego and the ego ideal. Yet, here we also gain an opportunity to trace back one of the familiar psychoneuroses to its original form in phylogenesis. We are thinking of melancholia, and should like immediately to state that here we are following up the speculation of Freud, who has expanded upon the idea in private conversation. It will be helpful to start with Freud's (1917) study "Mourning and Melancholia." In it he finds a number of similarities and differences between these two psychic disturbances. We shall see that when we compare the mourning of civilized man to that of the primitive, the similarity of the two affects increases while the discrepant features disappear step by step. The self-accusations and self-punishing tendencies which come to the fore in the clinical situation (Freud, 1917, pp. 246–248) can be equally well observed in primitive mourning rites. In the case of melancholia, the picture is "completed by sleeplessness and refusal to take nourishment, and — what is psychologically very remarkable — by an overcoming of the instinct which compels every living thing to cling to life" (p. 252), exactly as the primitive will torment himself in mourning in all ways imaginable, or inflict punishment or symbolic death upon himself. The self-accusations of the melancholic start from a critical tension within the ego, which leads to conflict between the two main tendencies of the ego. Seen in the proper light, it becomes clear that these self-accusations are really complaints. Originally directed at another person, they were included within the ego, thus being identified with a part of the ego (p. 248). Similarly the inflictions of self-punishment in primitive mourning rites are in the first instance addressed to the deceased, i.e., the father, and are only secondarily redirected to the person himself. We get somewhat closer to primitive mourning in the compulsive accusations of neurotics after a death: "Of the three preconditions of melancholia — loss of the object, ambivalence, and regression of libido into the ego — the first two are also found in the obsessional self-reproaches arising after a death has occurred" (p. 248). The narcissistic regression of the libido is expressed, in melancholia, especially in the form of refusing to take in food, and in stubborn silence. The origin of this private taboo can be studied in the mourning rites of the primitives to great advantage. In Australia, the widow and the blood avenger who has eaten the flesh of the deceased must not speak, and, linked vicariously with this taboo on speaking, we find the eating of red-blooded animals (Howitt, 1886; Ling-Roth, 1896; Spencer and Gillen, 1899, 1904).

In Melanesia, we find that abstinence after a bereavement is explained by the deceased's having turned himself into the food concerned (Codrington, 1891, p. 33; Rivers, 1914, Vol. 2, p. 361), and if the food tabooed is the same as is otherwise eaten at the feast (Seligman, 1910, pp. 164, 165), it follows that in that food the deceased is incorporated so that to eat it is to repeat the sin of anthropophagy. We are now on the track of answering the question: What is the actual sin of the melancholic? Or, expressed in a different way: In what situations did the mechanisms originate that are still active in melancholia? After the death of the primal father, both the tribal organization and the psychic unity of the "confederated" brothers fell apart. Outside raged the fraternal war of the rivals; inside, the fight between the newly gained ego ideal representing the father, and the "actual ego" of before. The sons had eaten the father, and they tended constantly to repeat that act, yet something within themselves had become a father and inhibited a repetition of the sin. Tabooed food — the Maoris say — is one in which a supernatural creature is contained, and if eating a man is the greatest insult that can be done him, then how much greater an offense it is to eat the gods (Shortland, 1882, pp. 25, 26).

Thus, the prohibition of anthropophagy gradually spreads to other foodstuffs, and we gain the picture of increasing refusal to take in food that is so characteristic of melancholia. We may therefore derive the injunctions against eating during the mourning period from the same source as the totemic interdiction of food, or see, in the latter, prohibitions of the mourning period which have become permanent. In the same way, we have to look upon the great feast that terminates the mourning period as a breaking of the prohibitions analogous to the totem sacrament. The melancholic refuses to take in food and punishes himself in all kinds of ways because he has committed the great sin of having killed his father and eaten him (Abraham, 1916, pp. 276–278). By that act, he has introjected his father as an ego ideal and has so brought inward the fight between father and son, brother and brother — a conflict between actual and ideal ego. Yet what explains the periodicity in the lapses of mania and melancholia? Once we have found melancholia, mania cannot be far off.

Freud in his well-known study of the subject (1917) says that the phase of triumph, which corresponds to mania, is not to be found in normal mourning. This is correct for the mourning activities we find in our observations of everyday life, but not for the primitives. On the contrary, we can establish that the mourning period for them frequently ends in an orgy, a great feast, or even a warlike expedition.[4] Let us turn to these possibilities.

The period of mourning is terminated when the deceased is avenged, i.e., killed for a second time in the person of his assumed murderer. Here is a case from the Leprose Islands: A father sinks into a genuine depression after the death of his son, and refuses all food unless he can have human flesh. After he does, the period of mourning comes to an end (Codrington, 1891, p. 344). In Australia we find two variants. The mourning periods last until the deceased is avenged, i.e., until someone, usually a stranger with dark color (whom the medicine men have described as the cause of death), has been killed, or until the bones are ceremoniously collected, smashed, and broken into small pieces. In Africa, to choose another example, an animal may be sacrificed in place of a man at the graveside. All the same, what began with death must end in death. The murder that unconsciously lurks behind every death must be repeated, either on the corpse itself (breaking up the bones) or on a substitute.

We shall now summarize the description that is given by Forbes (1884) of the feasts after conclusion of the mourning period in Timor: Animals are killed in masses in order to placate the insatiable avarice of the people for food. They devour the meat in a half-raw state, and while doing this, drink nothing but the strongest arrack. Under the influence of the alcohol the women start a round dance, with drums beating. First, all goes slowly, then the rhythm grows faster and ends amid general orgies of clamoring at a breathless speed. The men, too, are infected by the excitement and dress up in their war apparel to join in the dance. The excitement grows more and more intense until the dancers collapse exhausted. The manic phase here follows the spell of melancholia, as is found in clinical practice.[5] In melancholia, all relations are withdrawn into the ego, objects lose their significance, and even the aggressive impulse turns away from the outside world, finding its object within the ego. In mania, these fixed relations turn back to their objects and a tendency develops to cathect a great many objects in turn. The melancholic attacks himself, while in the manic state projection takes place and he attacks others. In the period of mourning, the primitive will inflict wounds on himself, but the end is that he kills

---

4. See Hertz (1907) and the conditions in the well-known Australian sources.

5. The situation is more complicated than would appear from the text. The narcissistic-infantile ideal ego is projected onto the father with the formation of the first mass of animals, only to be included again in consequence of theophagy (eating of the father) in the ego, or introjected. Thus the ego becomes "double-layered," and in this our speculations above have their starting point.

others. There is a curious condition at work here: After he has avenged his father or relative and killed the foe, the son will identify himself, as he had done before, with his father. From the hair of the deceased the Warramunga make a *Tana,* a cigar-shaped emblem of the blood avenger. Since the hair otherwise plays a great part in the marital rites of the tribe, we must look upon the *Tana* as a phallic symbol. Now the blood avengers have achieved their goal and the enemy is dead. His kidney fat is excised so that his strength can be inherited by others. Wundt (1914) has seen a sexual significance in the magic importance of the fat: Among the powers for which primitives yearn is included sexual strength to a very important degree. If one's own dead are eaten, this means that one wants to inherit their qualities. In the case of the enemy, it also means that his strength in turn should pass on to the eater. The magic bones which are made up from the shinbone or forearm of the dead man serve to kill his murderer by magic means, by merely being pointed at him; the murderer can also die by being consumed by fire when these bones are cast into it. That is to say, the murderer is identified with the dead man (Kleiweg de Zwaan, 1913, p. 32).

Now let us turn to the ideology of the headhunt. The period of mourning is, in Indonesia, terminated by the return of warriors who have succeeded in capturing enemy heads. When in Nias a chieftain dies, a number of heads must be cut off. Once these heads are at hand, the party goes to the grave and the eldest son offers the deceased his sacrfices with these words, as translated by Friess: "Free of reproach is the man; free of guilt is now your son; you have received your share, your honor, your reward." The party then returns home where the priest implores the dead man's spirit: "Strangle our youths no longer, your recompense is given you; strangle no longer our sons, you have your fame and honor now" (p. 32). The enemy falls in substitution for the sons whom the dead man would strangle. The relationship between blood revenge, or the headhunt, and the Oedipus complex is clear, even if we have to postpone the exact explanation for a while yet. For now it remains the most important thing to know that the headhunter regards the skulls of the conquered enemies as his protective spirits, that he keeps them together with the skulls of his own ancestors, that he even expects from them, as from his ancestors, the fertilization of the women of his own tribe. The Dayak are even so obliging as to tell us the true meaning of the headhunt, by means of a not quite "accidental" comparison: "When during an expedition, we have arrived outside our tribal borders and want to conquer some heads, then we kill any man, even if he should be our own father" (Ling-Roth, 1896, Vol. 1, p. 159). The case is even clearer in Melanesia; on the Solomon Islands a headhunting expedition is launched after a chieftain's death. In due course a slave is captured and that slave is the rightful heir to the throne of the dead chieftain (Rivers, 1914, Vol. 2, pp. 100, 161). In order to evaluate this, one has to know that the conquest of slaves on a headhunting expedition usually represents a mitigated form of beheading; and if the person captured takes the place of the chieftain, then it is in fact the dead chieftain whom they wish to behead (or castrate). The Tugeri in New Guinea ask their victim's name before cutting his head off. Having this, they thus possess the person's soul and give it to their sons or kin as a protecting spirit. This is accomplished by renaming the child, giving it from that moment onward the name of the killed enemy (Wilken, 1912, Vol. 4, pp. 79–81). In other words, child and foe become identified, the enemy is killed in place of the son, as above in place of the father. The murderous deed that liberates one from the melancholia of mourning is thus a repetition of that primal deed which first caused the mourning, but displaced onto a new subject. *It is not the primal deed that is repeated in the manic state, but that deed as displaced, hence the delay after the original melancholia.* We now have the complete picture before us, quite as Freud assumed. The sons slew their father in a phase of manic excitement, after which they would fall into the first melancholia, resulting from the conflict between the newly acquired ego ideal and the ego, and from the neurotic inhibition of the oral functions after having eaten the primal father.

In some parts of Indonesia the mourning period lasts until an emeny's head has been taken; in Australia until a foe has been slain in expiation of the magic murder. In the manic phase of these warlike expeditions the substance of the conflict of melancholia is again expressed but now as it represents the way in which the phylogenetic period of the fraternal wars (endopsychic conflict of melancholia) came to a close — with the entry of a strange clan. Only those clans could survive in the struggle for existence which could create an organization of some size, and their bond was based upon the homoerotic pleasure of owning women in common (group marriage). Conflict with others now ensued, and in killing the enemy, the murder of the father was repeated, along with incest in the act of raping the strange women. The manic phase is not actually a direct repetition of the primal act of the murder of the father, but it is the repeat of a repetition, acted out on a substitute. Thus mania, clinically speaking, comes after melancholia. As an individual in the first place only knows the libidinous ties of the family, then afterward lives during puberty with other men in common ownership of women (free love, prostitution), and finally acquires a strange wife for himself, so in phylogenetic history group marriage follows the primal clan, and eventually exogamy develops.[6]

---

6. With reference to the sequence of social forms, partly divergent and partly similar theories are to be found in Flügel (1912) and Freud (1921).

The period following mourning represents the repetition of that phase of human history from the death of a clan member (the father) to the death of a stranger; from the Oedipus struggle, through primal melancholia, to the repeated act of the Oedipus conflict on a new object in the primal mania. Theophagy, the consumption of the dead divine father, means the beginning, and the repetition of the act on an animal or on an enemy signifies the end of the period. We find this primal scene in reverse form in reports on the initiation of the Australian shaman. The shaman is cut up like a deer, then put together again and resurrected to life in a new, supernatural form. The spirits accomplishing this are ancestral spirits, i.e., representatives of the father image.

As with initiation rites generally, this legend is handed to us in a disguised form; it should read that the sons killed and ate their father and, by identifying themselves with him, broke through the limitations of the group and gained a new superinfantile or supernatural strength from the father who had been resurrected within them as part of their own selves.[7] But one feature of the reports on shamanism remains unexplained — the quartz crystal. Two tools characterize the Australian shaman — the magic bone and the magic quartz crystal. If we are able to prove that these tools are symbols of man's psyche, then we will have solved the riddle of the Australian medicine man, and gained some insight into the psychogenesis of medicine and science. The quartz crystal must somehow be linked with the intestines, and must be an object into which the flesh of the consumed father has been transformed, for it is regularly stated that spirits disembowel the future doctor of medicine (shaman) and replace the perishable human bowels with new spirit-digesting organs, as well as with a crystal which also resides in the stomach or intestines of the medicine man. In accordance with our presuppositions we shall say that the flesh of the eaten father has turned into an excremental symbol, or, as some Australian tribes would put it, the quartz crystals are the excreta of the god of heavens (Angas, 1847, Vol. 2, p. 224; Koch-Grünberg, 1910, Vol. 2, p. 155; Palmer, 1884, p. 296; Róheim, 1921b, p. 524).

We can readily understand the belief that the quartz crystal can be propelled by a whirlwind (Howitt, 1886, p. 90, 1904, p. 365) when we know that it resides inside the medicine man as a source of his power and can be projected from him as a lethal weapon (Howitt, 1904, p. 553; Parker, 1905, pp. 35ff.). In Western Australia, according to Salvado (1851, p. 291), the magician *boglia-gadak* obtained the magic substance *boglia* only after his father's death, that is to say, after he had killed him. In the same way, in the Awabakal, the magician obtains his human bone

---

7. Concerning the initiation of the shaman in Australia see Hubert and Mauss (1909, p. 131).

when sleeping at a graveside (Threlkeld, 1892, p. 48). The *boglia* resides in his abdomen and is shot by him into people he wishes to kill (Grey, 1841, Vol. 2, pp. 84, 321, 337; Salvado, 1851, p. 299). According to Oldfield (1865, p. 235), the only source of the *boglia* is the human body, especially the anus. Analogues can be found in different parts of the world, e.g., New Guinea. Here, the *Labuni,* a sickness germ like the *boglia,* leaves the magician's body *per rectum* (Seligmann, 1910, p. 640). The significance of the quartz crystal is indeed an ambivalent one, for the medicine man of the Arunta throws his *atnongara* stones into his patients, not, as is usual, to make them sick, but to destroy the effect of the evil missiles and to cure the patient (Spencer and Gillen, 1899, p. 525). Yet, the lethal effect predominates, and the power to heal must be regarded as a reaction formation. The Anula in the North of Central Australia know only evil sorcerers and in serious cases call in the medicine men of neighboring tribes (Spencer and Gillen, 1904, pp. 488, 489). As doctor's fees the Kobeua would regard Carayura dye, capsicum, pots, hammocks, bows, but never arrows (Koch-Grüberg, 1910, Vol. 2, p. 156). But what is the matter with arrows? Most probably they are something of special interest to the doctor and characteristic of him, but something of which he is already ashamed since they symbolize an outated period in his development. For elsewhere the arrow is the weapon of evil magicians and sickness demons,[8] and it would indeed be an indelicate allusion to his murky past were one to present an arrow to the doctor. In fact it can be shown that in at least one case a weapon is first turned into a magic weapon, and then eventually into an instrument of healing. The bloodletting bows of the Papus are small flitting bows by means of which a small arrow is flung at a certain spot of the skin to hit a blood vessel. Among the Isthmus Indians the operator shoots a small arrow with a bow into different parts of the patient's body, until by chance a vein is opened. The arrow is held a short distance from the spot in order to prevent too deep a penetration (Bancroft, 1875, Vol. 1, p. 779; Bartels, 1893, p. 268; Buschan, 1909, p. 192,; Spix and Martius, 1823, Vol. 1, p. 385).

If we can then see in the lethal missiles of the wicked magician the prototypes of the healing activity, and in the evil or, as so often he is called, black magician the forerunner of the doctor, it will be of great importance to learn if we can also at this level discern the presence of anal-erotic mechanisms. The activity of the primitive magician is, basically, just as uniform as that of the medicine man. The medicine man is a being who sends sickness germs, quartz crystals into his fellow men and sucks them out again. It is the specialty of the black magician to burn the excreta, but also body dirt, saliva, blood, food remnants, foot tracks, etc., of other people in or-

---

8. See the sources in Róheim (1914, pp. 63, 240).

der to kill them thereby (Frazer, 1911a; Róheim, 1921c). The *bangal* (magician) kills people by burning their excreta. It is these excreta that the magician jumps on "like a miser upon a treasure" (Beveridge, 1883, p. 70).

The black magician is thus someone who kills his enemies by burning their excreta. In the magician, i.e., the black magician, we find a transitional form between anal-sadistic perversion and compulsion. A shifting of the direct anal-sadistic activity to hallucinatory wish fulfillment, and action carried out at a distance, has already occurred, but we cannot yet speak of a real repression of these desires. Such repression only occurs by the black magician turning into a white one, by a murderer, so to speak, turning into a master of the art of healing; and thus we can say that medical science, just as compulsion neurosis, owes its origin to the repression of the anal-sadistic drive components. The first obsessional neurotic was also the first doctor.

A case described by Brill (1914) provides an appropriate analogy. A patient, 39 years of age, suffered from compulsion neurosis. He was obsessed by a compulsion to brood over his fears and fantasies about someone being killed. His infantile sexual life was characterized by pronounced anal activity, but most remarkable of all was his inclination to cruelty. He learned early to use guns; he would shoot tiny birds, hares, and squirrels. In puberty he suddenly became full of pity, and one day felt pangs of remorse after having shot a squirrel dead. From that day onward he found it very hard to shoot. At 18, the actual compulsion neurosis set in; now he would suffer from persistent constipation. Medication would not help, until one day he invented the following game, which led to the desired result: He played with a spool of thread on which was the picture of a child. He would roll the spool and when seeing the child, stick a pin into it. After four or five minutes, he would have to go to the toilet. Later the game was shortened; he would draw a picture on a piece of paper and imagine it was a girl, and then throw his pen on the picture. When in the country, he would take his gun and fire a few shots, and when he imagined he was killing Indians, he had to go to the toilet immediately. In this case the parallel of shooting and defacating — inability to shoot and constipation — is quite clear. He even went so far as to repeat the rites of the primitive magicians, for they too would stick pins into an image, in which case the act, since it is a matter of a love charm or the revenge of a jilted lover, can also be seen as coitus (Róheim, 1921d, p. 325). The child that is rolled about on the spool signifies the feces, and the magical analogy is culminated with a bowel movement. From the game with the pen, the throwing about of the pin and pen, he had the compulsive idea that one day a pin had fallen into the garden and been swallowed by a child; originally, as is shown in the game, a desire which had turned into a tormenting fearful idea (Brill, 1914, p. 328). One step further and he could sense the compulsion to remove pins from the child's body, so as to save her from the death which he himself wished to cause.

It cannot be denied that in compulsion we have found the actual key to the beginnings of medicine. The main characteristic of this neurosis, the sensation of acting under the pressure of an irresistible compulsion, is found in two forms. First, in its original form: The medicine man thinks he wants to act differently but believes he cannot resist the dictate of an overwhelming force of spirits. In fact he observes a complicated ritual which has to be acted out at any price. If Freud occasionally refers to compulsion neurosis as the "taboo sickness," then we must say that the medicine man more than any primitive has to struggle through a primal thicket of taboos. Then there is the second form: Finding himself overcome by a sensation of irresistible compulsion, the medicine man projects this feeling onto the outside world; he conquers instead of being conquered. He cannot resist the dark desires in his unconscious, others are equally powerless to help him, and nature itself is helpless against his compulsive acts and rites. Here we come back to anality as the principle of explanation. Ferenczi (1916, p. 185) explains the infantile feeling of omnipotence as a projection of the fact that the anal urge cannot be resisted, and notes that the phase of magic words and gestures is chiefly in the service of the infant's excremental functions. In the case of the medicine man, the feeling of omnipotence is manifested in terms of an excremental symbol (the quartz crystal). Thus we should expect that the magical chants of the medicine man will be connected with excremental activity, as will his habit of collecting the most varied but useless objects in his medicine bag and investing them with libido, i.e., with magic force. The tendency of the compulsive personality to sink into deep thoughts stems from ambivalence, as well as from the far-reaching fixation of libido, and tells us a great deal about the origin of medicine and theoretical science itself.

By and large then we must say that all healing acts and methods of the primitive medicine man seem to go back to one common root. In all cases the body of the patient is cut, kneaded, or sucked; it is licked and breathed on; and an object now looked upon as a materialized form of the disease is removed.

It is difficult to imagine how this custom could have been created spontaneously and independently by a variety of peoples and races; but if we follow Tylor (1870, pp. 279–281),[9] we can understand that it must have evolved and migrated with mankind itself, and must be held to be a com-

---

9. Editors' note: At this point Róheim's subsequent theoretical shift is indicated: He alludes to the ontogenetic experience of the impact of prolonged dependence. Historically, it was under Abraham's influence that the Hungarian school (Ferenczi, Hermann, Róheim, Klein) elaborated the significance of pregenitality for character development.

mon heritage which different peoples brought with them from their prehuman ancestors. Such a view of the suction healing method as primal and prehuman is in thorough agreement with the basic biogenetic law, since we find the activity of sucking at the beginning of ontogenesis as well. Since the medicine man chiefly heals by means of sucking, we must assume a fixation at a very early stage when the chief pleasure activity of the child consists in the sucking of the mother's breast. The medicine man transfers his infantile desire for sucking onto the patient, and therefore we must say that the doctor's explorations of the patient's body in order to find the point of sickness are new editions, as it were, of the groping motions of the child seeking his mother's breast. Here we have the cultural equivalent of the well-known rescue fantasies described by psychoanalysis; owing life to mother, the doctor saves the sick.

Abraham has described the first form of libidinal development as the oral or cannibalistic phase, and what we are trying to suggest here is that the beginning of the medical profession can be found not only in prehistory, but in ontogenesis as well. Cannibalistic and sadistic fantasies in Abraham's patients could be traced back to the situation in which the child sucks blood, that is, the mother's milk, and possesses unlimited power over the passively offered breasts. A patient told me he had "cannibalistic ideas" ever since his childhood. In his fourth year he had had a nanny to whom he was very devoted. It was she who stood in the center of these cannibalistic fantasies. The patient later wished to bite into her and to swallow her whole, her hair and skin included. He would suddenly feel a desire for milk or meat, and it seemed to him as if he were looking for a substitute for human flesh. From there, the associative train of thought led him to the fantasy of biting a woman's breast, and here, we have a direct connection between meat and milk (Abraham, 1916, pp. 263–264). Similarly the medicine man just as consistently links the desire for sucking with cannibalism. We have already shown above that the medicine man or shaman incorporates his ego ideal by eating his father, and now we find that he heals the sick by sucking. Still more striking, however, is this connection in the instance of the evil sorcerer; again and again, he is described as a blood sucker and cannibal. In Central Afica the sorcerer turns himself by means of his magic into a hyena, a leopard, or any other animal that feeds on carrion. Magic and cannibalism are, in fact, described by the same term (Werner, 1906, pp. 84, 169), just as in the Botoya languages in Brazil there is only word for the sorcerer and the jaguar (Koch-Grünberg, 1910, Vol. 2, p. 105). With the Ba Thonga, the power of the evil magician is passed on through the mother and is taken in through the mother's milk. These Baloyi eat men, killing them by sucking their blood. The Baloyi has power only over his own kith and kin, and he supplies them to the other

Baloyi for the common cannibal feast. Not only the sorcerer and cannibal, but anyone who commits an act of incest is a Baloyi (Junod, 1913, Vol. 2, pp. 461-467). Among the Ewe, the witches are people who have a permanent lust for blood. They will sit upon a sleeping person and suck his blood until he is dead. Instead of blood they also drink coconut water or palm wine (Spieth, 1906, pp. 682, 724). Anal-erotic components can also be detected in the personality of the witch or *adze*, since this creature will steal people's property, and if there is nothing to steal, will eat the intestines of her victim. The "adze" also feels especially attracted to the dung heap (pp. 832, 850, 906). The system of the *subache* in the western Sudan consists of one member of a family being credited with the power of stealing the life of a fellow human being, and of being able to eat it in a cannibalistic manner (Frobenius, 1910, p. 76). A Subache cannot hold sway over anyone who is not related to him and so is by nature "owned" by him in a certain sense (p. 77). The same is the case with the Mande. But the Bosso know of another type, which is more of a blood-sucking than cannibalistic creature. This being not only sheds all its clothes, but also its own skin, and thus becomes a red creature that can enter a victim's body through any opening. In the anus the Subache has a suction device that is shaped like an elephant's trunk. This he lets out of his body, placing it into the victim's mouth or through his nostrils so as to suck out all his blood. Other Subaches have a little funnel shaped like a bloodletting cup, in which they collect blood (p. 82). In Europe we find cannibal witches and vampires, and in an Italian fairy tale the witches use a veritable bloodletting cup to suck their victim's blood (Leland, 1892; Róheim, 1920a).

We can now continue our comparison between the killing magician and the medicine man. The sorcerer steals excreta in order to burn them, and the medicine man makes people sick, but also heals them by injecting objects which symbolize excrement into their bodies and then removing them by suction. In the same way as the life-saving activity of the medicine man is a reversal of the life-giving activity of the mother, we can also notice here a partial reversal of the physiological processes. The child sucks the mother's milk and passes it out in the form of excreta; the medicine man shoots excreta into his victims and sucks back not milk but excreta. The medicine man and sorcerer belong to each other like the two sides of a coin; in the magician we find unsublimated sadistic desires, whereas in the medicine man these same desires appear in an inhibited form as a result of his identification with the victim, i.e., they appear as sublimations. The magician lets the blood of his victim flow from his veins, or sucks it until he dies; the medicine man actually does the same; he lets out the patient's blood, sucks the blood or other substances from the wound, and licks the sore spot — yet, instead of completely devouring his patient, after having prepared to do so, he heals him.[10] On the whole, the sorcerer may be taken to be an anal-erotic; the medicine man or doctor an anal character. The child plays with his excreta and reacts with hatred to any interference in his sphere of pleasure. In this hatred (directed first and foremost at the parents), Jones (1913) sees the prototype of ambivalent disturbance in later sexual life. The primitive sorcerer, repeating the course of phylogenesis, finds parental substitutes in the stranger, whose excreta he seeks and whom he simultaneously hates but also identifies with. He usually carries out magic as his main activity, and healing only as a subsidiary one; later on, the healing act alone becomes capable of entering consciousness, yet for a long time to come the sorcerer can be accused of murderous intent by those who have some sense of his unconscious wishes. "The cheapest gutter joke of all time and a constant trump card in the hands of all fools has been to declare the doctor the murderer of his patients," says Höllander (1905, p. 174). The doctor has even been envied, as it were, for his established right: "*Solis medicis licet impune occidere*" (p. 174). If Martial writes, "*Nuper erat medicus nunc est vespillo Diaulus, Quod vespillo facit, fercerat et medicus*" (p. 175), then here it is said in jest, but it was certainly a popular belief at one time that the evil magician and later the doctor could turn themselves into cadaver-eating animals. But the first doctor is also the first collector, for he is the only one among primitive people who exercises his craft and earns his livelihood not by directly killing an animal, but by receiving a fee or payment. As an anal character, he is the first capitalist; for even in the Middle Ages we read, "*dat Galenus opes,*" and what kind these "*opes*" were originally we can also find out: "*Stercus et urina medici sunt prandia prima, Ex aliis paleas existis collige grana*" (p. 181). In Australia, the quartz crystal (anal eroticism) and the lethal magic bone of a dead man (sadism) are the two attributes of a doctor; among the people of the Middle Ages, bloodletting was the primal form of surgery, and the purgative the alpha and omega of internal medicine. "The trifolium of therapeutics was the enema, bloodletting and purging," states Höllander (p. 220). Just as the aggressive acts of compulsive neurotics frequently are interpreted by them as protective devices springing from their concern for the lives of beloved relatives, so in the same way the sadistic acts of the medicine man are purported to serve to save the patient's life. Actually, both the magician and the medicine man should already be

---

10. Here my remarks converge most closely with those of Dr. Simmel who in his Berlin
     Congress paper said that the patient during analysis actually eats the doctor, i.e.,
     introjects him (assumes him to be his ego ideal), and then identifies the eaten one with
     his own excreta. The identification of an "eaten" love object with the feces was estab-
     lished by Dr. Abraham in melancholics in his discussion of that paper.

called compulsive neurotics, except that the obsession of the magician is still in a more primitive phase of development. In the case of the magician, we have an inhibition of anal-sadistic activity and a shift to a substitute;[11] in the case of the medicine man, however, the reversal or reaction formation is caused by identification with the patient, and we have already shown that eating the father must be seen as the primal form of this identification. Correspondingly, we find both the magician and the medicine man as representatives of the father imago, since they have, in the cannibal feast, identified themselves with the primal father, the father who gives life as the medicine man saves it. In actual fact, cannibalism plays an important part in the lives of the magician and the medicine man; they acquire ability and power by eating human flesh, or by indicating that they will eat the victim and thus heal him. It cannot be doubted that the application of the lips to a sore spot of a fellow being has to be regarded as a residue of the act of eating him, and from this destructive action has developed the great life-protecting organization of civilized humanity with all its medical faculties and associations.

We are now asking: Did all the brothers eat of the father's flesh? Surely only those who at the time of the father's murder were sufficiently strong to secure a bite for themselves; and this is why, in those who also took part in the subsequent fraternal war, repression by oral and anal countercathexis took place. These men formed the first male secret society, and the most repressed among them developed secret rituals and rites (Rivers, 1917–1918, p. 19). Within the group, there must already have existed dispositional differences, discrepancies in the distribution of libido over the partial instincts. Some, certainly, must have been more fixated on the oral level, and these would have maintained a lifelong fantasy investment in the eating of the father and identification with his decaying corpse; others, however, less orally fixated, would have overcome this preoccupation after the conclusion of the normal mourning phase. For the former, the father they had eaten had now become the source of repression within them, the block that inhibited them from carrying out their genitally based oedipal wishes and forced them to regress into pregenitality. The original susceptibility of these men to this form of repression provides the basis for compulsion neurosis today, just as historically it gave rise to medicine.

Let us hear what Parkinson (1907) has to say about the inhabitants of the Gazelle Peninsula: "The anatomic expertise of the natives is presumably due to cannibalism, and the knowledge of the human body and its organs, which was acquired in this way, is quite considerable; one could say

---

11. Burning the excreta in place of anal-sadistic coitus.

that their knowledge in this respect far surpasses that of an educated average European. They are able to give the exact position of the individual parts of the body, and can judge whether the liver, lungs, stomach, and other organs, are affected" (p. 107). If the knowledge of anatomy of primal man stems from the cannibal feast, we may well be on the right track in retracing medical science to that same source.

The magician is thus a cannibal and blood-sucker, blood becoming a substitute for mother's milk. When the brothers had killed the father, eaten his flesh, and drunk his blood, they regressed into the first phase of libido development, the cannibalistic oral-erotic phase.

By repeating the act of sucking in the theophagy of eating the father, the countercathexis of the father's corpse was created as a basis of the first inhibition of the Oedipus complex. The cathexis that served the libidinization of the corpse was, however, withdrawn from the mother, the primal object, and was to retain the traces of its primal goal even in its new place of application. If the Arunta let their blood flow on the rock underneath which the primal ancestor of the kangaroo totem is buried, the young kangaroo spirits jump forth from the rock. Yet we have seen that letting the blood flow freely symbolizes ejaculation, and the rocky grave of the ancestor from which the kangaroos are born is the vagina. Underneath the rock, however, the totemic father lies buried (Spencer and Gillen, 1904).[12] Thus it seems as if the corpse, by fixation of infantile oral-erotic libido in the cannibal feast, has been invested with maternal qualities. This libidinal shift also appears to be hidden behind the rebirth aspect of male initiation rites. The youths, it is said, are killed by a male creature and eaten; this means, by reversal, that they eat the murdered father, and since this meal revives the pleasurable traces of the first sucking act, they now become their father's children, reborn from the father, and identify with him instead of the mother. The rebirth is an absolution from the female, and is meant to draw the youths more closely to male company (Reik, 1919, p. 114).[13] There are, however, a number of rites in which the rebirth of the father, who is also the mother here, is represented. In his treatise on the Kol Nidre, Reik (1919) has pointed out the connection between birth and totemic sacrifice. He seems, however, to have missed the one point that passing through the insides of a killed animal is symbolic of

---

12. The description in the text naturally presupposes the result of Róheim's (1925) interpretation (translator's note).

13. Another source of a condensation of the father and mother imagoes can be shown in the development of genitality. In lower species, the male "weapons" serve to force coitus on the female (opponent and sexual object, father and mother, in one person); in higher species the males fight among each other for the female.

death. "Brotherhood may just have been the original sense of the rite in which a dissected animal, split tree or cleft rock would assume a motherly significance. Jahve's passing through the dismembered animals may well be equated to the Jews' passing through the Red Sea, and be taken as a birth rite" (Róheim, 1920, p. 398). Among the Basuto, an act of purification is followed by a man being pulled through a hole in a slaughtered animal (Frazer, 1919, Vol. 1, p. 408). When Peleus took the city of Jolcos, he killed its king, Akastos, and its queen, Astydameia, and let his army enter the city through the cut-up parts of her body. The king's wife, Astydameia, sometimes referred to as Hippolyte, was in love with Peleus and had been turned down by him; here we see a well-known means of defense against mother love, since the courtship is projected onto the mother. Incited by his spouse, the king now wants to kill Peleus and leaves him behind in the wilds as prey for the Centaurs, but Peleus is saved by them and Chiron (exposure formula). The saga therefore deals with the killing of the father, and the taking possession of the city-mother, and we have to look upon the killing of Astydameia and the passing through her cleft body as incestuous coitus and rebirth, respectively (Roscher & Seelinger, 1884–1886, p. 209). After giving birth, the Transylvanian gypsy gets rid of her impurity by countering the act of giving birth by being reborn; if she has had a son, she will cut up a cock, if a daughter, a hen; then she will walk through the pieces, whereupon the men eat the cock, or the women the hen (Frazer, 1919, Vol. 1, pp. 410, 411). In the primal horde, after the brothers had killed the father, they expiated their dead by making the hated father into a love object and transferring some of their libido to the corpse. They ate of the father as they had, as sucklings, drunk of mother's milk; and they may even have walked through a corpse in order to free themselves from the sin of incest, by a substitute fulfillment. Giraldus Cambrensis (Lynch, 1848–1852) tells of a wild tribe in old Ireland near Kenel Cunil, where he observed the following ceremonial at the investiture of a new king. The people gathered from all sides, and a white mare (mother symbol) was led into their midst. The king-to-be approached on all fours like a foal; the mare was slaughtered, then cut into pieces and cooked. The meat was eaten by the king and all present. He had to bathe in the broth and drink of it while doing so; drinking not in human but in animal fashion, with his tongue. Why did he behave in this beastlike manner?

Let us now briefly summarize the origins of totemism as we have discussed them elsewhere, in a few sentences. In his pioneering study Freud (1913) has already indicated that the choice of an animal as a substitute figure for the father could occur only after the murder, in a situation full of regret and fear. Without going into details, we have ourselves arrived at the following conclusions: (1) The oldest totemic animals are corpse-eating creatures,[14] and (2) the totemistic Intichiuma ceremonies are repetitions of the primal clan fight in the period of estrus, and subsequent period of mourning. In human prehistory there was no repression, but there were indeed two obstacles to protect the ego against the excessive claims of the libido — first, the mammalian condition of estrus and periodicity, and second, the primal father's resistance. When the human species, due to improved feeding conditions, lost the primate estrus pattern, the ego had to defend or protect itself against the dangers of the incessant claims of genitality. This problem arose especially after the death of the primal father, and its solution was achieved by means of the following psychosexual mechanism. The consumption of the father's flesh was a basic identification and allowed for the formation of an ego ideal which blocked the way to mother. In the act of theophagy, the corpse of the father was cathected with libido, just as the mother's breast had been. Thus the feared and hated live father turned into the beloved dead father; yet, since this love was denied an adequate requital, it was in turn changed into fear. The pivotal point of these shifts of libido was, however, the eating of the father, and this is why the guilt-laden conscience of the murderer sees in animals that have eaten of the corpse a representation of the dead father, since they too are identifying with him. Now he fears the punishment of being eaten up by these animals; and behind this phobia is hidden the wish to be used sexually by the father. This is the explanation of the wolf phobia in Freud's (1918) case history of an infantile neurosis, and we can see that infantile phobic hysteria is an attempt to fend off premature libido by the ego. In the history of the species, however, the need for this defense can have arisen only after the disappearance of the clear division that separates periods of genitality and ego instincts from one another. Thus we come to the conclusion that animal phobias are to be looked at not only in terms of their unconscious contents, but also in terms of libidinal economics as repetitions of phylogenetic totemism.

---

14. In agreement with this view, Dr. Simmel speaks of a pregenital totem animal, i.e., of the origin of totemism on an oral-erotic basis. The animals that feed on the father's corpse are father symbols, but at the same time mother symbols, since the corpse after death returns to the inside of a living being (uterus of the mother) (Rank, 1922, p. 160). The father's corpse had by being eaten turned into the mother, and vice versa — the animals that had fed on the father's corpse, the first totemic animals, were both mother and father symbols. From the father, the totemic animals have the forbidding side, from the mother, the protective side of their natures.

Editors' note: See also Boyer, 1979, pp. 21-22, 1980, pp. 268-269; Wallace, 1983.

The substitute formation of homosexual desires[15] is likewise the characteristic mechanism of paranoia. The paranoiac feels constantly endangered by the supernatural powers of certain people who can easily be identified as new representations of the father. In association with Freud's (1921) work on group psychology, I have already tried to find the clue to the relationship between feelings of being persecuted and the homoerotic impulses in the primal horde situation. The brothers, who loved each other while being banished, turned into enemies after the primal father's death, becoming rivals and hostile persecutors of each other; and in facing the sum of his enemies, each brother could behold the resurrection of the dead father's threat (Róheim, 1922, p. 209). He has in fact eaten his father, and the fear of him is now being projected outward as fear of the brothers. By devouring the father and killing him, he also has sexual relations with him (displacement upward), and here also may well lie the clue to the female attitude of the shaman toward his protective spirit (Czaplicka, 1914; Ling-Roth, 1896). The shaman identifies himself in an oral-erotic manner with his mother and loves his father whom he has eaten. In the manic state, this god will speak out of himself, and his hysterical fits, his fighting with the ancestral spirit, are presumably to be understood as representations of the coital act. Perhaps the role of the shaman originates not at the sickbed but at the burial place. For in Australia, after every death the medicine man is called in, and while laying his head on the corpse or rubbing himself with the liquid of the corpse, he proceeds to accuse an unknown double of himself, a strange medicine man, of having done just what he has done: causing the death of someone by evil magic, i.e., killing and eating the father. His aggressiveness against the father and against the corpse takes two forms: On the one hand, it becomes an unmitigated aggressiveness against the enemy, projected beyond the boundaries of the unity of the tribe (the avenging expedition); on the other, it appears in a mitigated form in the act of healing, directed toward the sick as semi-corpses of his own tribe.

Now we can see how the Egyptians are proved right. Every dead man is an Osiris, i.e., the death rites are repetitions of the deeply upsetting events after the death of the primal father. The libidinal tie that kept the group, i.e., the brother horde, united, ceases — and the first panic results (Freud, 1921).[16] Thus primitive peoples flee in senseless fear from the grave, and

---

15. Passively, the wish to be used sexually by the father; actively, the oral-erotic coitus of the father during theophagy.

16. I have commented elsewhere on the custom of the most primitive tribes to leave the corpse where it is and just run away from it.

Plutarch relates: "When first the pans and satyrs living in the environs of Chemnis learned of that sad event, the death of Osiris, and spread the news of that happening, the sudden terror and confusion of the mass broke out into a state of panic" (1850, Chap. 14, p. 23). The sons have now regained the narcissistic ego ideal of their childhood, which they had given up to a common object when entering the group; the man who has eaten the father now becomes a greater and higher being than he could have been in the group. And yet, he has also lost something: his libidinal tie with the group. He is on the way from group to individual psychology, to a role as leader, but he is nevertheless menaced by a great many threats from the hostile brothers standing in his path. After the death of an African god-king, a state of wild anarchy breaks out, a *bellum omnium contra omnes* (Frazer, 1910, Vol. 2, p. 350) that lasts until a new ruler assumes the throne (Frazer, 1911a, p. 117, 1911b; Frobenius, 1915, Vol. 3, p. 149). This was also the case in the primal horde, and during these repeated periods of unrest and upheaval the human species acquired the first of the psychic mechanisms that we can today observe in most neuroses. Libidinal gratification was inhibited by the other brothers and transformed into fear, then projected onto an animal as a representation of the father. The first animal phobia was the consequence, establishing a preliminary stage of totemism, and it was to return in the form of phobic hysteria. With the incorporation of the father in the cannibal feast, inhibition had become internalized; it was directed at first against the repetition of the act from which it had originated. One was thus not allowed to eat human flesh; later, in the totemistic phase, the meat of a certain animal species was prohibited, and finally, food of any kind. The war of the brothers at the graveside of the father is introjected, giving rise to a conflict within the ego — between the ego ideal (father's party) and the actual ego (revolutionary party) — and from the symptomatic acts of this conflict, or the shortened repetition of the brothers' war, emerged the rites of primitive mourning or primal melancholia. The mourning ends in a manic phase; the conflict, which had at first been real and then became intrapsychic, is again projected into the outside world by waging a campaign of vengeance against the enemy as murderer of the father. As at one time the horde was reunited by the approach of another horde, the fight between ego and ego ideal ceases in this manic phase, and both coincide, ostensibly as avengers of the father, but in reality in order to repeat the deed on a new object. For after the brothers had killed the enemy, they identified with him as they had with the father, and married his widows and daughters as during the aftermath in the primal horde. The war is followed by exogamy, sadism by object love. With the appearance of a second horde on the stage of prehistory, the compulsive repetition of the eternal oedipal conflicts is broken, and the horde becomes a tribe with two exogamous clans.[17] In some of the brothers, an anal-erotic disposition will dominate; these will identify the decaying corpse with excreta and regress to the anal-sadistic stage of organization, inhibited now by their newly gained ego ideal from a genital expression of the oedipal urges. The libido invested in the corpse transfers the properties of its primal aim onto the new one; the image of the nurturing mother is revived in the devoured father, but also in the swollen body of the patient. Inhibited by the positive mother fixation, the sadistic acts turn into healing methods, and the sublimation of anal eroticism leads ultimately to the development of antisepsis. The primitive medicine man should be looked upon as the father of religion and science, and he is the direct heir of the obsessional neurotics of the primal horde. The oral-erotically, anal-erotically, homoerotically tinged strivings attached to the cannibalistic feast formed the dynamic basis for repression, by inhibiting the genital incestuous drive and thus initiating morality. In a paranoid fashion these drives are projected by the shaman onto a band of alien and supernatural persecutors; and this paranoid projection, derived from the death of the father, gives rise to belief in the supernatural and to nationalism as a homoerotic identification among the brothers and a projection of their aggressiveness onto the alien.

As a result of conflict between one group and another, between one primal king and another, the members of the brother horde suffered a series of unwelcome traumata to which they reacted with certain shifts in their libidinal structure. These primordial reactions remain at the base of all human civilization, and are repeated in archaic form in the psychoneurosis. All these reactions once constituted powerful weapons in man's fight for existence; they led to the development of society, religion, and science. Numerous transitional phases of this kind, in the life of the individual until puberty, composed the great transitional phase or puberty of mankind, from the nursery of the primal horde to manhood in the encounter with an alien horde. The road leads from the primal horde to the tribe, from the compulsion incest rigid-conservation repetition to plasticity and progress through exogamy.

BIBLIOGRAPHY

ABRAHAM, K. (1916). The First Pregenital Stage of the Libido. *Selected Papers.* London: Hogarth Press, 1948, pp. 248–279.
ANGAS, G. F. (1847). *Savage Life and Scenes in Australia and New Zealand: Being an*

---

17.   As the men of the conquered tribe are killed off, two groups of women remain — the incestuous and non-incestuous love objects — as foundations of the two clans.

Artist's Impressions of Countries and People in the Antipodes, Vols. 1 & 2, 2nd ed. London: Smith, Elder.

ATKINSON, J. J. (1903). *Primal Law.* London: Longmans, Green.

BANCROFT, H. H. (1875). *The Native Races of the Pacific States of North America,* Vols. 1 & 2. New York: D. Appleton.

BARTELS, M. C. A. (1893). *Die Medizin der Naturvölker Ethnologische Beiträge zur Urgeschichte der Medizin.* Leipzig: T. Grieben (L. Fernau).

BEVERIDGE, P. (1883). On the Aborigines Inhabiting the Great Lacustrine and Riverine Depression of the Lower Murray, Lower Lachlan and Lower Darling. *Journal of the Royal Society of New South Wales,* Vol. 17.

BOYER, L. B. (1979). *Childhood and Folklore. A Psychoanalytic Study of Apache Personality.* New York: Library of Psychological Anthropology.

_____ (1980). Folklore, Anthropology and Psychoanalysis. *J. Psychoanal. Anthropology,* 3:259-279.

BRILL, A. A. (1914). *Psychoanalysis; its Theories and Practical Application,* 2nd ed. Philadelphia & London: W. B. Saunders.

BRUGSCH, H. K. (1891). *Religion und Mythologie der Alten Aegypter.* Leipzig: J. C. Hinrich'sche Buchhandlung.

BUDGE, E. A. T. W. (1904). *The Gods of the Egyptians; or, Studies in Egyptian Mythology,* Vols. 1 & 2. Chicago: Open Court.

BUSCHAN, G. H. T. (1909) (c. 1910). *Illustrierte Volkerkunde.* Stuttgart: Strecker & Schroder.

CODRINGTON, R. H. (1891). *The Melanesians: Studies in Their Anthropology and Folklore.* Oxford: Clarendon Press.

CRAWLEY, A. E. (1909). *The Idea of the Soul.* London: A. & C. Black.

CZAPLICKA, M. A. (1914). *Aboriginal Siberia: a Study in Social Anthropology.* Oxford: Clarendon Press.

ELHORST, H. J. (1914). Remarks in *Studien zur Semitischen Philologie und Religiongeschichte,* ed. K. Marti, abstr. M. Lambert. Giessen: Topelmann, pp. 117-128.

ERMAN, A. (1909). *Die Aegyptische Religion,* 2nd ed. Berlin: G. Reimer.

FERENCZI, S. (1916). Stages in the Development of the Sense of Reality. *Sex in Psychoanalysis.* New York: Basic Books, 1950, pp. 213-239.

FLÜGEL, J. C. (1921). *The Psycho-Analytical Study of the Family.* London: The International Psycho-Analytical Press.

FORBES, H. O. (1884). On Some of the Tribes of the Island of Tuma. *Journal of the Anthropological Institute,* 13:402-430.

FRAZER, J. G. (1906). *Adonis, Attis, Osiris: Studies in the History of Oriental Religion.* London: Macmillan.

_____ (1910). *Totemism and Exogamy: A Treatise on Certain Early Forms of Superstition and Society,* Vols. 1, 2, 3, & 4. London: Macmillan.

_____ (1911a). *Taboo and the Perils of the Soul.* London: Macmillan.

_____ (1911b). *The Dying God.* London: Macmillan.

_____ (1919). *Folk-Lore in the Old Testament: Studies in Comparative Religion, Legend and Law,* Vol. 1. London: Macmillan.

FREUD, S. (1900). The Interpretation of Dreams. *S.E.,* 4 & 5. London: Hogarth Press, 1953.

_____ (1913). Totem and Taboo. *S.E.,* 13:1-161. London: Hogarth Press, 1955.

_____ (1917). Mourning and Melancholia. *S.E.,* 14:237-258. London: Hogarth Press, 1957.

_____ (1918). From the History of an Infantile Neurosis. *S.E.*, 17:1–22. London: Hogarth Press, 1955.

_____ (1920). Beyond the Pleasure Principle. *S.E.*, 18:7–66. London: Hogarth Press, 1955.

_____ (1921). Group Psychology and the Analysis of the Ego. *S.E.*, 18:69–144. London: Hogarth Press, 1955.

_____ (1923). The Ego and the Id. *S.E.*, 19:12–67. London: Hogarth Press, 1961.

FROBENIUS, L. (1910). *Kulturtypen aus dem Westsudan... (Ergänzungsband XXXV, Petermanne Mitteilungen, no. 166).* Gotha: J. Perthes.

_____ (1915). *Und Afrika Sprach...,* Vols. 1, 2, & 3. Berlin: Vita.

GREY, G. (1841). *Journals of Two Expeditions of Discovery in North-West and Western Australia during the Years 1837, 1838, 1839...,* Vols. 1 & 2. London: T. & W. Boone.

HERTZ, R. (1907). Contribution à une Étude sur la Représentation Collective de la Mort. *L'Année Sociologique,* 10:48–137.

HÖLLANDER, E. (1905). *Die Karikatur und Satire in der Medizin.* Stuttgart: F. Enka.

HOWITT, A. W. (1886). On Australian Medicine Men; or Doctors and Wizards of Some Australian Tribes. *Journal of the Anthropological Institute of Great Britain and Ireland,* 16:23–59.

_____ (1904). *The Native Tribes of South-East Australia.* London: Macmillan.

HUBERT, H., & MAUSS, M. (1909). L'Origine des Pouvoirs Magiques dans les Sociétés Australiennes. In *Mélanges D'Histoire des Religions.* Paris: Alcan.

JONES, E. (1913). Hate and Anal Erotism in the Obessional Neurosis. *Papers on Psycho-Analysis,* 2nd ed. London: Baillière, Tindall & Cox, 1918, pp. 540–548.

JUNOD, H. A. (1913). *The Life of a South African Tribe,* Vols. 1 & 2. London: D. Nutt.

KLEIWEG DE ZWAAN, J. P. (1913). *Die Insel Nias bei Sumatra. Vol. I. Die Heilkunde der Niasser.* The Hague: M. Nijhoff.

KOCH-GRÜNBERG, T. (1910). *Zwei Jahre unter den Indianern. Reisen in Nordwest-Brasilien,* 1903/1905, Vols. 1 & 2. Berlin: E. Wasmuth.

LAMBERT, M. (1921). Review of *Studien zur semitischen Philologie und Religiongeschichte,* ed. J. Wellhausen. Giessen: Topelmann, 1914. *Revue des Études Juives,* 72:75–79, p. 78.

LELAND, C. G. (1892). *Etruscan Roman Remains in Popular Tradition.* London: T. Fisher Unwin.

LING-ROTH, H. (1896). *The Natives of Sarawak and British North Boreno,* Vol. 1. London: Truslove & Hanson.

LIPPERT, J. (1886–1887). *Kulturgeschichte der Menschheit,* Vols. 1 & 2. Leipzig.

LYNCH, J. (1848–1852). *Cambrensis Eversus, seu Portius Historica Fides in Rebus Hibernicis Giraldo Cambrensis Abrogata, in quo Plerasque Justi Historici Dotes Desiderari Plerosque Naevos Inesse, Ostendit Gratianus Lucius,* Vols. 1, 2, & 3. Dublin: Irish Celtic Society.

OLDFIELD, A. (1865). On the Aborigines of Australia. *Transactions of the Ethnological Society of London.* New Series, Vol. 3. London: John Murray.

PALMER, E. (1884). Notes on Some Australian Tribes. *Journal of the Anthropological Institute of Great Britain and Ireland,* Vol. 13.

PARKER, C. S. (1905). *The Euahlayi Tribe: Study of Aboriginal Life in Australia, by K. Langloh Parker.* London: A. Constable.

PARKINSON, R. H. R. (1907). *Dreissig Jahre in der Südsee...* Stuttgart: Strecker & Schroder.

PLUTARCH, M. (1850). *Über Isis und Osiris ... mit Übersetzung und Erläterungen von Gustav Parthey.* Berlin: Nicolais.

———— (1936). *Isis and Osiris*, trans. F. C. Babbitt. Cambridge: Harvard University Press.

PREUSS, K. T. (1896). Menschenopfer und Selbst verstümmelung bei der Totentrauer in Amerika. In *Festschrift für Adolf Bastian zu Seinem 70 Geburtstage, 26 Juni 1896*. Berlin: D. Reimer (E. Vohsen).

RANK, O. (1922). Die Don Juan Gestalt. Ein Beitrag zum Verständnis der sozialen Funktion der Dichtkunst. *Imago,* 8:142–196.

RAPP, A. (1884–1886). Die Erinyen als Huterinnen der Familienrechte. In *Ausführliches Lexikon der Griechischen und Römischen Mythologie,* ed. W. H. Roscher. Leipzig: B. G. Teubner.

REIK, T. (1919). *Probleme der Religionspsychologie.* Leipzig & Vienna: Internationaler Psychoanalytischer Verlag.

RIVERS, W. H. (1914). *The History of Melanesian Society,* Vols. 1 & 2. Cambridge: Cambridge University Press.

———— (1917–1918). *Dreams and Primitive Culture.* London: Longmans, Green.

ROEDER, G. (1909–1915). Tiere und Symbole des Set. III. Die Tiere des Set. In *Ausführliches Lexikon der Griechischen und Römischen Mythologie,* ed. W. H. Roscher. Leipzig: B. G. Teubner.

———— (1915). *Urkunden zur Religion des Alten Ägypten.* Jena: E. Diederichs.

RÓHEIM, G. (1914). *A Varazsero Fogalmának Eredete. [Origin of the Concept of Magic Power.]* Budapest: Posner Károly Lajos és Fia.

———— (1920a). *Adalékok a Magyar Néphithez (Második Sorozat). [Contributions on Hungarian Folklore.]* Budapest: V. Hornyánszky.

———— (1920b). Zur Psychologie der Bundesriten. *Imago,* 6:397–399.

———— (1921a). Das Selbst. (Eine Vorläufige Mitteilung Schluss.) IV. Aussenseele. *Imago,* 7:453–504.

———— (1921b). Steinheiligtum und Grab. Ethnologische Bemerkungen über Totemismus und Kulturschichten in Australien. *Internationale Zeitschrift für Psychoanalyse,* 7:522–525.

———— (1921c). Das Selbst. (Eine Vorläufige Mitteilung.) I. Die Magische Bedeutung des Menschlichen Körpers. *Imago,* 7:1–39.

———— (1921d). Das Selbst. (Eine Vorläufige Mitteilung). III. Eidolon. *Imago,* 7:310–348.

———— (1922). Völkerpsychologisches. In *Massenpsychologie und Ich-Analyse,* by S. Freud. *Internationale Zeitschrift für Psychoanalyse,* 8:209–218.

———— (1925). *Australian Totemism: A Psycho-Analytic Study in Anthropology.* London: G. Allen & Unwin.

———— (1950). Oedipus Complex Magic and Culture. *Psychoanalysis and the Social Sciences,* 2:173–228. New York: International Universities Press.

ROSCHER, W. H., & SEELINGER, F. K. (1884–1886). "Akostas." In *Ausführliches Lexikon der Griechischen und Römischen Mythologie,* ed. W. H. Roscher. Leipzig: B. G. Teubner.

SALVADO, R. (1851). *Memorie Storiche dell' Australia, Particolarmente della Missione Benedettina di Nuova Norcia e degli Usi e Costumi delgi Australiani.* Rome: S. Congregazione de Propaganda Fide.

SELIGMANN, C. G. (1910). *The Melanesians of British New Guinea.* Cambridge: Cambridge University Press.

SHORTLAND, E. (1882). *Maori Religion and Mythology.* London: Longmans, Green.

SPENCER, H. (1879–1896). *The Principles of Sociology,* Vols. 1, 2, & 3. London.

SPENCER, W. B., & GILLEN, F. J. (1899). *The Native Tribes of Central Australia.* London: Macmillan.

————, & ———— (1904). *Northern Tribes of Central Australia.* London: Macmillan.

SPIETH, J. (1906). *Die Éwe-Stämme: Material zur Kunde des Éwe-Volkes in Deutsch-Togo.* Berlin: D. Reimer (E. Vohsen).

SPIX, J. B., & MARTIUS, C. F. P. (1823). *Reise in Brasilien,* Vols. 1 & 2. Munich: M. Lindauer.

STOW, G. W. (1905). *The Native Races of South Africa; A History of the Intrusion of the Hottentots and Bantu into the Hunting Grounds of the Bushmen, the Aborigines of the Country.* London: S. Sonnenschein.

THRELKELD, L. E. (1892). *An Australian Language as Spoken by the Awabakal.* Sydney: C. Potter.

TYLOR, E. B. (1870). *Researches in the Early History of Mankind and the Development of Civilization,* 2nd ed. London: J. Murray.

WALLACE, E. R., IV (1983). *Freud and Anthropology: A History and Reappraisal.* New York: International Universities Press.

WERNER, A. (1906). *The Natives of British Central Africa.* London: A. Constable.

WILKEN, G. A. (1912). *De Verspreide Geschriften,* Vols. 1, 2, 3, & 4. Semarang: G. C. T. Van Dorp.

WUNDT, W. (1914). Totemismus und Stammesorganization in Australien. *Anthropos,* 9:299–325.

3
Crisis and Continuity in the Personality of an Apache Shaman

L. BRYCE BOYER, M.D., GEORGE A. DE VOS, Ph.D., and RUTH M. BOYER, Ph.D.

Recently, we wrote of the critical experiences, and the intrapsychic conflicts, of Dawnlight, an Apache woman, as she assumed the shamanic status (Boyer, Boyer, and De Vos, 1982). Her personal history with its problems and successes was presented in the context of the socialization patterns and social structure of her group from data amassed over a period of a quarter of a century.[1, 2] This information was completed by a

1. The Boyers have been engaged in a combined anthropological and psychoanalytic study of the Apaches of the Mescalero Indian Reservation in conjunction with other anthropologists and psychologists since 1957. Their longest period of continuous residence on the reservation lasted for almost 15 months in 1959–1960. They have spent some period of time there during each of the past 28 years. The ultimate purpose of the ongoing research is to delineate the interactions among social structure, socialization patterns, and personality organization. Their principal anthropological collaborator is Harry W. Basehart, Professor Emeritus of the University of New Mexico, who has mainly studied social structure. R. M. Boyer's major contribution has been an extensive and intensive study of socialization processes (R. M. Boyer, 1962). L. B. Boyer's initial research stratagem was to conduct psychotherapeutic interviews in which his actions were almost limited to interpreting transference and resistance. By the end of the 1959–1960 stay on the reservation, the researchers had concluded, in agreement with Devereux and La Barre (1961), that the study of expressive culture offered the best available means of understanding these interactions. In consequence, much of the Boyers' subsequent activities have been in that direction. Early on, the value for the research project of projective psychological test protocols became very evident, particularly those obtained by the Rorschach test. The principal psychological collaborator prior to De Vos's participation was the late Bruno Klopfer.
   The research has been partially supported by NIMH Grants M-2013 and M-3088 and Faculty Grants from the University of California at Berkeley.
2. Detailed data pertaining to Apache socialization and social structure are to be found in Basehart (1959, 1960), L. B. Boyer (1964a), R. M. Boyer (1962, 1964), Kunstadter (1960), MacLachlan (1962), and Opler (1933, 1941, 1969).

Rorschach protocol obtained from Dawnlight two days after her first public performance, during which she assumed a previously unreported, idiosyncratic role. This paper reexamines the issues raised in previous publications in the light of a Rorschach test administered two years later.

INTRODUCTION

The formal study of shaminism essentially began in northeast Asia,
where an ecstatic aspect is prominent (Ducey, 1976, 1979; Eliade, 1951;
Lommel, 1967). The Tungusic-Siberian shamans were found to have been
recruited from the "excitable," "the half crazy," and the "deviant"
(Bogoras, 1907; Czaplicka, 1914; Shirokogoroff (1924). Ackerknecht
(1943), extrapolating from the observations and formulation of the
above-named students of Siberian shamanism and generalizing on the basis of a simplistic cultural definition of normality, held the shaman to have
been "cured" of adolescent schizophrenia.[3] Howells (1956, pp. 129–144),
summarizing the popular view, found the shaman to belong to a "psychological type" combining features of the severe hysteric and the schizophrenic (see also Silverman, 1967).

The ecstatic aspect so prominent in Asian shamanism is largely absent in
the behavior of American Indians assuming a shamanic healing role
(Luckert, 1979, p. 12). All the same, in his classic article, Devereux (1956)
held the shamans with whom he had contact in the Southwest invariably to
be psychologically disturbed. He asked whether a "shamanistic and/or
ethnic psychosis" (1) is the opening gambit of an idiosyncratic psychosis,
(2) masks, "at the later stage," an underlying idiosyncratic psychosis, or
(3) represents the terminal, restitutive manifestations of an idiosyncratic
psychosis. In one of the few detailed investigations of individuals during
their accession to shamanic status, Day and Davidson (1976; Davidson
and Day, 1974), studying a Pilipina becoming a shaman, found evidence
supporting Devereux's third hypothesis.

Kroeber (1940) found not only shamans but the whole lay public of
"primitive societies" to be involved in psychopathology, noting that "the
psychopathologies which get rewarded among primitives are the mild or
transient ones," particularly of "the hysteric type, involving suggestibility

---

3. This formulation predates Freud's (1911) idea that the hallucinatory and delusional
symptoms of psychosis are attempts at reconstituting a shattered ego. He wrote: "[that]
which we take to be a pathological product, is in reality an attempt at recovery, a process
of reconstructions" (p. 71). Loewald (1979) has illustrated some of the complexities involved in defining psychological normality.

of half-conscious volition" (p. 318). "The rewards seem to be reserved for individuals who can claim abnormal powers and controls, not for those *who are controlled*" (p. 318). Kroeber's inference was clear: that the shaman is personally better organized and socially more effective, even though he shares whatever indigenous psychopathology may exist. Boyer (1961, 1962, 1964a) agreed with Kroeber primarily on the basis of fieldwork with Apaches. A Rorschach study (Boyer, Klopfer et al., 1964) indicated that shamans are not necessarily individuals who, through assuming the shaman's role, have reintegrated after a serious psychological illness. However, some manifest, as do some artists, an ability to use regression in the service of the ego (Kris, 1952). They have integrative capacities that not only allow them to adapt, but are socially useful and are sought after by others. The protocols of the Apache shamans varied in their manifestations of creativity, liveliness, and hysterical traits. The record of the one shaman who was experiencing a life and professional crisis, as was Dawnlight, revealed perseverative qualities reminiscent of schizophrenia, but other responsive manifestations pointed instead to hysterical characterological features with oral and phallic fixations (Klopfer and Boyer, 1961). There was also evidence of sexual identity confusion in his record, another feature in common with the protocol of Dawnlight. The variability found in the Rorschachs of Apache shamans was similar to that found in the Rorschachs of a series of Okinawan shamans collected by Lebra and studied by De Vos (n.d.).

Our present case, Dawnlight, gives clinical evidence of having functioned previously with a more stable personality pattern, which decompensated somewhat under the stress of social circumstances such that some underlying weaknesses were exacerbated. Nevertheless, she has also been able to compensate by calling on inner resources, directed toward a form of social integration, that were strengthened by the social expectations of her group, which needed someone to take on the role of healer.

As do other Apaches of the Mescalero Indian Reservation, Dawnlight believes that the shaman may use his[4] supernatural power at will for culture-supporting purposes or in the service of witchcraft. She was convinced that she might unintentionally harm her patients. She conceptualized herself as a parent with the capacity to be alternately totally good or totally evil. At some level of consciousness she clearly equated shamanism with parenthood.

Dawnlight's record, like those of some other Apache shamans, revealed emotionally expressive content that was notably symbolic in nature. Typically, Apache records are relatively bland and commonplace and their

---

4.   For the sake of brevity, the male pronoun is used generically in this paper.

"psychopathology," if the term may be used, is expressed by heightened emotional constriction (Boyer, De Vos, and Boyer, 1983; Day, Boyer, and De Vos, 1975). Dawnlight's protocol revealed that in the depth of her regression there was a resemblance to psychosis in a fashion similar to the shaman whose Rorschach was discussed earlier (Klopfer and Boyer, 1961).

The record revealed a content of preoccupation with a homosexual conflict and reflected her conscious anxiety lest her internal badness prevail and cause her unintentionally to become a witch; it also portrayed her equation of shamanism with parenthood.

This paper summarizes relevant information concerning Apache religiomedical philosophies and practices and the information provided previously. It also supplies clinical data obtained during the two subsequent years, and presents a second Rorschach protocol and a discussion comparing the two protocols.

Although Dawnlight's position as a shaman and her possession of supernatural power appear to be strongly credited by members of her and her husband's extended families, other culture mates are less supportive and she herself now seems to be somewhat less certain of her shamanic capacity. Her second Rorschach protocol is much more constricted than was the first; her psychological integrity has diminished. We assume the reduction of integrity to be the result of overdetermined environmental and intrapsychic factors. Her self-chosen idiosyncratic shamanic role is one that involved the transgression of a strong taboo — her assumption of a function traditionally performed only by men — thereby risking putative supernatural and/or public censure. This remains true, although it now appears that an ancient and currently little-known Apache custom did provide a place in religiomedical practices for the assumption by a woman of a traditionally masculine function; and did so despite the fact that Apache custom did not provide, as was common among Plains Indians, an approved position for *berdaches* (Driver, 1961; Lowie, 1935). Interestingly, the homosexual conflict was absent in the more constricted second record. Instead, there was a preoccupation with fear of incapacity.

APACHE SHAMANISM

Here we present but the barest essentials of Apache religiomedical philosophies and practice. For more information, the reader is referred to other studies (Bourke, 1892; Boyer, 1964a, 1964c, 1979a; Boyer, Boyer, and De Vos, 1982; Mails, 1974; Opler, 1941, 1947).

The basic concept of Apache religion is that of a vague, diffuse, supernatural power that pervades the universe and may enliven inanimate objects. To become effective, it must "work through" humankind. Inhabiting some animal, plant, natural object or phenomenon, it will approach a human being when he is in an altered ego state, usually during a period of involuntary ordeal. If the person who has been approached accepts the power with its prescribed prayers, songs, and rituals, he is entitled to practice shamanism. As a shaman, he may use his supernatural power to intervene with powers or spirits who have been affronted by the actions of humans or to counteract the malevolent efforts of witches and ghosts.[5] However, to "own" supernatural power is an awesome responsibility. While power has no intrinsic quality of good or evil, its human possessor may voluntarily use it for good, shamanic, culture-supporting purposes or evil, witchcraft purposes. If he chooses the latter route, his life and the lives of his family members are endangered. Additionally, since people are inherently both moral and immoral and sometimes perform actions involuntarily or think unbidden thoughts, those who own power might unwittingly use it for sinful purposes, thus inadvertently harming others or reaping personal supernatural retribution. Finally, the practicing healer and his family are vulnerable as a result of his shamanic activities. A power that has been especially affronted will demand a death. If the person who insulted it is cured due to shamanic intervention, the power will find a way to kill the curer himself or, if he chooses to deflect the vengeance onto one of his loved ones, that person will die. Inferentially, then, every shaman is also a witch.

Although in some Indian groups shamans perform ceremonies cooperatively, among these Apaches each shaman owns his powers individually and acts alone. He fears that his powers might be stolen from him and is careful to guard against the possibility of such theft by uttering only part of his prescribed ceremonies aloud when performing his rites. He is also afraid nonqualified listeners will be harmed by what they have taken in through their ears. While other tribes could join forces in the Peyote Religion (Gusinde, 1939, pp. 401–499; Hollander, 1935; La Barre, 1938; Slotkin, 1956), when these Apaches sought to practice shamanism as teams, violence and murder resulted and peyote use was proscribed (Boyer, Boyer, and Basehart, 1973; Opler, 1936a).

The Apaches have another set of individuals who possess supernatural power that is used in a culture-supporting way, ordinarily to alleviate

---

5. The notion that insanity is the result of the influence of ghosts is widespread (Barrett, 1917; Best, 1922; Boyer and Boyer, 1983; Gifford, 1917; Steward, 1929).

problems confronting either the tribe as a whole or small groups. These men are known in Chiricahua as $ga^n heh$, in Mescalero as *jajadeh*, and in English as Crown Dancers, Mountain Spirits, Masked Dancers, Devil Dancers, Horn Dancers, and Mountain God Dancers (Bourke, 1892; Boyer, 1964a, 1979a, 1979b; Boyer and Boyer, 1983; Goddard, 1916; Harrington, 1912; Hoijer, 1938; Kane, 1937; Mails, 1974; Opler, 1941, 1946a). While both males and females may become shamans, in recorded times only men have been *jajadeh*.

The Horn Dancers constitute an addition to Southern Athabaskan religion that has diffused from the Pueblo Indians (Luckert, 1979). They are "made" $ga^n heh$, mortals who represent the "true" underground supernaturals of the same name. Each team consists of at least six men, the singer or leader, four masked dancers, and one or more clowns. Ideally, the singer has been approached by a "true" *jajadeh* while in an altered ego state and accepted the songs, rituals, and designs for a team of "made" Crown Dancers. Generally, the singership and thereby the ownership of a team is handed to a younger relative when the singer retires or is deemed to have become incompetent or immoral. If a shaman's solitary actions have been ineffective, Mountain Spirits are hired occasionally to assist him in the cure of an individual. Very rarely, in the absence of a shaman, the Spirits are employed to act for a single individual.

DAWNLIGHT'S ACQUISITION OF THE SHAMINISTIC STATUS

Dawnlight, now a middle-aged woman, underwent typical Apache childrearing experiences and her life has followed the average expectable pattern for native residents of the Mescalero Indian Reservation.[6] Since her mother and several other members of her extended family were shamans and her father owned the songs, ceremonies, and paraphernalia of a Crown Dance team, she was heavily exposed to traditional folklore and religiomedical philosophies and practices. Following the pattern of the great majority of modern young Apaches, she lost her early interest in such matters, despite her knowledge that were she to pursue them, she was highly eligible to become a shaman. As a singularly beautiful teenager, she became interested almost solely in self-indulgence. She "stole" a handsome, hardworking man some dozen years her senior from his wife and children. Within a few months after they began to live together, she and Wide Eyes had become drunkards. They remained so, living from hand to

---

6. See footnote 2; for details concerning Dawnlight's early life, see Boyer, Boyer, and De Vos (1982).

mouth in filth for some 15 years. She states, "We were just disgusting." As is true also for other Apaches (Freeman, 1968), these Indians typically have a prolonged period of functional adolescence: The majority of them do not become responsible adults until they are of grandparental age (Boyer and Boyer, 1976). Before their marriage, Dawnlight and Wide Eyes gave up attendance at their childhood Christian church. Soon after their oldest daughter had a baby, they joined an evangelistic, fundamentalist sect which forbade alcohol consumption and strongly censured involvement in native religious practices. As abruptly as they had become drunkards, they now renounced drinking and became model citizens and parents. Just before Dawnlight first performed publicly as a shaman, she and Wide Eyes proudly celebrated 15 years of teetotalism.

Wide Eyes, too, had come from a family steeped in traditional ways. When he and Dawnlight changed into responsible people, they turned strongly to oldtime activities. Dawnlight became a proficient beadworker. She was much sought after as a seamstress of ceremonial costumes, tipis, and the like. She also turned her attention to native herbs, learning more about others' uses of them in addition to recalling her mother's practices. At first she used herbs only for members of her own nuclear family, but later her services were sought by members of her extended family. Indian music, live or recorded, was to be heard in their house at all hours of the day and night. Dawnlight and Wide Eyes gave no evidence that they were troubled by being deeply involved both in such traditional pursuits and the Christian sect which strongly censured native religious practices.

As mentioned earlier, Dawnlight's father, Smiles, had been the singer for a team of Crown Dancers, owning its ceremonies, songs, designs, and sacred paraphernalia. The singership had been owned by his mother's family for generations. The aged Smiles earlier had transferred the role to James, one of his sons, after James, a recent grandparent, had renounced drunkenness.

Within a year after James became the singer, his and Dawnlight's parents died and he quickly reverted to drunkenness. His performances were undependable, "shameful," and he stopped caring for the sacred paraphernalia, which became shoddy and filthy. The extended family members were concerned, fearing both supernatural retribution and loss of face. Although an older sister was living, she was a drunkard so that Dawnlight held herself responsible for the welfare of her extended family. Accordingly, after her counseling and exhortations failed to rehabilitate James, she made an unusually courageous decision. Aboriginally, it was believed that if a female were even to *watch* as the singer painted and costumed the team's dancers before their holy performance, the "real" *jajadeh* would harm her. If she were to *handle* the sacred paraphernalia, she could expect serious retribution. In an illustrative story, a girl watched the painting and costuming and touched the "sword" and headdress; the following day she was found burned to a crisp in the ashes of the ceremonial fire around which the ga^nheh always dance. Nevertheless, after much trepidation, Dawnlight decided to take the paraphernalia under her own care, to clean and repair them, and to return them to James only when he became morally responsible once again.

James did not improve and Dawnlight and other family members prevailed upon him to transfer the singership to his son John although the latter was only a little more than 30 years old. About a year after James handed down the singership to John, James died in an accident associated with drinking and soon thereafter the oldest sister was murdered in a drunken brawl.

As mentioned earlier, Dawnlight's use of native herbs had increased following her renunciation of alcohol. For some years she had remembered having watched in girlhood her Lipan Apache mother's use of Lightning Power in a ceremony to cure a "paralyzed" woman. However, it had not occurred to her that she would ever believe herself to possess any supernatural power except perhaps that inherent in the prayers to the spirits of the herbs.

Following an injury, Wide Eyes had suffered debilitating arthritis of one knee for many months. He had undergone several fruitless curing ceremonies and received much Western medical care without effect. He had great pain, always used a cane or crutches, and was "paralyzed." About six weeks following the death of her older sister, Dawnlight, probably remembering that the handling of the Crown Dance paraphernalia had not resulted in "bad luck," used her mother's "Lightning Medicine" ceremony in an attempt to cure Wide Eyes.[7] The effort was remarkably successful.

During the next year, many misfortunes befell members of Dawnlight's extended family. In the most disastrous event, Navaho Man, her paternal

---

7. In a Lipan version of "Coyote Steals Fire," after Coyote stole fire from the Firefly People, they tried in every way to get the fire back and force the Apaches to continue to eat raw meat (Opler, 1940, pp. 111–114). When the forest was ablaze, the Firefly People prayed for rain and all of the fire was put out except some embers which Turtle protected with his shell. Lightning struck Turtle many times in unsuccessful attempts to make him drop the fire and have it extinguished by the rain. The marks of the shell of the turtle came from the striking of the lightning. The first step of the ceremony used by Dawnlight to treat Wide Eyes' pain and "paralysis" involved her putting "coal or ashes" left on a tree which had been struck by lightning into her turtle shell and then mixing them with pure water. Four round, flat stones emblemizing Turtle were heated white hot, and cold water was dripped onto them. If one or more of them had chipped or broken, the ceremony would have been stopped. The breakage would probably have meant either that Turtle Power or Lightning Power was displeased and, if used, would have "turned back" on Dawnlight or one of her loved ones.

cousin and a shaman, suffered spastic quadriplegia as a result of a broken neck. He was confined to a wheelchair. After each unfortunate occurrence affecting some family member, Dawnlight suffered episodes of anxiety that included apprehension of attack by unknown people or agents. We may assume that on some level of consciousness she feared that the unfortunate events had been the result of supernatural retribution because of her transgression of the taboo against handling the sacred regalia and/or her having practiced shamanism without first having had a "power dream." Dawnlight received transitory relief from her anxiety attacks following most of the tragic events via ceremonies conducted by local shamans. However, her reaction to Navaho Man's calamity was deeper and prolonged. It was finally relieved through the ministrations of a famous shaman in a distant Pueblo. Following his having obtained sufficient autobiographical data from Dawnlight, he effected a cure by explaining to her that her extended family was being hexed by a powerful but unidentified witch who had been hired by Apaches envious of her and Wide Eyes because they had been able to renounce drunkenness and become highly successful in traditional ways.[8] The astute shaman had supported Dawnlight's own defensive posture.

With the death of her sister, Dawnlight became the oldest member of the extended family and as such was accorded much respect. After her having handled the sacred paraphernalia without incurring supernatural retribution and having successfully treated Wide Eyes' "paralysis," she received increasing esteem and was in constant demand as a counselor.

Soon John and Dawnlight developed a relationship which has been unrecorded and which had not been disclosed to the Boyers. John's dance team was respected and hired frequently for the purposes which are usual for the Mountain Gods. Additionally, the team came to be employed to assist shamans whose previous ministrations had not effected cures.[9] Before the team danced on such occasions, John regularly consulted with Dawnlight, seeking and receiving advice from her regarding diagnoses and modifications of ceremonies, inferentially adding her power to that of the shaman in charge while also effectively making her consultant singer, and having her assume a masculine ceremonial role. Tribal members began to say that Dawnlight was the "power behind" the team; some even postulated that she actually owned the team. It should be recalled that historic-

8. To be outstandingly successful incurs resentment on the parts of others, as reflected in some folklore (R. M. Boyer, 1972). In a representative example, a high school boy did very well scholastically to which a gang of his Apache peers responded by beating him up and torturing and killing his dog before him while holding him helpless.

9. This may be recent religiomedical behavior and we do not know its frequency. We had heard of its occurrence in the remote past but did not learn of or observe it during the years 1957–1980.

ally the *jajadeh* or *ga^{n}heh* and the singers of their teams have been men and only men.

Then Dawnlight had an experience which she interpreted to be a power dream. Sometime following Navaho Man's tragic accident, she began to think that she would soon need to use the Lightning Medicine ceremony once again. Accordingly she obtained coals from a tree which had been struck by lightning. Then she dreamed that John came to her, recounting a dream of his own and seeking its interpretation.[10] In the first part of John's dream within her dream, a Crown Dance team were the protagonists. The team consisted of four shamans, including her father, and a clown. They went tandem to the sacred fire and blessed it, the clown going last as usual. In the second part of John's dream within her dream, the clown went first to the fire and blessed it, being followed by the other members of the team. Dawnlight knew she had had a power dream when soon thereafter John came to her in reality, first telling her that he and his dance team had been requested to perform a ceremony for Navaho Man and then recounting a dream of his own which was identical in both parts to the dream within her dream. Dawnlight interpreted his dream to be a supernatural message which prescribed the actions of the dance team during the forthcoming ceremony, directing John to conduct it in a manner which constituted an unrecorded departure from the usual pattern and one new to the Boyers, in which the *clown* was to lead the dancers and be the first individual to bless the fire and the sufferer, Navaho Man.

Following John's having consulted Dawnlight and her having interpreted his dream, her and Wide Eyes' extended families expected *her* to take charge of the planning and conduct of the curing ceremony, and she did so. During the rite, the clown did indeed lead the dancers and first bless the fire and Navaho Man. The ceremony was the most solemn, peaceful, and beautiful the Boyers have ever attended. As far as they could observe, no participant or audience member entered an altered ego state.[11]

In light of the Rorschach protocol to follow, Dawnlight's spontaneous associations two days after the ceremony are highly relevant. She was ea-

---

10. Ordinarily, Chiricahua and Mescalero Apaches believe that individual manifest dream contents have culturally defined symbolic meanings, signifying good or back luck, and that they can be used to prescribe behavior in general. An occasional shaman is thought to have the power to use their own or others' dreams as vision experiences. They are called dream shamans and are said to be able to dictate specific behavior from their understanding of manifest dreams. Dawnlight's experience may constitute the first evidence that Lipan Apaches have held a similar belief.

11. The Boyers have never observed any participant in a public or private religiomedical ceremony to enter into a discernible altered ego state.

ger to talk about the ceremony and its implications for her and invited the Boyers to her house for that purpose.[12]

After the amenities, Dawnlight talked immediately of her fear of witchcraft and of the duplicity of witches who, motivated by jealousy, pretended to be friendly but secretly sought to harm. Her illustrative story depicted the actions of a witch who was part of the audience of the puberty ceremony of one of Dawnlight's daughters and, although smiling and offering assistance, really wanted to harm that daughter.[13] While talking of witchcraft Dawnlight spoke of a previously unrecorded and perhaps idiosyncratically derived means whereby one might become a witch: by smelling the corpse of a witch, inspiring and incorporating his or her evil. This apparently new idea is a logical extension of the Apache view that witchcraft is accomplished through the invisible shooting of arrows which have been tipped with tiny pieces of human cadavers or other offal into intended victims, arrows which may be sucked or grabbed out of a sufferer from witchcraft by a shaman.[14]

There are psychological resemblances between the puberty ceremony and Dawnlight's debut as a shaman. The basic function of the ceremony is to assist the nubile maiden to become a moral woman who will take re-

---

12. LBB had for some years been viewed as the shaman for Dawnlight and Wide Eyes' nuclear family and a year previously had successfully treated an episode of ghost sickness suffered by the former solely by means of interpretations pertaining to her hostility and guilt. Her transference toward him was mixed, of course, with close realistic object relations, and included his serving for her as an omniscient, omnipotent, and predominantly loving father surrogate.

13. It may be that Dawnlight expressed in this way a fear, perhaps unconscious, that LBB might seek to harm her although pretending to be friendly. When the Boyers were first met by her after arriving on the reservation, she hugged LBB, tearfully saying, "I wouldn't be standing here if you hadn't saved my life." Soon thereafter, however, she had tactfully told him his services as family shaman were no longer required. The year following Dawnlight's assumption of the shamanistic status, RMB informed her that she would come to the reservation alone; Dawnlight agreed to meet with her on an appointed date. However, when RMB arrived, Dawnlight and her family were in another state, having decided at the last moment to attend a powwow there. We may suppose that the sudden decision was related to LBB's absence. Some years previously, while he served as the family shaman, he had not gone to the reservation at a time when the family expected him; they had assumed that he knew without having been informed by human communication that Dawnlight was suffering from ghost sickness and expected his assistance. She was bitterly disappointed and unforgiving when it became necessary for her to get her help during a long-distance telephone conversation, help achieved through interpretation of guilt related to her feelings toward a person whose murder had provoked her ghost sickness.

14. This means of curing an individual who suffers from witchcraft is very widespread among American Indians (Ackerknecht, 1949; Kroeber, 1925; Murphy, 1958).

sponsible care of her future family (Opler, 1941, pp. 82–134). Dawnlight's first public shamanic performance constituted a statement that she deemed herself to be responsible for the welfare of her extended family. The maiden is to be assisted by supernatural power through the mediation of her singer and her sponsor. Dawnlight was to be helped by supernatural power which she had come to possess. It is possible that, in her complex transference relationship with the Boyers, she viewed them as being her singer and sponsor. She was very eager to impart to them all of her recently acquired ideas and her behavior and to gain their blessing and support.

Following her talking of witches and their dangers, Dawnlight turned to the subject of death. She recounted a previously unreported means of avoiding ghost sickness, that of throwing the soles of the deceased person's shoes into his grave. She said the action was intended to enable the soul of the dead individual easier access into the promised land and thereby diminish its resentfulness and/or loneliness, so that the ghost would not be so likely to seek vengeance on loved ones, or be lonely for them, and therefore would be less likely to drive them mad in order that they would commit suicide or act foolishly and be killed. The Boyers have attended many funerals and have never observed this action; no other informant has mentioned it. This may be yet another idiosyncratic idea introduced by this highly imaginative woman that may later come to be an accepted part of Apache folklore, as a result of her shamanic authority (Opler, 1946b). The homophony of sole and soul can scarcely be ignored. The two words in Apache have no similar homophony but Dawnlight thought automatically in either English or Mescalero.

In her spontaneous progression of associations, Dawnlight then spoke of her physical reactions following the curing ceremony for Navaho Man. Her arms had become so stiff she could scarcely move them and only after a long period of massage and exercise could she use them easily once again. She said she had taken Navaho Man's stiffness into her and because of that, she was even more certain that his spastic paralysis would be cured. It will be recalled that in the cure of an individual who has been bewitched, the shaman may suck or grab out the witch's arrow which has caused the illness or misfortune.

Next, Dawnlight turned to the subject of parental transmission of their own good or evil aspects to their children. She and Wide Eyes had had four children while they were still "disgusting" drunkards and each child had turned out badly, having predominantly immoral, irresponsible, and "mean" aspects. To the contrary, the three children who were born after their parents' renunciation of alcohol were thoughtful, loving, gentle, and good. Although she used different words to express herself, Dawnlight's explanation for this phenomenon was that children incorporate the parental model that is offered to them. As we shall see from her first Rorschach protocol, obtained following her having expressed the foregoing thoughts, Dawnlight is cognizant of a fear that she might as a shaman transmit evil as well as good to others, as she believed she had done as a parent. Her conceptualization of the shaman-witch duo was clearly that of the mother who would be viewed alternately by her baby and herself as totally good or totally bad.

THE SYMBOLIC ANALYSIS OF DAWNLIGHT'S FIRST PROTOCOL

The following is an outstanding example of how symbolism on the Rorschach test, in addition to reflecting the structural dynamics of an individual's personality, can be helpful in understanding underlying attitudes. Dawnlight reveals an exceptional intelligence, a very strong motivation for personal achievement, a vital active personality; but more than anything else, through a rather open symbolic expression with content directly derivative from her culture, she presents both the positives and negatives of being invested with the power of a shaman. In the tables that follow we shall present in the first column the responses given spontaneously with the presentation of the Rorschach cards. That column also includes the brief inquiry about the responses conducted by L. B. Boyer after the completion of free association to all ten cards, and his comments. The standard scoring categories of a modified Klopfer system resembling that now used by Exner (1974) are presented in the second column, alongside, in the third column, a response-by-response analysis of the content symbolism using De Vos's scoring for Rorschach symbolism as a point of departure.[15]

The Affective Symbol Scoring System is based on psychoanalytic assumptions. It classifies all responses into seven categories and sub-

---

15. The special scoring first used by De Vos was reported initially in 1952 (De Vos, 1952). It was applied to samples of normal, neurotic, and schizophrenic subjects utilized by Beck in his research on schizophrenia (Beck, Grinker, and Stephenson, 1954). This system was subsequently used by Singer and others (Singer, n.d.; Speisman and Singer, 1961; Streitfelt, 1954; Weiner, Thaler, and Reiser, 1957; Wynne and Singer, 1966) in clinical diagnostic studies. Subsequent cross-cultural use was reported in various publications (Boyer, De Vos, Borders, and Tani-Borders, 1978; Day, Boyer, and De Vos, 1975; De Vos, 1961, 1966; De Vos and Borders, 1979; De Vos and Miner, 1959; Helm, De Vos, and Carterette, 1960). For a revised detailed manual, one may write to Professor George A. De Vos, Department of Anthropology, University of California at Berkeley, Berkeley, California, 94720.

classifies the responses in each category. For example, among responses which suggest hostility one can subclassify responses into symbols of oral aggression (e.g., teeth, chewing, biting), direct aggression (fighting), or indirect aggression (knives, spears). Responses may symbolize a combination of hostile and anxious content (worms with pincers, the claws of a crab) or hostility and inner tension (a nozzle shooting flame, a spinning top, eruption of a volcano). Sadomasochistic fantasy may be represented by attention to deformities, missing body parts, or mutilations. Anxiety responses are subdivided into those evidencing oral or tactile disgust (a slimy reptile), diffuse, evasive, or threatening images (clouds, maps, a gargoyle, respectively), or depressive components (a dried-up tree). There is a category for body preoccupation, with subcategories (bone, flesh, nerves, sexual anatomy); one of socially conforming or dependent responses (a newborn babe, a praying figure, a policeman's badge). There is a general category of positive affect, which includes responses pertaining to nature, food, sensual pleasure, recreational activities, and so forth; a miscellaneous category, which includes responses that do not fit well into any of the above; and a final category of neutral responses in which underlying affective determination seems minimal.

This classification system makes it possible to make quantitative comparisons of a relatively objective nature: One can compare clinical groups (e.g., schizophrenics) with cultural groups, and cultural groups with each other. One can compare an individual with his own social group or clinically definable groups.

The affective scoring system, in other words, permits some generalizations as to how the individual functions in comparison to group norms. For example, in Dawnlight's case, she gives relatively less hostile content than the general norm (4%), whereas her anxiety content (36%) and body preoccupation (14%) are higher than the general norms. The total (54%) of unpleasant affect is significantly higher than that so far found generally in nonclinical groups (De Vos, 1952). However, at the same time that she gives such a high percentage of negatively weighted content material, she produces positively toned symbolic material suggesting good social adaptation. She has a total of 10% dependency responses and 14% positive content for a combined total of dependent and positive material of 24%, which is also higher than the general norms and contraindicates pathological social withdrawal. Her Rorschach protocol, in sum, is a very rich, affectively open record in which we find both more positive and more negative material than is the general expectancy. The fact that there is a balance in symbolic content is contraindicative to a pathological interpretation of her negative, regressively toned symbolic material. We have found in the past that it is most infrequent that any such large percentage of positive symbolic material is given by individuals classified as either schizophrenic or neurotic.

The commentary is a result of discussions between the Boyers and De Vos in which the Boyers delineated the specific cultural background suggested by the symbolic content. Thus, cultural referents, as well as psychodynamic considerations, are taken into account in the scoring of the material. For example, an "owl" in the Apache Rorschach context suggests a special meaning of disaster since we know that the presence of the owl is seen by the Apaches as indicative of a threat of death.[16] By contrast, a response of an owl given by another Native American may not have the same threatening implications.

CARD I

RESPONSES (Replies During Inquiry) /Tester's Comments/	Modified Klopfer Scoring	De Vos Symbolic Affective Scoring
1. 90″ pause. A DESIGN OF A DANCER. A CROWN DANCER. (He's dancing, the darkness, the shading is important.)	$D_2FY + M + H$	Drel, Dauth Athr, Prec, Porn
2. CROWN DANCER. HIS FACE, BENDING DOWN. (His face is covered with a mask.)	dd FY − H	Drel, Dauth, Aobs, Athr, Prec, Porn
3. CROCODILE. (The shape of it and the shading.)	$D_1FY + A$	Hor
4. TAILBONE, WITH THE ANUS. (Of the crocodile. I can't see the parts between.)	dd, FY − Ad (arbitrary)	Ban
5. 120″ pause. BAT WINGS. (Flying. Black and the shading.)	D FM FY FC′ + Ad	Athr
6. TEDDY BEAR, ITS FACE. (Furry and the eyes.)	dd Fc + A	Acnph, Pch Aobs

Commentary — Card I

On Card I we have already found the major themes that are to characterize this record throughout — themes of a positive and negative nature re-

---

16. When an owl flies nearby at night, the Apache hears him say, "I am going to drink your blood." When the Apache is angry, he often says *shi zhade shi nah-i-shish,* "You make the blood rise to my throat." The owl clearly serves as a culturally supported bogy onto which oral aggression in all its omnipotent primitivity can be projected.

lated to power and witchcraft. The Crown Dancer is viewed by the Boyers as a symbol of social control with both positive and negative features. Seen religiously, the Crown Dancer represents communal authority, but he is also a threatening figure to participants in ceremonies. To the children, he is especially awesome. Seen secularly, the response has both aesthetic and recreational aspects. It is, therefore, from the standpoint of its symbolic implications, very complex. The second response is again a Crown Dancer but with emphasis on his mask. The mask on the Rorschach is very often seen in the context of some implied threat. Should the response show preoccupation with eyes as well as masks we infer obsessional, even paranoid, features to be present in the respondent.

Dawnlight's third response is to an area very often seen as a naked human body, usually a woman's. She sees a crocodile, an oral aggressive response. Note that this early theme, hostile threatening orality, is not a usual feature of this record and that it drops out later on.

The next response, the anus and tailbone, is more characteristic of Dawnlight's later preoccupations. The small area on the top of the card evokes for her the shape of buttocks. This type of response will appear again on Card III where she again gives anal and sexual material. Here on Card I, therefore, is the first indication of what appears later more directly as concern with the disavowed which has homosexual implications. As communicated in her associations to L. B. Boyer during the course of the Rorschach, Dawnlight, in her conscious thoughts, directly relates anal concerns and homosexuality to individuals practicing witchcraft. It is interesting to observe that similar disavowed anal and homosexual material in the Middle Ages in Europe was also directly related to beliefs about the practice of witchcraft. Similarly, the association of witchcraft, homosexuality, and/or anal preoccupation is common among other cultures (Bogoras, 1907; Czaplicka, 1914; Eliade, 1951; Housse, 1939; Maestes and Anaya, 1982, pp. 142–151; Parin-Matthèy, 1971; Poole, 1983).

The fifth response, bat wings, is not to the whole area of the blot as it usually is on this card. She picks out instead only a specific part. Had she seen the more usual bat, one would tend to consider it a more neutral type of response prompted by the suggestive shape of the entire blot, but since she goes to some trouble to pick out an unusual area we must code the response as suggestive of a more threatening meaning. The Boyers maintain that in Apache folklore the bat serves a dual role, a projection of both good and bad maternal images (Boyer, 1979a, Chapter 6; R. M. Boyer and Boyer, 1981). The final response to the card, a teddy bear, is an affective reversal in that it suggests childlike innocence — a stuffed animal, harmless, even comforting. At the same time one must note that it is in a seldom used area and that she emphasizes the eyes — a rare small detail. This response and the previous mask are obsessional-type responses of which one finds other examples in the following cards. "Bear" is one of the most irascible of the "powers" of these Apaches, a fact which makes us even more aware of the counterphobic nature of the teddy bear response.

Let us summarize Dawnlight's responses to this card in the light of her entire record. Her very first response is that of the Crown Dancer, a ritual figure that represents social control in both its positive and negative aspects, a theme repeated throughout. Her preoccupation with anal-sexual material is also repeated, as is the pattern whereby a response suggesting threat is followed by some kind of counterphobic reassurance — benign percepts replacing the possibility of threat as in the use of the teddy bear. This defensive maneuver is one that she uses successfully throughout her record, suggesting socially adaptive integrative capacity. This first card, therefore, evokes the internal ambivalences associated with the assumption of power as a shaman, and suggests adaptive integrative capacity sufficient to remain in good contact with her social group. Compared with most Athabaskan and other American Indian protocols, this record is exceedingly rich and highly symbolic.[17] More characteristic for Native Americans records are rather matter-of-fact, concrete protocols that give evidence of a good sense of reality testing, but provide very little symbolic elaboration.

Commentary — Card II

The first response to Card II is a fairly curious one. The Boyers note that totem poles are as esoteric to Apaches as to whites and have no traditional religious meaning within Apache culture. However, today a totem pole may be a somewhat indirect indication of a pan-Indian identity. Note, nevertheless, that it is the faces on the totem poles that are important to her. Faces and eyes are a continuing theme in her record.

The second response is a fairly popular response to this card, but for Dawnlight it has specific associations. The Bear Dance is related to Bear Power and its magical connotations.

The third, fourth, and sixth responses repeat her obsessional concern with faces. Note that the fourth response is a crying face, indicating concern with sadness. Among these faces she intersperses in her fifth response a butterfly, which is a positive-type response. A final obsessional sheep's

---

17. Although we possess and have examined many hundreds of protocols from Apaches, Navajos, several groups of northern Athabaskans, and other American Indian groups, we have elected not to present statistical validation for this statement in the present communication.

CARD II

RESPONSES (Replies During Inquiry) /Tester's Comments/	Modified Klopfer Scoring	De Vos Symbolic Affective Scoring
7. 30″ pause. FACES ON TOTEM POLES. (Looking some way. The color is important.)	D₂FC + Rel. Art	Aobs, Porn, Drel
8. 120″ pause. BEARS DANCE. LIKE IN A STORY. /She refers to a story she and her husband had told LBB earlier, having to do with Bear Power and its magical connotations./ (Just the shape.)	D₃FM + A P	Drel
9. 30″ pause. DEER FACE. (The shape and the shading.)	dd Fy − Ad	Aobs
10. 60″ pause. SOMEBODY SAD, CRYING. THE TEARS ARE RUNNING DOWN. JUST HER FACE. (You can see the tears running down.)	D₁ Fm − Hd	Aobs, Hgl
11. /Holding card with arm fully extended./ FLYING BUTTERFLY OR MOTH. (It is colorful.)	D₁ FM FC + A P	Acnph, Pnat
12. FROM CLOSE UP. A SHEEP FACE. /Could not relocate./		(Aobs)

face is not relocated in the inquiry so the last acknowledged percept is a colorful butterfly.

Commentary — Card III

The response to Card III shows a loss of reality testing. It is what might be considered in the classical tradition a psychotic-type response. The form has some reality but the assembly of the parts is unreal. She produces an incipient childbirth concept, seeing the entire card as the insides of a woman pregnant with two babies. There is an arbitrary nature to what is seen inside — the percept of the pelvis moves from being located in the center red area to the outside black area during the inquiry, in which she seeks to describe how and where she saw things on the card. The stomach also does not hold its position well as she attempts to justify her perception. Nonpsychotic people rarely respond to Card III as a representation of pregnancy and childbirth. Note that, in contrast to her performance on the previous cards, she does not give a second response; she remains fixed

CARD III

RESPONSES (Replies During Inquiry) /Tester's Comments/	Modified Klopfer Scoring	De Vos Symbolic Affective Scoring
13. 24″ pause. THE FIGURE OF A LADY, PREGNANT. HER STOM-ACH IS UP TOP. /Indicates the white area above the figures./ THE PELVIS AND THE BABY, TWO BABIES. (It's the inside of a woman's body, bearing twins.) /During the inquiry she changed the location of the stomach from the white area to the red of D_2. The red D_1 remained the pelvis although she also used D_3 as a pelvis and used D_4 as the babies./	WS FC− H Anat, Sex	Bch

on the entire card as representing pregnancy. As will be seen, subsequent responses will deal with childbirth directly. From Card III on, she shifts her style to focus on the total blot area, whereas in the first two cards she picked up some rare details and gave responses to separate regions of the cards. From Card III on, she takes a different approach in which she attempts an integration of the entire card area, at least in the first response.

CARD IV

RESPONSES (Replies During Inquiry) /Tester's Comments/	Modified Klopfer Scoring	De Vos Symbolic Affective Scoring
14. /Her arm is extended./ 30″ pause. THE BACKBONE OF SOME ANIMAL. (Looking down on the furry animal's back from the top.)	W Fc + Ad P	N
15. 60″ pause. A CROWN DANCER. (Dancing. In his mask.)	W Fc M + H Rel	Drel, Dauth, Athr Pcom, Porn

Commentary — Card IV

On Card IV she first sees the entire card as a furry animal's back as viewed from the top. She is thus highly responsive to the texture of the card, suggesting social sensitivity. The Crown Dancer on Card IV is well perceived, repeating the theme of Card I. This card, often symbolic of oppressive dominance of masculine authority, is handled without stress and with a socially adaptive symbol.

CARD V

RESPONSES (Replies During Inquiry) /Tester's Comments/	Modified Klopfer Scoring	De Vos Symbolic Affective Scoring
16. GRASSHOPPER, FLYING	W FM + A	Athr
17. BAT WITH WEBBED WINGS. (Black, flying, furry.)	W FC' M + A P	N
18. 60″ pause. SOMETHING ELSE FLIES. (A black owl.)	W FC' − FM A	Athr

Commentary — Card V

On Card V she picks up the most frequently perceived bat but she adds two alternate responses. Her first response is a flying grasshopper, her third a black owl. It must be noted that the Apaches are worried about grasshoppers since they have been literally plagued with them in the past; as a matter of fact, at the time of the test there was a grasshopper invasion of the area. Note also that the owl heralds death in Apache thinking. These are therefore symbols of threat and anxiety. Since Card III she has continued to give whole responses.

Commentary — Card VI

Her first response to Card VI is intellectual and evasive. She says it is a design but cannot elaborate. Her second response, feathers, she associates to the feathers worn in Indian headdresses during dances which may be ceremonial and then tells Boyer a story in which an Indian uses a headdress feather to guide a tornado away from his property and over a hill to destroy a city. In scoring the feather for its symbolic content, we note religious and ornamental value but also that the story suggests a counterphobic theme in which the feather is used magically to deflect a threat. It must be remarked that Card VI is commonly considered to have phallic content and that while she uses the phallic area first, for the feathers and plumes, she then veers away from phallic implications, saying that the area consists of a crawling creature with its eyes turned away to the side. Clearly, the phallic area disturbed her, and we may suspect that her own phallic strivings make her anxious.

It may be, too, that inasmuch as the destroyed city of the story was a white man's city, and her feelings at the time for Boyer, the recently discharged (white) family shaman (see footnotes 12 and 13), were ambivalent, part of her interpolated response was determined by suppressed or repressed hostility toward him.

CARD VI

RESPONSES (Replies During Inquiry) /Tester's Comments/	Modified Klopfer Scoring	De Vos Symbolic Affective Scoring
19. 30″ pause. IT WAS FOLDED UP BUT I'M ONLY SEEING HALF. IT'S SOME DESIGN. /Unable to amplify./	W Card Description	Aev
20. 180″ pause. PLUMES WITH FEATHERS. /She means they are feathers such as are worn in Indian headdresses during ceremonial but not necessarily religious dances. They are unrelated to the Crown Dancers. At this time she told a story in which an Indian used a feather from a headdress to guide a tornado away from his property and over the hill to destroy a city./	D₅ Fc + Aobj	Drel, Porn, Acnph
21. Rotated for 60″. RAWHIDE. (The smooth side.)	W Fc + Aobj P	Psen, Acnph, Aobs
22. 30″ pause. SOME CRAWLING CREATURE. EYES AT SIDES. IT'S TURNED AWAY TO SEE.	D₃ FY + A	Acnph

CARD VII

RESPONSES (Replies During Inquiry) /Tester's Comments/	Modified Klopfer Scoring	De Vos Symbolic Affective Scoring
23. 60″ pause. IT'S TWO WOMEN, ONE WITH A BLACK MOUTH, TALKING DIRTY. SHE'S A WITCH AND THE OTHER WOMAN IS AFRAID OF HER. THE WITCH'S BREAST IS DOWN THERE. /At this time she told a story of a female witch who made a witch of another woman by dancing naked with her./ (The women are turned away from each other although they are looking at each other.)	W M + H (sex) P Arbitrary	Asex, Athr, Drel, Bso

Commentary — Card VII

Card VII gives us unusually direct material. Although the response of dancing women to the overall area is common, Dawnlight responds atypically by locating the witch's breast on a part of the blot that is usually perceived by others as a buttock area.[18] In this card she is making direct reference to an activity which she describes in other associations as being of a homosexual nature and related to witchcraft: two women dancing together. Being a shaman allows for some sex-role reversal in many regions of the world. The Apache female witch whom she pictures as involved in homosexual relations is seen as the dominant or male partner in the relationship. Perhaps Dawnlight's Crown Dancer responses reflect both her unconscious wish for and fear of the assumption of masculine powers. We may presume that a major psychological problem with which she is dealing at this time is how to handle the hostile homosexual impulses related to her supernatural power. She projects her homosexual and aggressive wishes, and fears victimization.[19] At the time of the Rorschach administration she was convinced that she and her extended family were being victimized by witchcraft and also afraid that her supernatural power might not be adequate to protect her family and herself. At the same time, she counterphobically challenged an unknown witch who had caused another shaman, Dawnlight's paternal cousin Navaho Man, to become quadriplegic in an accident, despite not only Navaho Man's shamanic power but the power ascribed to Boyer as the family shaman. We also see in some of the responses a paranoid quality which may indicate that her paranoid

---

18. This unusual Rorschach response — the association of a breast with a buttock — is common in the associations of regressed patients in the analytic situation and those of young children (Isaacs, 1948; Klein, 1932). To them, the buttock represents the anus, the agent of expression of primitive, omnipotent, and omnidestructive aggression which has resulted from the frustration of being orally deprived (of the breast). Such ideas are thought to be present side by side with the idea that one is alternately totally bad or totally good, an idea clearly present in the thinking of those who perceive their healers to be inevitably alternatively all good (shamans) or all bad (witches), such as the Apaches and others who project onto their curers totally good and totally bad self-representations. As an example, many Latin Americans alternatively call their healers (curanderos) witches (brujos), as we and many others have observed (Gillin, 1948; Hudson, 1951; Kiev, 1968).

19. Today, most psychoanalysts believe that paranoia serves fundamentally as a means of dealing with primitive aggression rather than homosexuality per se (Meissner, 1978). This would be a logical extension of the ideas of van Ophuijsen (1920) and Stärcke (1920) that the earliest roots of paranoia stem from the infant's notion that his expelled feces would attack him, and the Kleinians' view that feces become persecutory symbolic equivalents of the bad breast of the schizoid position (Segal, 1957).

ideation is an alternative to the breakthrough into consciousness of a direct homosexual wish to be victimized and thereby passively obtain the witch's means of dealing powerfully and relatively safely with his or her internal, omnipotently destructive self-representation. The assumption of the shaman's role heightens underlying homosexual anxiety. Locating a breast in the region of the buttocks suggests ambivalence about whether women are generative and nurturant or, conversely, poisonous and destructive. Many authors have suggested that witches are socially sanctioned projections of the "bad mother" introject (Hippler, 1971; Parin, 1971). The supernatural power Dawnlight has gained is obviously perceived by her to be a two-edged sword which may threaten her with certain inner potentials that she had not had to face previously.

CARD VIII

RESPONSES (Replies During Inquiry) /Tester's Comments/	Modified Klopfer Scoring	De Vos Symbolic Affective Scoring
24. THESE COLORS MEAN THE DAY. THE GRAY IS THE DAWN, THEN MORNING, THEN EVENING AND DUSK. SOME ANIMAL TRAVELS DURING THE DAY. WHAT IS IT? THE ANIMAL GETS AHOLD OF THE DAY IN THE MORNING – YOU CAN SEE THE HAND – AND LETS IT GO DURING THE NIGHT. THE FOOT IS DOWN THERE.	W. Csymb FM + A Anat P O +	Pnat

Commentary – Card VIII

After the disturbing material of Card VII, Card VIII appears as a poetically symbolic liberating response. It is a beautifully organized representation of an integrated use of nature. Once again, it is unusual to find this type of symbolic response by American Indians. The colors are directly, consciously symbolic. She sees the day as being traversed by animals from gray dawn to red dusk. The Boyers know of no folktales that could be the source of this poetic thought. The response seems to be totally original – a creation of Dawnlight. Following the anxious implications of the previous card, color and its underlying affectivity come as a relief. It is indicative of her sense of reality and her social adaptation that she is able to integrate both the common percepts of the animals which are popularly seen on the sides of this card and the varying colors in a type of response which is only possible for a person of high intelligence with creative capacity. We find here a graphic example of the counterbalancing which goes on in the entire record between negative and positive content. In her artistic use of primary process thinking, one finds constructive positive features as well as fears of the disavowed and the destructive.

CARD IX

RESPONSES (Replies During Inquiry) /Tester's Comments/	Modified Klopfer Scoring	De Vos Symbolic Affective Scoring
25. THREE COLORS, GREEN IN THE MIDDLE. 120″ pause. A DIFFICULT ONE. THE COLORS MAKE THE DIFFERENCE. GREEN, RED, ORANGE.	W Color naming	Aev
26. IT'S A PICTURE OF CHILDBIRTH. THE BABY IS BORNING. THE WOMAN'S BEHIND, THE I-DON'T-KNOW-WHAT-YOU-CALL-IT-IN ENGLISH. AND PART OF THE BLOOD/Means the vagina and womb combined./	W FC Fm− Hd Anat Sex	Anat, Bch, BS

Commentary − Card IX

Dawnlight first responds to Card IX with intellectual evasiveness, naming the colors rather than giving a true response. Then she repeats her affective reaction to Card III. The symbolism of childbirth and generativity are given again but in this instance the content is not handled with the intellectual disruption of the previous response. There is no disorganized shifting of the contents of her percepts.

Commentary − Card X

On Card X Dawnlight responds with enthusiasm, expressed in thinking heavily influenced by the primary process. The woman's body is emitting her parts all over, giving good things to others, but she is afraid she is giving bad things too. A baby's face is found, and then a rabbit, and then, in the last response, a woman's tailbone represents her anxiety about the witchcraft temptations connected with the role of a shaman. She tells Boyer a story illustrating how a person can become a witch through smelling the corpse of a witch, by inspiring the evil aura. Again she refers to women who dance naked together. It is interesting that she leaves out an orange part in the center because it reminds her of something male − a

RESPONSES (Replies During Inquiry) /Tester's Comments/	Modified Klopfer Scoring	De Vos Symbolic Affective Scoring
27. OH, MY LORD, IT'S BEAUTIFUL. BLUE, GRAY, COLORS ALL OVER AND ALL CONNECTED TO THE RED PART, EXCEPT THE ORANGE. WHAT'S THE RED PART? IT'S A WOMAN'S BODY. EMITTING HER PARTS ALL OVER, GIVING GOOD THINGS TO OTHERS AND AFRAID SHE'S GIVING BAD PARTS TOO. /By woman's body means vagina and uterus. She excluded the orange area because it reminded her of a scrotum, full of seeds. She then spoke of how one's children might turn out to be good or bad. She said her children who were born when she was a drunkard had turned out badly, being irresponsible, immoral, and, in at least one case, dangerous and possibly murderous. She then shifted to talking about shamanism and how a medicine woman feared that her medicines and ceremonies might not only cause good for others, but might also cause others and maybe herself evil rather than good./	W FC Fm+ H	Psex, Hba, Bch, Bs
28. BABY'S FACE, WITH A BIG EYE.	D F− Hd	Df, Aobs
29. RABBIT. (Its head.)	D$_7$ F+ Ad P	N
30. A WOMAN'S TAILBONE. IT'S CONNECTED WITH WITCH-CRAFT. /At this time she repeated the story illustrating that a person can become a witch through smelling the corpse of a witch, by inspiration of the evil aura. She again referred to women who danced naked together. When she first viewed the area she saw it as naked buttocks but then changed the concept to a pelvis viewed from the rear./	D$_8$ F− Anat Sex	Asex, Drel Dauth, Bg

scrotum full of seeds. There's a rejection of male generativity in her concept of herself.

All of Card X becomes a mystical representation of the role of the female shaman with its positive and negative features. This style of primary process thinking has no general cultural license, but given the context of her assuming the shaman's role there is specific license for regression in the service of the ego. Dawnlight is attempting to master an internal crisis which involves the irruption of unconscious material. At the same time, this threatening material is contained socially, and positively expressed in her ritual practice rather than in a private retreat into some form of psychosis. Rorschach records with generativity responses such as rebirth, eggs, unfolding of inchoate forces, are not infrequent among individuals classified as acute catatonic-schizophrenics. In the instance of Dawnlight, however, there is no attendant manifest retreat from social adaptation nor any indication in her daily life that she has been overwhelmed by the content of her unconscious.

Dawnlight has summarized for us on her last cards the epigrammatic meaning of female shamanism to some Apache. She equates the power of female generativity and its possible evil consequences with the female shaman's role. She is obviously fearful of her own evil potential which unconsciously involves homosexuality. She is afraid that her power will come back to harm her as well as others if she does not keep careful control over it. It is noteworthy that she leaves the record almost where she started, with a symbol that has anal implications, and that in her subsequent free associations she mentions a way of becoming a witch, through smelling his or her decaying corpse. One may, in other words, become a witch inadvertently, through no desire of one's own. But the dancing together of naked witches certainly is an intentional act — one by means of which one woman can sexually seduce another into the practice of witchcraft.

Summarizing this protocol in accord with Standard Rorschach Scoring, Dawnlight reveals an intellectual approach that shifts after the first two cards. She starts out selecting details, even rarely used areas, manifesting an initial inhibition which is overcome on Card III. Most subsequent responses are to the entire blot area (W% = 45). This latter approach suggests that she is ambitious, committed to tasks even beyond her capacity. She can overcome an initial constrictive anxiety; she can expand her perceptions to holistic imaginative concepts. She is fanciful and original, even idiosyncratic. There are moments of failure. She again becomes constricted when she cannot give more than a description of the blot, without true content. Her use of enriched determinants of shading (FY = 7, FC' = 1, FC = 4) and the ratio of color and movement responses (M = 3, FC = 8) suggest unusual responsiveness to social environment.

Her use of color and shading throughout the record suggests a quick emotional responsiveness. The balance is passive in that continued attention to the shading (FY = 7, FC' = 1) and the texture (Fc = 4) suggest wariness and sensitivity and a tendency to anxiety. Her inner life shows tensions and immaturity (M = 3, FM = 4), but it is strongly directed toward role responsibilities as represented by the human content of her responses. The overall form level of her responses (F + = 66%) is low. Only three of her 20 responses utilize pure form, suggesting a person swept up by her inner processes — to the extent of endangering her grasp of reality. She produces seven popular responses in the midst of others of poor form that suggest autistic proclivities. Thus one presumes there is a continual awareness of and a need to return from her own preoccupations to share the perceptions of her social world. Although potentially imaginative, she does not extend her interests out into a wider realm (A% = 51). There can be a banality in her thought as well as an intense preoccupation with inner tensions.

The Boyers' behavioral observation would indicate that whatever the internal crisis which is being expressed symbolically on the Rorschach, certain reintegrative social processes are also at work. Homosexuality for the Apaches specifically implies witchcraft, whereas in some of the other cultural instances where shamanism and homosexuality coincide, witchcraft is not necessarily inferred. Being a shaman gives license for sex-role reversal in many regions of the world (Eliade, 1951). However, there is no indication that Dawnlight is consciously using the role for purposes of sexual inversion. Note well how Dawnlight feels responsible for the paraphernalia of the Crown Dancer, a masculine role, but tries to stay away from participating directly in that role. She tries, as best as possible, to maintain her role as a woman.

We observe that there are certain areas of paranoid ideation, but again these are socially and culturally licensed. Dawnlight is convinced that she and her extended family are being victimized by witchcraft and at some level is worried about this. What seems to be occurring here is a projection of homosexual wishes into a fear of victimization triggered at least in part by several factual tragic events. On a personal level, these can be seen as possible paranoid fantasies; on a social level, they are so well accepted and well defined that they draw no attention to her.

She counterphobically undertakes to battle a witch who is so powerful that he or she caused another shaman, Dawnlight's relative, to become a quadriplegic. The degree to which she is threatened by her own homosexual strivings determines the degree to which she is paranoid, according to Freud's (1911) classical concept. While she may assume the shamanistic role defensively, the assumption of the role itself heightens her homosexual anxiety. While the culture allows for certain paranoid beliefs to be institutionalized, her protocol suggests that paranoid defensiveness may be exacerbated by the social possibility of having supernatural power. We may well ask how a person can continue in this role should his desire to cure magically not be realized in particular cases. The system itself perhaps, with its emphasis on the duality of power, the duality of good and evil, helps explain failure as well as create illusions of success. Since the system of belief has within it methods of avoiding failure, shamans can continue to believe in themselves. There is one concern, however, with this particular person which we will have to watch over the long run. Dawnlight has been precipitated into becoming a shaman by an ardent desire to cure a quadriplegic family member whose obvious physical problems do not lend themselves to the possibility of psychological cure. Opler (1936b) and Boyer (1964a) have observed that in most instances shamans are careful to direct their attention to the types of problems which may be defined physically but in actuality are usually of psychological origin. Dawnlight had taken on a problem which cannot be resolved by shifts of a psychotherapeutic nature. Only the future will disclose how the situation will be resolved and explained in Apache as well as in personal terms.[20]

TWO YEARS LATER

Wide Eyes' recovery from his painful knee affliction, his "paralysis," had been maintained. However, Navaho Man's quadriplegia was unchanged. Nevertheless, the curing ceremony at which Dawnlight made her public debut was considered uniformly to have been successful by the members of Dawnlight's and Wide Eyes' extended families. Their wholehearted belief in her possession of supernatural power had led them subsequently to seek her shamanic assistance for various problems and they were well satisfied with the results of her ministrations. Other Apaches were skeptical, disbelieving that Navaho Man would eventually recover. Opler (1936b) noted that Apache custom provided many loopholes which could be used by shamans to explain their failures, and commented that wise shamans usually avoided assuming the responsibility of treating either the chronically insane or the physically incurable. Dawnlight was thought to have been foolish to have undertaken the cure of a

---

20.   We are indebted to Milton Lozoff, M.D., for an interesting suggestion. Dr. Lozoff, recalling Freud's (1917) "Mourning and Melancholia," hypothesized that Dawnlight's assumption of the shamanistic role may have had as one of its roots an attempt to mourn the loss of LBB, both as a real and a transference object through identification with his shamanistic status.

quadriplegic, but she also had potential loopholes: (1) Navaho Man had previously undergone curing ceremonies by renowned shamans from other tribes. If their ministrations were ineffective, at worst she was no more powerful than they. (2) Navaho Man had been an immoral shaman and his supernatural powers might have been so affronted that they would not be mollified by shamanic intervention. (3) A very powerful unidentified witch, probably a member of some other tribe, had been hired by jealous Apaches who wanted to harm Dawnlight, now the oldest member of her extended family, by harming an important member of that family. Until that witch could be identified and his hex counteracted, no cure could be expected. (4) It might appear that Navaho Man's recovery was at best slow, but that did not obviate the certainty that cure was imminent.

Dawnlight had not become a shaman of the usual kind. On her own she never performed ceremonies for the treatment of individuals. Although she had been a relatively sophisticated Apache herbalist before she assumed the shamanic role, she had renounced the usage of native medicines. She never used her supernatural power except in conjunction with John's Mountain God dance team. She explained this specific choice of a shamanic role by her fear that if she treated individuals unassisted, she might inadvertently do something wrong which would result in supernaturally determined harm to her family or herself.

Dawnlight limited her shamanic activities to being what she called John's "aide." John consulted her before leading his dance team for any function, whether directed to the welfare of the tribe as a whole, families, or individuals. She had advised him as to the optimal conduct of a wide variety of ceremonies, including dedications of public buildings both on and off the reservation, dancing for maidens at their puberty ceremonies, seeking to reduce marital discord, and cures of afflicted individuals. The means of his requesting assistance followed the pattern described above. After she had a dream within a dream, John brought a matching dream of his own which was to be interpreted in terms of its prescription of a ceremony. Dawnlight was the periodic custodian of the dance team paraphernalia, keeping them clean and repaired. She attended and quietly supervised each dance team ceremony.

Apaches try to believe they can fool the supernaturals. Thus, they assume that both mortals and supernaturals will be envious or jealous if they have a beautiful child, and proclaim a particularly healthy and handsome baby to be ugly, to avoid having the child harmed or stolen. They share widespread beliefs about the evil eye (Róheim, 1952; Servadio, 1936; Vereecken, 1968). Dawnlight's fear of being a shaman is reflected in her claim to be but an "aide," to deny that she is practicing shamanism while she is obviously doing not only that but leading a Crown Dance team — that is, assuming masculine powers. She hides behind the presumed omnipotent protection of John, the brother and father surrogate who quite literally took over her father's magical powers.

Dawnlight appeared to be less certain than she had been two years previously of her possession of supernatural power and of her shamanic capacity. Her protestations that Navaho Man had improved were too vehement and defensive and she was reticent to discuss her activities and share her ideas with the Boyers, in contrast with her previous spontaneous eagerness. She was clearly conflicted. At the same time, though she sought to project onto them her self-accusations of incompetency if not chicanery, her reality testing capacity kept her aware that they remained her noncritical friends.

Until our field trip in 1983, we believed that Dawnlight had assumed a totally idiosyncratic shamanic role: To our knowledge it is unrecorded and we had not heard of anything resembling it in 28 years of gathering data pertaining to Apache religiomedical practices and philosophies. It is a role which is unusual, entailing a woman's challenge of taboos pertaining to powerful roles traditionally restricted to men.

In 1981, every Apache with whom the Boyers spoke agreed that the shamanic role assumed by Dawnlight was idiosyncratic and that there had been no historical precedent. Fears were expressed by others as well as Dawnlight that her choice of that role might lead to harm to herself and/or her family. By 1983, her assumption of that role appeared to have been accepted and such fears were no longer expressed by her culture mates. Now Dawnlight said that as John's "aide" she was performing a traditional role in which a female relative of a somewhat undependable singer assumed the advisory function of the clown to him and the dance team, and the messenger role of the clown to the people. She said that she remembered having seen many times as a child her mother helping her father care for the dance team paraphernalia and helping with the painting of the dancers, "just like she was the clown." A tribal leader, Dawnlight's half sister by a different mother, who had previously asserted that she believed Dawnlight's shamanic role to be idiosyncratic, now said that she had taken over the traditional functions of the team's clown and stated in a matter-of-fact manner that Dawnlight was the "power behind the team." All of our other informants were in agreement with her.

Other data that had been obtained in 1981 were modified substantially in 1983. Previously, the Boyers understood that Dawnlight's shamanic intervention in behalf of Navaho Man commenced with the ceremony described above. Now they were told that immediately following his hospitalization, when the doctors said he was incurable, she visited him nightly four times, each time blessing him with her Lightning and Turtle Power. She saw improvement after each evening, so she knew before performing it that the public ceremony was destined to be successful. Earlier, she said she became John's helper only because he'd come to her after she'd had her dream within a dream and that she had known that it had been a power dream only after John came to her, asking for an interpretation of his identical dream. Now she said she had to become his "aide" because he periodically lapsed into drunkenness despite her efforts and those of others.

In 1981, she and Wide Eyes still attended services at the evangelistic, fundamentalist church whose help they had credited with the responsibility for their having been able to renounce drunkenness. Perhaps a year following her being involved in the public ceremony for Navaho Man, she and Wide Eyes renounced attendance at that church, giving as the reason that church's hostility toward Indian religion. We might suspect that inasmuch as no apparent harm had come to her or her family as a result of her actions, they felt less need of support. Now they attended certain services such as funerals and marriages in every other Christian church on the reservation, but disclaimed any need to do so in search of help for themselves.

Dawnlight gave further examples of her new capacity to foretell the future. As an example, a year previously she had a dream or a vision which informed her that John's team would be asked to participate in an important Catholic dedication ceremony at Mescalero. Soon thereafter a Catholic nun who is the daughter of a tribal member and who lived in a distant city came to see her, claiming that she had had a vision while in her city home in which God enfolded Dawnlight in his arms. Then John went to Dawnlight, telling her he'd dreamed he'd be asked to do something for the Catholic church in Mescalero. She advised him to accept the charge. No word came from the church for several months but then the nun, commissioned by the new bishop for the diocese, which includes not only Mescalero but an area comprising most of southern New Mexico, approached Dawnlight as the power behind the dance team to obtain John's agreement to dedicate a new cathedral in a city a hundred miles away. The Boyers were present when Dawnlight told the nun that she accepted the commission on John's behalf, and agreed to attend and supervise the ceremony which was to take place on the first of four nights of ceremonies involving Hispanic, Anglo, and Pueblo participation as well as Apache.

Although the Boyers continued to be beloved extended family members, there was increasing evidence of ambivalence on the part of Dawnlight toward L. B. Boyer. Before her assumption of the shamanic status, his religiomedical assistance was sought, especially by her, both in person when he was on the reservation and by telephone when he was not. After she became a shaman, his shamanic assistance was no longer requested. The day before the Boyers arrived in 1983, Dawnlight learned that one of her daughters was probably suffering from an incurable blood disease and might die within a few months. The family, including Dawnlight, obviously hoped for miraculous intervention on the part of L. B. Boyer and when none was volunteered reacted with mixed emotions.

An older daughter, one of the children born to Dawnlight and Wide Eyes while they were drunkards and whom Dawnlight had previously described as having inherited her badness, had been "getting into trouble." The next evening Dawnlight was scheduled to perform a ceremony intended to exorcise her daughter's badness. The Boyers were not invited to attend the ceremony, ostensibly because some relative had wondered whether L. B. Boyer's presence might be harmful in some way. It was his impression that the hostility ascribed to the relative was Dawnlight's own and that it had resulted in part from his not having given hope of miraculous cure for the daughter with the blood dyscrasia. However, there were other reasons for hostility toward him. He had failed her expectations on several occasions. He had not gone to the reservation one time when she had been severely troubled and had expected him to know of her need omnisciently (see footnote 13). He had not magically killed the witch who was purportedly hexing her extended family at the time he had been the family shaman. But it is probable that the most important reason that she distrusted him to the degree that she did was because she had projected onto him her own self-criticism for having dared to take over a masculine shamanistic role, thus symbolically replacing her father in her extended family. These Apaches sometimes equate knowledge with possession of the phallus. Thus a woman who doubted a man's protestation of ignorance said, "I thought you knew everything. Your third leg hangs to the ground."

COMPARISON OF DAWNLIGHT'S TWO RORSCHACH
PROTOCOLS

In comparing Dawnlight's two records, we find in the second protocol considerable evidence of a constrictive process, scarcely present in the initial Rorschach taken during the liminal period when she had just entered the role of shaman. Before directly examining the second record, let us note that, while there is a continuation of symbolism related to supernatural power, certain themes evoked in the first record have been much diminished or are now totally absent.

The first theme that has almost disappeared is that of the Crown Dancer. A second theme no longer present is pregnancy, generativity, and female functions related to childbirth. A third theme now missing is concern with being homosexual and thereby becoming a witch.

An obsessional preoccupation with faces remains evident in both records. In the second protocol, however, her anatomical concern with the spine is modified to become a concern with the absence of spines as well. In the second record the previous concern with masculine authority has disappeared. Turning to religious themes, in the second record concern with exorcism becomes explicit, but the ritual of religious authority of the masculine type, represented in the first record, disappears.

In both records there is a responsiveness to color on the Rorschach blots which can be imaginative, even poetic. It is in her responses to the black and white cards that one especially notes the greater constriction of the second record.

Summarizing what is very apparent: The first record was a more open one, elicited at a time of crisis and change. The second record suggests that she has assumed a more chronic defensive posture in which she is more constricted in coping with everyday reality. In the second record, a dangerously overt and florid concern with homosexuality, as well as other potential evils of the shaman's role, disappear from view. Nevertheless, we should note that her very last response to Rorschach blot X raises the question of whether religious singing is good or bad. We assume that her concern with spinelessness represents an expression of fear either that she lacks masculine authoritativeness, a quality which she perceives to be required of her shamanic role, or that she has it but is ambivalent about it and is therefore afraid.

CARD I

RESPONSES (Replies During Inquiry) /Tester's Comments/	Modified Klopfer Scoring	De Vos Symbolic Affective Scoring
1. 20″ pause. A SPINE. (Of some animal.)	dd F − Bone	Acon, Bb
2. HEAD OF A LIZARD. (Just there.)	dd F ad	Acon
3. CUTE OWL WITH TWO EYES, HANG ONTO SOMETHING. (I saw the eyes first.)	dd FY	Acon, Aobs (potential)
4. HEAD, WITH ARMS OUT. (Maybe Crown Dancer.)	dd Hd F − Y	Acon Drel, Dauth Prec, Porn

Looking at the areas selected in her several responses to Card I we note an evident ego constriction. She refuses to cope with the totality of the blot but selects instead little-used small locations. She starts with an anatomical response. Although she may have been stimulated to see the figure of a woman in the central area that is apparent to many, she does not respond overtly with this answer but goes in deeper and picks out only a central line and makes a spine of it. Then she selects another small area to see the head of a lizard. From this affectively ambiguous response, she goes to a third area, giving a more reassuring, positively turned response of a "cute" owl. The owl response is determined by its two large eyes that she finds in the deeply shaded area. There is thus both a counterphobic denial of anxiety indicated by insisting that the owl is "cute" and, at the same time, a concern with eyes and faces which is to characterize a number of subsequent responses. She then selects the upper center of the blot to represent a head with the arms out. If we compare this with the previous record, we see that the upper portion of the Crown Dancer perceived in record one was located here. Her response to this area in the second record is much diminished. She now utilizes only a small blot area. This response continues the massive constriction that characterizes her responses to the first card. Instead of going in the direction of potentially pathological symbolism, she utilizes denial and an intellectually constrictive process, severely limiting her imagining potential.

CARD II

RESPONSES (Replies During Inquiry) /Tester's Comments/	Modified Klopfer Scoring	De Vos Symbolic Affective Scoring
5. TWO BEARS, DANCING.	D_3 Ma A P	Prec
6. SAD FACE. (I see tears dripping down.)	D_1 F – Y Fm	Aobs
7. TWO FACES, WITH MUSTACHE, ON TOP. (Man's face, look at each other.)	D_2 FC Fy Mp Hd	Aobs

On the second card she is able to respond quickly with a conventional movement percept. We must note that this card has red color, and as in her previous Rorschach, she gives evidence of a labile but positive reactivity to the warm colors. One can interpret this as a readiness for a positive warm response in social relationships. She then returns to her obsessional concern with faces. She again sees a sad face, very dramatically, with tears dripping down. Here again, as on the first card, there is attention to eyes. The face does not threaten but is sorrowful. We can assume that in her shamanic role she is aware of others' helpless expectations of her more than of their potential hostility toward her. The third response to Card II is also faces.

CARD III

RESPONSES (Replies During Inquiry) /Tester's Comments/	Modified Klopfer Scoring	De Vos Symbolic Affective Scoring
8. TWO PEOPLE, BEAT ON A DRUM. (That's all.)	W Ma F P	Drel, Dauth, Prec
9. IT'S GOT NO SPINE OR TAILBONE. IT'S IN THE MIDDLE. THE STOMACH IS UP TOP AND MISSING FROM BELOW IN THERE. (The inside of a person or animal. The tailbone /D$_1$/ *should* be there /pointing to the area in the space just behind and below the buttocks of one of the drum beaters/ and the stomach /D$_2$/ there in the space between the lap of a drum beater and the drum.)	W F − Anat	Aobs, psychotic confabulation, arbitrary paranoid forcing

On the third card Dawnlight quickly sees the ordinary human figures. They are envisioned as beating drums, suggesting a ceremonial setting. As in her previous record, she indicates her active stance toward life in her characteristically kinesthetic motion response. The response is integrative, positive in nature. By it she gives evidence of her social adaptability. She shares awareness of common reality with others.

However, her next responses become psychopathological. She is preoccupied with the idea that something is missing, complaining that there is no spine or tailbone in the middle of the person or animal. She arbitrarily rearranges her percepts, first seeing a stomach in the space at the top of the card and subsequently changing its location, thereby demonstrating a logical deformation in her thinking. There is a conceptual disorientation as well as an incapacity to deal with the blot areas as they are on the card. She attempts to put the tailbone in the middle white space. This associative chain constitutes, in Rorschach language, a contamination. We assume the alogical transposition of the location of the stomach to have been stimulated at least in part by an affect-laden response to the red area. The internal logic of her needs supersedes the limitations of reality.

We can note here a "confabulatory" movement from a partial perception of a tailbone in the central area to a tailbone which becomes the whole blot. In this process, the stomach is moved into another position to be part of the internal anatomy. We can find sufficient evidence of the forcing of logic and association to suggest the same type of process involved in paranoid thinking.

A second observation we can make about the content is that, compared with the childbirth response elicited on the previous protocol, her present responses are far removed from possible sexual implications. She continues to be concerned with the inside of the body, but she concentrates mainly on the spine. The spine, a hard object, indicates firmness, perhaps authority, and may well represent qualities she fears she cannot have as a female. One can surmise that her concern with the lack of a spine symbolizes an abiding sense of inner capacity. It may be that she retains suppressed or regressed knowledge that her cure of the quadriplegic shaman was unsuccessful and thus symbolizes her inner feeling of powerlessness. On this record she pays no attention to female generativity. The symbolism throughout is focused on incapacity.

CARD IV

RESPONSES (Replies During Inquiry) /Tester's Comments/	Modified Klopfer Scoring	De Vos Symbolic Affective Scoring
10. 180″ pause. RAWHIDE. (The shading is important.)	W FY P	
11. BULL HEAD. (Two eyes, looking at me.)	D₁ Ad FSh FM	Aobs
12. SPINE, IN THE MIDDLE. (Back part of an animal hide.)	dd F − Y	Aobs, Bb

On the fourth card she again manifests associative blocking to a black and white card on which there is no reassuring color. Nevertheless, after a silence of three minutes, she is able to give a global percept of an animal hide, a very common response to this card. This is the third of four cards to which she has been able to give a popular, conventional response. Again, despite her ideational problems of paranoid arbitrariness, she is very much aware of the ordinary perceptions of reality. Then she goes to the center of the blot, to an area that is commonly perceived as a head. She perceives a bull's head, the head of an active, massive figure. She again attends to the eyes looking out at her. The eyes of the bull are very clearly perceived. The repetitive face response indicates the continuity of her obsessive wariness. And again obsessionally, she focuses on the spine in the middle of the card. Once more we observe evidence both of anxiety and constriction and the continual concern with incapacity as represented by the spine. We interpret her anxiety to be related both to the impossible task of having to cure a quadriplegic client and to the continual more general anxiety evoked by the necessity to perform well in her accepted role as shaman, to fulfill others' dependent demands on her.

CARD V

RESPONSES (Replies During Inquiry) /Tester's Comments/	Modified Klopfer Scoring	De Vos Symbolic Affective Scoring
13. BAT. (Flying.)	W FMa P	
14. GRASSHOPPER, NO SPINE. /Unable to clarify what she meant./ (Flying.)	W FMa	Aobs

When Dawnlight first took the Rorschach Test, she reacted to Card V with two responses that we interpreted to indicate anxiety. First she saw the dangerous owl, a very unusual response to this card although one of adequate form, and then a grasshopper. As noted, there was then a plague of grasshoppers and she was acutely worried about her garden. This time she promptly gives the popular bat response but then sees a spineless grasshopper. The continuing anxiety pertains now to a feeling of incapacity. She attempts to deal with it obsessively, by displacing it from its source. As we find elsewhere in the second protocol, her defensive postures against anxiety do not work very well.

CARD VI

RESPONSES (Replies During Inquiry) /Tester's Comments/	Modified Klopfer Scoring	De Vos Symbolic Affective Scoring
15. 22″ pause. A SHIELD. (Indian shield with feathers on it.)	D₂ F obj	Porn
16. TWO HANDS, PUT TOGETHER. (Praying.)	dd Hd M F	Drel
17. 180″ pause. AN ARROW, SHOT INTO THE HEAD OR NECK OF SOMETHING. /Couldn't identify the object being shot into./	dd F Ma	Hh

On Card VI, she first gives a positive response, a decorated (Indian) shield, well perceived in its ornamentation. Then she gives a religious response, two hands praying. Card VI is used constructively, to indicate ethnic symbolism, a protective shield and a supplication for power from the outside, a type of response De Vos views as a "dependency" response in his system of scoring. What continues throughout her record is a sufficient number of positive responses, or responses indicative of the investment in positive features of living, that are usually absent in clinical patients when they are tested with the Rorschach. She gives a number of responses either scored as positive or as dependent. These categories usually appear to individuals who are not clinically disturbed. The next response, an arrow that is being shot into the neck or head of something unidentifiable, is the first response to be categorized under the direct hostility heading.

CARD VII

RESPONSES (Replies During Inquiry) /Tester's Comments/	Modified Klopfer Scoring	De Vos Symbolic Affective Scoring
18. A WITCH-LADY WITH A BLACK, DIRTY MOUTH, WITCHING A PERSON. JUST THEIR HEADS. (One on either side; both have bad mouths.)	D₃ Hd M FY P	Aobs, Athr, Acon.

On Card VII, Dawnlight comes closest to a theme found in the previous record. In this instance it is only the heads of two witches with dirty mouths that are perceived. In the previous testing, this particular response was more elaborated, both in regard to the blot area covered and the associated comments given to the tester. In that protocol, she utilized the entire blot, and opened a discussion about the homosexual possibilities of induction into becoming a witch. Structurally, the constrictive tendency here narrows down the area of the blot used, and leads to the lack of further association. We also note that this particular use of the two heads gives her another popular response, so that she now has given popular responses on five of the seven cards.

On Card VIII, she uses the two commonly perceived animals as part of a theme of exorcism. The animals represent shamanistic practice in that the central part of the blot is being relieved of some evil that possesses it. She further elaborates that the animals are representative of Bear Power. This is an associative elaboration; since the animals look like bears, they represent Bear Power. She again uses the popular blot area, but in this instance gives some indication of the type of imaginative response she gave in the first Rorschach series. Note also that there are faces in the center, a reintroduction of her concern with faces that we noted in the earlier cards. The faces are observing the exorcism that is being conducted. The colder colors are used to represent evil and the warmer colors good, so that the

CARD VIII

RESPONSES (Replies During Inquiry) /Tester's Comments/	Modified Klopfer Scoring	De Vos Symbolic Affective Scoring
19. ALL THE COLORS. /Names them./	W C naming	Aev
20. TWO FACES. FACE UP THE MIDDLE. SOMETHING GOES UP INTO THE AIR. ANIMAL AT THE SIDE. PERSON BEING RELIEVED OF SOMETHING. IT'S A GOOD ONE. (The animals are medicine men relieving the persons of evil. I see it moving up in the turquoise and gray. The animals are pushing it out of the people below in the pink. They are Bear Power. Smoke and fire in the background.) /Could not relocate the face in the middle. The something going up was D_5 and the cylinder in D_3./	D_6 W F $-$ FC M P O	Drel, Pstr

gray and the pastel blue of Card VIII represent the evil that is being exor-cised. There is smoke and fire in the background. We remember that all of the Crown Dance ceremonies are conducted in the presence of fire and smoke and that, in the past, the same was true of most other shamanistic rites.

Another interesting note in respect to this response is that she does not herself possess Bear Power. We can assume, given her feelings of incapac-ity, that she aspires to other powers in addition to the Lightning and Turtle power she has borrowed from her mother.[21] In the De Vos scoring system, this response, motivated by her wish to obtain Bear Power, constitutes an active striving. Combined with the other movement responses in her rec-ord, it indicates an active, assertive attitude, characteristic of her stance toward life.

Card IX gives her some difficulty but she manages to produce a total in-tegrated response to it. She sees the head of a baby in the pink area of the bottom, an evil monster threatening it in the green, and a shaman in the orange who seeks to protect the baby from harm. Once again, the warm colors (pink and orange) are used affirmatively and the cool (green) nega-tively. So the colors symbolically represent interaction between good and evil, more specifically, the shaman's protection of a child from the influ-ence of the monster-witch. One must note that the form level is fairly poor

---

21. Another shaman was observed to acquire a new supernatural power when she was des-perate about her physical incapacity (Boyer and Boyer, 1977).

CARD IX

RESPONSES (Replies During Inquiry) /Tester's Comments/	Modified Klopfer Scoring	De Vos Symbolic Affective Scoring
21. 180″ pause. IT DON'T MAKE SENSE. THE GREEN MAN (D₁) LOOKS DOWN AT THE BABY'S HEAD (D₄). HE'S A MONSTER. THE TOP ONE (D₂). I DON'T KNOW. (The orange one/ diyiⁿ/ up top, good because of the color, is fighting the monster-witch and the bottom /D₄, D₅/ is the fallen person. Someone will pray for my daughter tonight.) /This last remark pertained to an actual planned ceremony to exorcise evil from a daughter who was born during the time she was a drunkard./	D W FC M O	Drel, Pstr, Athr

but the colors are used to delineate areas that have some form neverthe-less. A baby is very often seen in the red area below and some kind of per-son or magician in the orange area. Her capacity to see warm colors in a positive light on a symbolic level suggests the drawing of sustenance from her social reactivity which is used to combat the anxieties that are directly stimulated by the black colors on the achromatic cards and by the colder colors on the tinted cards. One might say that she draws sustenance from the outside and that this can be turned defensively against the anxiety to which she is prone. The bright colors overcome, they are strong affect that can be used integratively to overcome danger and anxiety. Although as a shaman she is constantly preoccupied with the themes of good and evil, potentially emanating from herself, as manifested so unmistakably on the first protocol, at this moment she is acutely occupied with that theme, in-asmuch as on the evening of the day when the test was administered for the second time, she was to take part in a ceremony intended to exorcise evil from one of the daughters who were born before she renounced drunken-ness. She recently restated her belief that she had imparted evil to all of the children she had then. Taking this into consideration we may assume that the green monster and its destructive wish toward the child was a projec-tion of an aspect of her self-representations, although she consciously feared that her daughter was being bewitched as the result of hostility to-ward her and, by extension, her family, hostility motivated by others' envy of her various successes, such as her capacity to renounce drunkenness and to have become a shaman in her particular idiosyncratic manner.

CARD X

RESPONSES (Replies During Inquiry) /Tester's Comments/	Modified Klopfer Scoring	De Vos Symbolic Affective Scoring
22. BABY'S FACE IN YELLOW ONE.	D_{10}, Hd F – C	Aobs
23. A MAN UP THERE.	D_{14} F – Mp	
24. SPIDERS UP THERE.	D_1 A F P	
25. BUTTERFLIES.	D_{15} AM FM FC	Pnat
26. RABBIT FACE.	D_7 AdP	
27. YOU GOT ALL YOUR COLORS THERE.	W Color naming	Aev
28. 120″ pause. FACE WITH OPEN (From the singing of the person). SAYING THAT BLUE THING (D_1). /The face was at the top of D_9./	dd Hd M	Aobs, arbitrary,
29. A MUSIC SIGN. (The red one in the middle.)	D_{12} Obj	Prec
30. THE PERSON IS SINGING AND ALL THE REST ARE REJOICING, DANCING. THE MAN UP THERE (D_9) IS MOVING BETWEEN THE ANIMALS; YOU CAN SEE HIS EYES AND THE STICK (D_{14}) IN HIS HAND. THE BLUE MONSTER ANIMAL HAS AN OPEN MOUTH AND IS MEAN. THE BUTTERFLIES (D_{15}) ARE HAPPY AND YELLOW. THE RABBIT IS AS CALM AS HE SHOULD BE. IS THE SINGING GOOD OR BAD? *(Diyi^n or Enti^n?)* /Apaches generally believe red, "the color of sunrise," and yellow, "the color of pollen," to be "good," meaning that they may bring "good luck."/	D W M P O	Drel, Athr, Porn, Auth, arbitrary

The last card starts with individual responses that are eventually turned into a total integration. The theme of the child is picked up again by seeing a baby's face in one of the yellow areas. In the blue she sees spiders, then goes to more innocuous butterflies and the face of a rabbit. The face of the rabbit is a very common response, as are the spiders in the blue area. Then she gives a rather peculiar response in that another part of the blot is "saying" the blue part. The blue area of the blot is words, just as one finds words being encircled by a balloon in a cartoon. She also sees a music symbol in the tiny center area. It is interesting that in the inquiry, omitted above, she does not find the rabbit's face but goes to some alternative responses about dancing, singing, and rejoicing and that a man in the center is moving between the animals on each side of the blot. The cool blue again becomes a monster with an open mouth but the butterflies of the warm yellow are happy. The center of the black area is a person singing; again this is related, as her other responses, to some kind of ceremonial activity. She ends handling this card by asking herself the question, "Is the singing good or bad?" Previously, on Card X, we had a much more global concept of the card as the representation of generativity of women who give birth to both good and evil objects. The question of good or evil here remains but the response is much toned down and the reference to generativity is not forthcoming.

If we look at the second record, we see that the identification with religious practice has now for her an integrative quality and gives her a feeling of adaptive participation rather than isolation. The last three cards all imply in one way or another some positive shamanistic functioning, but doubt is revealed about whether singing is really good or possibly could be evil. There is no such doubt on Card VIII where evil is being driven out, or on Card IX where the shaman is counteracting the monster that is attacking a fallen person, or a child. The shaman on Card IX is unambivalently a protector. The central figure of Card X carries a stick, a scepter, a "sword" of the ga^nheh, a symbol of potency, but the question remains whether his singing is good or evil, that is, whether he is practicing shamanism or witchcraft.

In summarizing a second time, colors are used symbolically as they were in the initial Rorschach, but the record is much more constricted. Nevertheless, under the stimulus of color she recovers her ability to give imaginative, holistic conceptions of very difficult, complex cards. The generativity of the shaman who can give birth to evil as well as good is replaced by the figure of the shaman in Cards VIII and IX as protective, exorcistic of evil, and the combatant of evil. The child we can readily identify as her daughter, born during Dawnlight's drunken period and thus "bad." Subsequently, when she was no longer a drunkard, Dawnlight believed she had imparted good things to the children who were born then, resembling her conceptualization of the shamanistic versus witchcraft roles. One might suppose on a deep level the monster on Card IX is her disavowed self which is being combated by her present, professional self as shaman. The openness and crisis of the first record two years previously have been replaced by constriction and anxiety. The second time through we find no overt or florid concern with homosexuality, but concern with evil and its potential remains.

Given the inconsistencies and other traumatizing elements of their socialization experiences, it is surprising that many of these Apaches are able to meet cultural expectations and become responsible people when they reach grandparental age. Both James and Dawnlight were able to do so, renouncing their drunkenness at that time. James assumed the singership handed down to him by Smiles and was able to handle that role adequately, although he required Smile's continual support to do so. Dawnlight became more and more like her mother in that she turned to traditionalism, including progressive involvement with her mother's religiomedical practices. We probably have here identification with her mother as part of healthy mourning (Freud, 1917), made easier by cultural expectations.

James apparently did not share his sister's level of psychological maturity. When Smiles died, James was unable to continue to function adequately as the singer. Although there was an older sister, she had been unable to renounce her drunkenness and could not serve as counselor and model for the extended family, as the oldest member is expected to do. Dawnlight assumed the responsibility of being the elder leader of the extended family and her functioning in that role was welcomed. In doing so, however, she undertook a responsibility which had been assumed in the past very rarely if at all by women, namely, the care of the *jajadeh* team paraphernalia, despite her anxieties that she would be criticized by other Apaches or punished by the "real" *ga^{n}heh*. It seems likely that in her assuming this unusual role, she could mourn her father by identification with his religiomedical role.

When her anxieties that she might be punished or criticized were found to be unfounded, Dawnlight allowed herself to perform a curing ceremony for her husband's "paralysis," although she had never had a power dream. With trepidation once again concerning supernatural retribution, that is, projected guilt, she used her mother's lightning ceremony. To her amazement, the ceremony was successful and she was not punished. Subsequently, however, she became much more actively involved in assuming a masculine role, becoming John's adviser and the power behind the singership, assuming very literally her father's role as James's "aide." However, the Rorschach data suggest that her bisexual identification had been established earlier and was the source of intrapsychic conflict.

The first protocol, obtained when she had felt so anxious about her having assumed the idiosyncratic shamanic role, revealed much anxiety and creativity, in addition to her capacity to regress to, and quickly recover from, a psychotic-like state. She had anxiety connected with a self-picture of being potentially either all good or all bad and specifically equated the power of female generativity and its possible evil consequences with the female shaman's role. She revealed a fear that her own evil potential resulted from her bisexual identification, her unconscious homosexuality. Ultimately, she thus revealed anxiety lest her aggression get out of control. Such a fear is reasonably realistic for these Apaches. Sometimes the best controlled of them become almost unimaginably cruel and lewd when in states of regression, often caused by intoxication.

During the ensuing two years, Dawnlight was confronted with little if any social disapprobation. Even though Navaho Man failed to improve, almost everyone used massive denial and believed Dawnlight's intervention to have been successful. People now claimed they knew that in the old days women had been the power behind the Crown Dance team when the singer felt insecure. That is, her personally selected shamanic role now received historical validation.[22] The services of John's dance team were sought both frequently and far and wide. Although ostensibly people were asking for assistance from John as the owner of the power associated with his singership, everyone believed Dawnlight to be the power behind the dance team, and to be factually in charge. They were seeking, if not primarily the use of her supernatural power, at least their combined powers.

One would think that with such public support Dawnlight's anxieties would have been relieved. To the contrary, she seemed to be more fearful of the Boyers' disapproval, and her second Rorschach revealed a typical Apache manner of handling anxiety, that is, by greater emotional constriction. A specific fear was symbolically portrayed, that of spinelessness, of incapacity. We have interpreted this to mean that she unconsciously recognized very well that Navaho Man had failed to improve and regarded herself as being also spineless, that is, to be incapable as a shaman. We would assume that she on some level of consciousness saw this as retribution for her having had the temerity to take over a masculine shamanic role, but we do not have direct evidence to support this assumption.

Stating the case differently, we observe that Dawnlight is anxious because, through a sense of responsibility and inner unconscious pressures, she has usurped the ritual role of a man by becoming the power behind the

---

22. When an individual is accredited as a shaman, in general the people ascribe good intentions to his every behavior and rationalize it, often in historical terms, even though those terms at times might be quite fanciful.

jajadeh team. This is probably the first time in Apache history that a woman has presumed such power. To do so runs the risk of supernatural retribution and public censure and one would say that she has presumed a form of masculine authority while knowing unconsciously that she is not equipped for the masculine role. We observe that a combination of social pressure and intrapsychic conflict-laden homosexual desires is the stimulus for the efflorescence of her paranoia.

To be promoted or to be put in a position by others to assume a role for which one does not internally feel capable can lead to a personal decomposition of the type that Freud (1911) described in the Schreber case. That case became the classic exposition of paranoia. When promoted to the role of judge, Schreber came face to face with a deep sense of inner insufficiency as well as the dangers of usurpation, and regressed to his paranoid psychosis. In a similar fashion, we may say that Dawnlight does not truly feel capable of assuming the role which she has been accorded by her society. This sense of incapacity deepens the need to worry about possible discovery by others of her insufficiency — she sees observing eyes throughout her Rorscharch record. On a deeper level, her incapacity is related to a concept of usurpation similar to that experienced by Schreber. Symbolically his promotion usurped a father's position.

The female shaman here usurps the masculine authority role with all its implications. In both cases, the defense structure of the individual has within it a defense against an acknowledgment of homosexual impulses. We would term this a success psychosis. One observes that a success neurosis or psychosis may derive from one's being incapable of performing a role or, in other instances, from the fear that one's success may result in castration or annihilation (Boyer, in press). Of course, an alternate fear is that one's being successful may result in one's becoming a murderer or, in Dawnlight's case, a witch.

Moreover, when one assumes the authority role, one becomes subject to the hostility and envy that is directed to this status position. It is the experience of the hostility of the subordinate or the rival which is projected at the time the individual assumes an authority position. It must be stated here that Dawnlight is not manifesting a fear of persecution; rather, she is afraid of her own incapacity. And unlike what is evident in most paranoid records, there is a socially integrative capacity to respond positively to others suggested in her Rorschach protocol. This responsiveness may be the reason that there are no overt signs of delusions that separate her from the others clinically. On the contrary, others believe in her and forego any questioning that may bring her into social disrepute.

Usually, when a person is seen as being paranoid, he has no social support. When an individual who may also be paranoid structurally has social

support he is protected from direct confrontation. As long as there is a social need to believe, the person maintains a social adaptability. In such circumstances one need not have an immediate crisis in the testing of one's
beliefs. To a certain degree, the individual remains socially adaptive.
There is no social withdrawal or withdrawal from the beliefs being espoused. Therefore Dawnlight's behavior would not be interpreted negatively, as if she were in a kind of where the crisis would be exacerbated by
being socially alone and isolated. People can have a potentially unstable
structure but if they continue to receive sustaining social support, they
cannot be considered as psychopathological.

Let us return to the popular idea that the shaman is a very disturbed individual or has been "cured" from psychosis by assuming the schamanic
role. Actually, Rorschach protocols reveal that shamans who show psychotic propensities are in the distinct minority. Dawnlight clearly was not
seriously psychologically disturbed before becoming a shaman. To the degree that her subsequent Rorschach protocols reveal psychotic propensities, her "psychosis" can be judged to be a "success psychosis."

Clearly, the findings in the case of Dawnlight are not generalizable, suggestive though they certainly are.

BIBLIOGRAPHY

ACKERKNECHT, E. H. (1943). Psychopathology, Primitive Medicine and Primitive Cul-
ture. *Bull. Hist. Med.,* 14:20–67.
_____ (1949). Medical Practices. In *Handbook of South American Indians,* Vol. 5, ed. J. H.
Steward. [Bureau of American Ethnology, Bulletin 143.] Washington: U.S. Government
Printing Office, pp. 621–643.
BARRETT, S. A. (1917). Ceremonies of the Pomo Indians. [*University of California
Publications in American Archaeology and Ethnology,* 12:397–441.] Berkeley & Los
Angeles: University of California Press.
BASEHART, H. W. (1959). *Chiricahua Apache Subsistence and Socio-Political Organi-
zation.* The University of New Mexico Mescalero-Chiricahua Land Claims Project.
Mimeographed.
_____ (1960). *Mescalero Apache Subsistence Patterns and Socio-Political Organization.*
The University of New Mexico Mescalero-Chiricahua Land Claims Project. Mimeo-
graphed.
BECK, S. J., GRINKER, R. R., & STEPHENSON, W. (1954). *The Six Schizophrenias.
Reaction Patterns in Children and Adults.* New York: The American Orthopsychiatric
Association.
BEST, E. (1922). *Spiritual and Mental Concepts of the Maori.* Wellington, N.Z.: Govern-
ment Printer.
BOGORAS, W. (1907). The Chuckchee: Religion. *Memoirs of the American Museum of
Natural History,* 11:277–536.
BOURKE, J. G. (1892). *The Medicine-Men of the Apache.* Ninth Annual Report, Bureau of
American Ethnology. Reprinted by The Rio Grande Press, Glorietta, N.M., 1970.

BOYER, L. B. (1961). Notes on the Personality Structure of a North American Indian Shaman. *J. Hillside Hosp.,* 10:14-33.

_____ (1962). Remarks on the Personality of Shamans, with Special Reference to the Apache of the Mescalero Indian Reservation. *The Psychoanalytic Study of Society,* 2:233-254, eds. W. Muensterberger and S. Axelrad. New York: International Universities Press.

_____ (1964a). Further Remarks Concerning Shamans and Shamanism. *Israel Annals of Psychiatry and Related Disciplines,* 2:235-257.

_____ (1964b). Psychological Problems of a Group of Apaches: Alcoholic Hallucinosis and Latent Homosexuality Among Typical Men. *The Psychoanalytic Study of Society,* 3:203-277, eds. W. Muensterberger and S. Axelrad. New York: International Universities Press.

_____ (1964c). Folk Psychiatry of the Apaches of the Mescalero Indian Reservation. In *Magic, Faith and Healing, Studies in Primitive Psychiatry Today,* ed. A. Keiv. Glencoe, Ill.: Free Press, pp. 384-419.

_____ (1979a). *Childhood and Folklore. A Psychoanalytic Study of Apache Personality.* New York: The Library of Psychological Anthropology.

_____ (1979b). Stone as a Symbol in Apache Folklore. In *Fantasy and Symbol: Studies in Anthropological Interpretation,* ed. R. H. Hook. London: Academic Press, pp. 207-232.

_____ (in press). Christmas "Neurosis" Reconsidered. In *Depressive States,* ed. V. D. Volkan. New York: Aronson.

_____, & BOYER, R. M. (1976). Prolonged Adolescence and Early Identification: A Cross-Cultural Study. *The Psychoanalytic Study of Society,* 7:95-106, eds. W. Muensterberger, A. H. Esman, and L. B. Boyer. New Haven: Yale University Press.

_____, & _____ (1977). Understanding the Patient through Folklore. *Contemp. Psychoanal.,* 13:50-51.

_____, & _____ (1983). The Sacred Clown of the Chiricahua and Mescalero Apaches: Additional Data. *Western Folklore,* 42:46-54.

_____, _____, & De VOS, G. A. (1982). An Apache Woman's Account of Her Recent Acquisition of the Shamanistic Status. *J. Psychoanal. Anthropology,* 5:299-331.

BOYER, L. B., De VOS, G. A., BORDERS, O., & TANI-BORDERS, A. (1978). The "Burnt Child Syndrome" among the Yukon Eskimos. *J. Psychol. Anthropology,* 1:7-56.

_____, _____, & BOYER, R. M. (1983). A Longitudinal Study of Three Apache Brothers as Reflected in Their Rorschach Protocols. *J. Psychoanal. Anthropology,* 6:125-162.

_____, KLOPFER, B., BRAWER, F. B., & KAWAI, H. (1964). Comparisons of the Shamans and Pseudoshamans of the Apaches of the Mescalero Indian Reservation. *J. Projective Techniques and Personality Assessment,* 28:173-180.

BOYER, R. M. (1962). *Social Structure and Socialization Among the Apache of the Mescalero Indian Reservation.* Unpublished doctoral dissertation, University of California at Berkeley.

_____ (1964). The Matrifocal Family among the Mescalero: Additional Information. *Amer. Anthropologist,* 66:593-602.

_____ (1972). A Mescalero Apache Tale: The Bat and the Flood. *Western Folklore,* 31:189-197.

_____, & BOYER, L. B. (1981). Apache Lore of the Bat. *The Psychoanalytic Study of Society,* 9:263-299, eds. W. Muensterberger, L. B. Boyer, and S. A. Grolnick. New York: Psychohistory Press.

CZAPLICKA, M. A. (1914). *Aboriginal Siberia: A Study in Social Anthropology.* Oxford: Clarendon Press.

DAVIDSON, R. H., & DAY, R. (1974). *Symbol and Realization: A Contribution to the*

Study of Magic and Healing. Berkeley: Center for South & Southeast Asia Studies, University of California.

DAY, R., BOYER, L. B., & De VOS, G. A. (1975). Two Styles of Ego Development: A Cross-Cultural, Longitudinal Comparison of Apache and Anglo School Children. *Ethos,* 3:345–379.

DAY, R., & DAVIDSON, R. H. (1976). Magic and Healing: An Ethnopsychoanalytic Study. *The Psychoanalytic Study of Society,* 7:231–292, eds. W. Muensterberger, A. H. Esman, and L. B. Boyer. New Haven: Yale University Press.

DEVEREUX, G. (1956). Normal and Abnormal: The Key Problem of Psychiatric Anthropology. In *Some Uses of Anthropology, Theoretical and Applied,* eds. J. Casagrande & T. Galwin. Washington: Anthropological Society of Washington, pp. 23–48.

_____, & La BARRE, W. (1961). Art and Mythology. In *Studying Personality Cross-Culturally,* ed. B. Kaplan. Evanston, Ill., & Elmsford, N.Y.: Row, Peterson, pp. 361–403.

De VOS, G. A. (1952). A Quantitative Approach to Affective Symbolism in Rorschach Responses. *J. Projective Techniques,* 16:133–150.

_____ (1961). Symbolic Analysis in the Cross-Cultural Study of Personality. In *Studying Personality Cross-Culturally,* ed. B. Kaplan. Evanston, Ill.: Row, Peterson, pp. 599–634.

_____ (1966). Comparison of Personality Differences in Two Generations of Japanese Americans by Means of the Rorschach Test. University of Hawaii, Social Science Research Institute, Reprint #14.

_____, & BORDERS, O. (1979). A Rorschach Comparison of Delinquent and Non-Delinquent Japanese Family Members. *J. Psychological Anthropology,* 2:425–442.

_____, & MINER, H. (1959). Oasis and Casbah: A Study in Acculturative Stress. In *Culture and Mental Health,* ed. M. K. Opler. New York: Macmillan, pp. 333–350.

DRIVER, H. E. (1961). *Indians of North America.* Chicago: University of Chicago Press.

DUCEY, C. (1976). The Life History and Creative Psychopathology of the Shaman: Ethnopsychoanalytic Perspectives. *The Psychoanalytic Study of Society,* 7:173–230, eds. W. Muensterberger, A. H. Esman, and L. B. Boyer. New Haven: Yale University Press.

_____ (1979). The Shaman's Dream Journey: Psychoanalytic and Structural Complementarity in Myth Interpretation. *The Psychoanalytic Study of Society,* 8:71–118, eds. W. Muensterberger and L. B. Boyer; assoc. ed. G. J. Rose. New Haven: Yale University Press.

ELIADE, M. (1951). *Shamanism: Archaic Techniques of Ecstasy,* trans. W. R. Trask. New York: Bollingen Foundation, 1964.

EXNER, J. E., Jr. (1974). *The Rorschach. A Comprehensive System,* Vol. 1. New York: John Wiley & Sons.

FREEMAN, D. M. A. (1968). Adolescent Crises of the Kiowa-Apache Indian Male. In *Minority Group Adolescents in the United States,* ed. E. B. Brody. Baltimore: Williams & Wilkins, pp. 157–204.

FREUD, S. (1911). Psycho-Analytic Notes on an Autobiographical Account of a Case of Paranoia (Dementia Paranoides). *S.E.,* 12:1–82. London: Hogarth Press, 1958.

_____ (1917). Mourning and Melancholia. *S.E.,* 14:237–258. London: Hogarth Press, 1957.

GIFFORD, E. W. (1927). Southern Maidu Ceremonies. *Amer. Anthropologist,* 29:214–257.

GILLIN, J. P. (1948). Magical Fright. *Psychiatry,* 12:387–400.

GODDARD, P. E. (1916). The Masked Dancers of the Apache. In *The Holmes Anniversary Volume.* Washington: James William Bryan Press, pp. 132–136.

GUSINDE, H. (1939). *Der Peyote Kult. Mölding, Sankt Gabriel, Festschrift.* Vienna: Missions-Druckerei St. Gabriel.

HARRINGTON, M. R. (1912). The Devil Dance of the Apaches. *Museum J.,* (Philadelphia), 3:6–9.

HELM, J., De VOS, G. A., & CARTERETTE, T. (1960). Variations in Personality and Ego Identification within a Slave Indian Kin-Community. [National Museum of Canada, Bulletin 1920, Contributions to Anthropology, Part 2.]

HIPPLER, A. E. (1971). Shamans, Curers and Personality Suggestions toward a Theoretical Model. *Transcultural Psychiatric Research,* 8:190–193 (abstr.).

HOIJER, H. J. (1938). *Chiricahua and Mescalero Texts.* Chicago: University of Chicago Press.

HOLLANDER, A. N. J. (1935). De Peyote Cultur der Nooramerikaansche Indianen. *Mensch en Maatschapij,* 11:17–29, 123–131.

HOUSSE, E. (1939). *Une Epopée Indienne. Les Araucans du Chili.* Paris: Plon.

HOWELLS, W. (1956). *The Heathens.* New York: Doubleday.

HUDSON, W. M., ed. (1951). *The Healer of Los Olmos and Other Mexican Lore.* [Texas Folklore Society Publication 24.] Dallas: Southern Methodist University Press.

ISAACS, S. (1948). The Nature and Function of Phantasy. *Internat. J. Psycho-Anal.,* 29:73–97.

KANE, H. (1937). The Apache Secret Devil Dance. *El Palacio,* 42:93–94.

KIEV, A. (1968). *Curanderismo. Mexican-American Folk Psychiatry.* New York: Free Press.

KLEIN, M. (1932). *The Psycho-Analysis of Children.* London: Hogarth Press.

KLOPFER, B., & BOYER, L. B. (1961). Notes on the Personality Structure of a North American Indian Shaman: Rorschach Interpretation. *J. Projective Techniques,* 25: 170–178.

KRIS, E. (1952). *Psychoanalytic Explorations in Art.* New York: International Universities Press.

KROEBER, A. L. (1925). *Handbook of the Indians of California.* [Bureau of American Ethnology, Bulletin 78.] Washington: U.S. Government Printing Office.

_____ (1940). Psychosis or Social Sanction. *The Nature of Culture.* Chicago: University of Chicago Press, 1952.

KUNSTADTER, P. (1960). *Culture Change, Social Structure and Health Service: A Quantitative Study of Clinic Use Among the Apache of the Mescalero Reservation.* Unpublished doctoral dissertation, University of Michigan.

LA BARRE, WESTON (1938). *The Peyote Cult.* [*University Publications in Anthropology,* No. 13.] New Haven: Yale University Press.

LEBRA, W., & De VOS, G. A. (n.d.). A Rorschach Study of Okinawan Shamans. Unpublished manuscript.

LOMMEL, A. (1967). *Shamanism: The Beginnings of Art,* trans. M. Bulloch. New York: MacGraw-Hill.

LOWIE, R. H. (1935). *The Crow Indians.* New York: Rinehart & Co. Reissued 1956.

LUCKERT, K. W. (1979). *Coyoteway. A Navajo Holyway Ceremonial.* Tucson: The University of Arizona Press; & Flagstaff: The Museum of Northern Arizona Press.

MacLACHLAN, B. B. (1962). *The Mescalero Apache Tribal Court: A Study of the Manifestation of the Adjudicative Function of a Concrete Judicial Institution.* Unpublished doctoral dissertation, University of Chicago.

MAESTES, J. G., & ANAYA, R. A. (1982). *Cuentos. Tales from the Hispanic Southwest.* Santa Fe: Museum of New Mexico Press.

MAILS, T. E. (1974). *The People Called Apache.* Englewood Cliffs, N.J.: Prentice-Hall.

MEISSNER, W. W. (1978). *The Paranoid Process.* New York: Aronson.

MURPHY, R. F. (1958). *Mundurucú Religion.* [*University of California Publications in*

American Archeaology and Ethnology, 49:1–154.] Berkeley & Los Angeles: University of California Press.

OPLER, M. E. (1933). *An Analysis of Mescalero and Chiricahua Apache Social Organization in the Light of Their Systems of Relationship.* Chicago: University of Chicago Press, 1936.

_____ (1936a). The Influence of Aboriginal Pattern and White Contact on a Recently Introduced Ceremony, the Mescalero Peyote Rite. *J. Amer. Folklore,* 49:143–166.

_____ (1936b). Some Points of Comparison and Contrast between the Treatment of Functional Disorders by Apache Shamans and Modern Psychiatric Trends. *Amer. J. Psychiatry,* 92:1371–1387.

_____ (1940). *Myths and Legends of the Lipan Apaches.* [Memoirs of the American Folklore Society, Vol. 36.] New York: J. J. Augustin.

_____ (1941). *An Apache Life-Way.* Chicago: University of Chicago Press.

_____ (1946a). The Mountain Spirits of the Chiricahua Apache. *The Masterkey,* 20: 125–131.

_____ (1946b). The Creative Role of Shamanism in Apache Mythology. *J. Amer. Folklore,* 59:269–281.

_____ (1947). Notes on Chiricahua Apache Culture. I. Supernatural Power and the Shaman. *Primitive Man,* 2:1–14.

_____ (1969). *Apache Odyssey. A Journey Between Two Worlds.* New York: Holt, Rinehart & Winston.

PARIN, P. (1971). Fantasy and Communication. In *Fear Thy Neighbor as Thyself. Psychoanalysis and Society Among the Anyi of West Africa,* by P. Parin, F. Morgenthaler, & G. Parin-Matthèy; trans. P. Klamerth. Chicago & London: University of Chicago Press, 1980, pp. 248–313.

PARIN-MATTHÈY, G. (1971). Witches, Female Shamans and Healers. In *Fear Thy Neighbor as Thyself. Psychoanalysis and Society Among the Anyi of West Africa,* by P. Parin, F. Morgenthaler, & G. Parin-Matthèy, trans. P. Klamerth. Chicago & London: University of Chicago Press, 1980, pp. 212–247.

POOLE, F. J. P. (1983). Cannibals, Tricksters and Witches. Anthropophagic Images Among Bimin-Kuskusmin. In *The Ethnography of Canibalism,* eds. P. Brown & D. Tuzin. Washington: D.C.: Society for Psychological Anthropology, pp. 6–32.

RÓHEIM, GÉZA (1952). The Evil Eye. *Amer. Imago,* 9:351–363.

SEGAL, H. (1957). Notes on Symbol Formation. *Internat. J. Psycho-Anal.,* 38:391–397.

SERVADIO, E. (1936). Die Angst vor dem bösen Blick. *Imago,* 22:396–408.

SHIROKOGOROFF, S. M. (1924). *Psychomental Complex of the Tungus.* London: Kegan Paul, Trench, Trubner.

SILVERMAN, J. (1967). Shamans and Acute Schizophrenia. *Amer. Anthropologist,* 69:21–31.

SINGER, M. T. (n.d.). Personality Measurement in the Aging. In *Human Aging: Biological, Social and Psychological,* ed. J. Birran. Washington: U.S. Government Printing Office.

SLOTKIN, J. S. (1956). *The Peyote Religion.* Glencoe, Ill.: Free Press.

SPEISMAN, J., & SINGER, M. (1961). Rorschach Content, Correlates in Five Groups with Organic Pathology. *J. Projective Techniques,* 25:356–359.

STÄRCKE, A. (1920). The Reversal of the Libido-Sign in Delusions of Persecution. *Internat. J. Psycho-Anal.,* 1:231–234.

STEWARD, J. H. (1929).*The Clown in Native North America.* Doctoral Publication, University of California, Berkeley. Unpublished.

STREITFELT, H. S. (1954). Specificity of Peptic Ulcer to Intense Oral Conflicts. *Psychosomatic Med.*, 16:315–326.

VAN OPHUIJSEN, J. H. W. (1920). On the Origin of the Feeling of Persecution. *Internat. J. Psycho-Anal.*, 1:235–239.

VEREECKEN, J. L. T. (1928). A propos du Mauvais Oeil. *Hygiène Mentale*, 57:25–38.

WEINER, H., THALER, M., & REISER, M. (1957). Etiology of the Peptic Ulcer. Part I: Relation of Specific Psychological Characteristics to Gastric Secretion (Serum-Pepsinogen). *Psychosomatic Med.*, 19.

WYNNE, L., & SINGER, M. T. (1966). Principles of Scoring Communication Defects and Deviances in Parents of Schizophrenics. *Psychiatry*, 29:260–288.

4
Sakulambei—A Hermaphrodite's Secret: An Example of Clinical Ethnography

GILBERT H. HERDT, Ph.D. and
ROBERT J. STOLLER, M.D.

INTRODUCTION

H.:* This study is an experiment in doing and writing ethnography. We present interviews done jointly by an anthropologist and a psychoanalyst with a man of the Sambia tribe in the Eastern Highlands of Papua New Guinea. We are concerned with exploring how to study subjective experience across cultural boundaries. Our aim is not to discuss theory or treatment; we did not do psychoanalysis or therapy in the field. Rather, we present the following dialogues as an example of what I have designated clinical ethnography: the use of clinical skills and concepts, focused empathy, and the explication of interpersonal relationships with informants in order to collect more precise information on the inner thoughts and feelings of others.

One of our larger aims is to show that clinically trained ethnographers *are* able to collect sensitive information about feelings and fantasies in another culture. From time to time, anthropologists have suggested that such data can be elicited under the right circumstances with the right person (reviewed by LeVine, 1982, pp. 285–304). But these reports sometimes omit the specific nuances of meaning surrounding peoples' beliefs, emotional responses, images, values, goals, and the related states of awareness

For research support, Herdt thanks the Australian-American Education Foundation, the Australian National University, the National Institute of Mental Health, the Department of Psychiatry of the University of California at Los Angeles, the Wenner-Gren Foundation for Anthropological Research, and Stanford University. The writing of this paper was supported in part by the Anne Lederer Foundation.

The paper will appear in a somewhat different form in a forthcoming book by the authors entitled *Intimate Communications: Method and Interpretation in Clinical Ethnogrphy.*

*Throughout the text, H. is Herdt, S. is Stoller, Sa. is Sakulambei.

(conscious, subliminal, unconscious) underlying the intersubjectively shared or idiosyncratic elements included in communication. Indeed, theorists such as Geertz (1968, pp. 107–114; 1976) have questioned whether it is possible for anthropologic investigators to describe and understand these subtle nuances. We hope to show that it is possible when clinical skill is combined with an in-depth cultural and linguistic understanding of a person and his personality. Others have questioned the reliability and/or "naturalness" of the ethnographic data collected in the manner (Kracke, 1980). In our summary, we return briefly to this problem within psychoanalytic and cross-cultural perspective.

Let us indicate the particular aims of our methodologic approach and research collaboration.

S.: We need not review here the advantages and limitations of experiments, those hallmarks of careful thinking. At this point, we shall only note that an experiment informs us more if the experimenter and his techniques do not contaminate the experiment. The laboratory ideal, however, is not only impossible in much behavioral research but, in the case of intimate communications, *cannot* produce the needed data. Only communication can do that, and communication requires a minimum of two interacting objects. Still, "social scientists" (the quotation marks indicate my belief that there is little science in some of these scientists) yearn to be scientists; science is the ideal. So what emerges? Innumerable deceptions that are meant to simulate someone's idea of science: an ugly, misshapen vocabulary; stuffy sentence structure; reference to authorities in place of data; questionnaires and attitudinal scales for probing privacy plus untold other ways to avoid intimacy with those we would study; scorn of the single case studied in depth; fear of subjectivity. These scientists want us to voyage encased in space suits, untouched by the environment.

We have all seen objectivity corrupted by its need to avoid or disparage what it cannot objectify. It is bad enough that it is sustained by a kind of dishonesty; even worse, it ruins the search.

(*H.:* Our aim is not to be iconclastic or polemical; rather, we hope to stir people to look more seriously at the quality of ethnography.)

S.: This paper is thus (1) a communication on experiments in ethnography, (2) in itself an experiment, and (3) a first run-through of a new way of teaching in ethnography. Let me begin with the paper as a communication. It reports experiments in which we tried out new techniques. First, from 1975 on—initially in letters, and from 1977 on, in person—a psychoanalyst supervised an ethnographer to enrich the ethnography. Second, at the same time, an ethnographer taught an analyst ethnography to enrich the analyst (but not his analytic technique). Third, the two specialists worked together in the field, extending the ethnographer's interviews but also introducing a clinician (medical practitioner: diagnostician and therapist) into the final data collecting. Fourth, as the interviews unfolded, there were (both during and between interviews) continuous discussions of the clinical findings, methodology, underlying dynamics of the participants and the processes going on among them, implications for theory in ethnography and analysis, a bit of theory making and breaking (braking), and problem solving (therapeutics; psychodynamics; personal histories, e.g., data on gender and erotic elements; how to interview skillfully, etc.).

Now let us discuss the paper as experiment. We are trying to create a better method of reporting clinical data – data gathered from individuals talking intimately about matters important to them. First, we have presented our transcripts in an unadorned manner and have preserved our original tapes if a colleague should want to check the printed version with that from New Guinea. Second, we have tried to present ourselves as close to the way we really were as a text permits. Third, we have added commentary to the transcripts to better reveal that which we believe was occurring that cannot be recorded on an audiotape. Fourth, we both wrote the paper and have indicated the parts for which each of us was primarily responsible. Beyond that, we have each edited and added to the other's writing, sometimes heavily, sometimes painfully, and always openly, without much defensiveness; we also tried to do this without homogenizing our styles too much. Fifth, we have inserted asides to the other's commentaries so the reader can share our disagreements. Sixth, we have retained the ambience of uncertainty that is the reality of fieldwork, thinking, and theory, for we believe almost everyone cheats in this regard.

Teaching is the next one of the paper's functions. We have let you see how H. taught me ethnography and I taught H. about clinical skills and psychodynamics.

In this report, then, we are examining two questions: Do intimate communications provide data that are valuable in studying human behavior; and, if so, what should we know in order to improve the power of those communications? Our purpose is not so much to answer these questions as to encourage colleagues to acknowledge that they are fundamental questions that must be answered.

THE SETTING

H.: Because descriptive materials on the Sambia are available elsewhere (Herdt, 1981, 1982a, 1982b; Stoller and Herdt, 1982), we shall describe their society briefly.

The Sambia number about 2,300 people scattered through rugged and isolated mountains on the fringes of the Eastern Highlands. Hunting and sedentary horticulture are their main economic activities, sweet potatoes being the staple. Patrilineality is marked at all levels of social grouping, and postmarital residence is patrivirilocal. All marriages (primarily infant betrothal or sister exchange) are arranged by elders. Sexual antagonism pervades male/female relations, and men fear women's bodily fluids. Warfare was traditionally rampant. All males are initiated into a secret male cult. Starting from ages seven-ten years, six initiations lead the boys through intense ordeals and warriorhood training from childhood to young adulthood. Ritualized (oral) homosexual contacts are obligatory and frequent for all males during this period of initiation development. Initiates live in men's clubhouses off limits to women and children. Married men live in separate family huts with their wives and children.

Sambia were forcibly pacified by the Australian government in 1964, but, aside from gradual social changes, no major disruptions occurred in their traditional life until the mid- to late 1970s when outside contacts increased. I began research in 1974–1976, and returned in 1979 for further fieldwork. S. joined me in 1979 for a few days, when the following interviews were done.

BIOGRAPHIC PORTRAIT

H.: In a society that prizes maleness, in which men emphasize phallicness and exhibitionistic performances, in which ritual and myth give highest value to penis, semen, and many progeny for admission into adult masculine personhood, there could hardly be a condition more anomalous or sensitive than hermaphrodism.[1] When I began fieldwork among the Sambia I was not aware of this. Nor did I know that there are intersexed Sambias: hermaphroditic males who are treated differently from birth, who are said to have microscopic penises, and who are apparently sterile. Sakulambei is such a person. This paper reflects on his life, its public and secret stigmata, especially the private secret he dared not share with anyone, and the relationship with us that allowed him to share it.

---

1. Apparently, hermaphrodism (familial idiopathic pseudohermaphrodism in chromosomal males) is more frequent in some Melanesian populations than in other parts of the world. At present there are several such males in the Sambia Valley proper, with a population of about 1000, and others, now dead, have been reported. Even stranger would be institutionalized transvestism with permanent cross-dressing and living in the opposite sex role (like the Mohave *alyu* or Tahitian *mahu* [Devereux, 1937; Levy, 1973]). However, Sambia and other Melanesians have no cross-dressing behavior or customary social role outlet of this kind (Herdt, 1984). The psychosocial dynamics of Melanesian groups make institutionalized cross-dressing among them implausible.

By 1979 Saku was in his late twenties, already established as a powerful shaman. He was married but childless. I had known him since 1974, when he was just an acquaintance who looked and acted a little odd in the first months of our relationship. In 1975, I interviewed him several times concerning his shamanism. He was warm, knowledgeable, and articulate, but I felt there were things he was hiding. At that time I was not interested in his hermaphrodism and did not discuss it. Soon thereafter I saw him belatedly initiated into third-stage bachelorhood, years behind his agemates. Then a few months later, he was married, surprising everyone. In early 1979, to understand his gender identity, I began to interview him in depth. When S. joined us after four months of constant work, dramatic results emerged.

I am uncomfortable condensing Saku's biography. He and his history are easily distorted. My materials on Saku and several other Sambia are rich and cover years. I worked alone with each, without an interpreter. I studied Saku's dreams, which facilitated the strong transference attachment he formed to me. Saku liked me, and I him; during these years my respect and admiration for him grew as I learned more of his struggle to be himself. But he never completely trusted me, even though in his distrust I sensed a desire to trust. It was not until the sessions with S. that I understood his mistrust.

Let me first sketch Saku's history and discuss the progress of our work in 1979, when S. entered the picture.

Saku was born about 1953. Warfare was still raging throughout his childhood. Although, during our 1979 interviews, I did not know the details of his birth, I did know that, though assigned to the male sex, he had been labeled at birth a hermaphrodite. Saku was so touchy discussing the subject that I could not learn the particulars from him. But once he opened up to S. and me, I was able later, in 1981, to investigate the details of his birth, and even interviewed the old woman who had served as midwife and who made the sex assignment.[2] He had been born with a tiny penis and an odd-looking scrotum. As were all male hermaphrodites there, he had been assigned to the male sex because people knew that later sexual differentiation in the genitals would occur around puberty.[3] Hermaphrodism is a

---

2. I finished my case study of Saku in 1981 after seven years of interviews. The old woman (and his sister) with whom I talked confirmed that at birth he was labeled a hermaphrodite but marked "male," because his glans was just visible, protruding from the top of his scrotal area.

3. Sambia believe that further growth of the male hermaphrodites' penises and secondary sex traits such as facial hair occur around puberty. They therefore assign them to the male sex in anticipation of these later developments (cf. Imperato-McGinley et al., 1974). Saku's development confirms these views. The underlying physical mechanisms in him are unknown.

mystery to Sambia. It has magical associations. But mysterious or magical, hermaphrodites are stigmatized. No different in appearance at birth from other hermaphrodites, Saku has made himself different. He is a powerful shaman. I know of no other Sambia hermaphrodites, past or present, who became shamans, let alone great shamans. Saku's achievement is unique.

It is Sakulambei's fate to have been the son of the greatest living Sambia war leader. Mon, his father, just died, in 1983. But until his death, in his late sixties, he was rough and tough, still acknowledged as *the* leading elder of Pundei hamlet. He killed at least eight men and was involved in countless battles. He married six times (outliving three of his wives) and fathered more than 20 children. Before his death, Mon was among the three or four oldest Sambia in the Valley – survivor of wars, epidemics, and famines, and the last of virtually all his brothers, age-mates, friends, and enemies. To the end, he was the ruthless, cold-blooded warrior, for some 40 years holding leadership through bluster, guile, intelligence, threat, and his special warlike skills. For instance, he proved himself a master of treachery, not above killing a clan brother.[4] At one time, with his brother Erujundei, he held shamanic powers, and throughout his life practiced sorcery to support his leadership. But Mon was never a successful shaman and had not practiced for years. Still, for longer than anyone, Mon firmly controlled his world – for nearly half a century.

Saku was the third and last child of Mon's third wife. She was much younger than Mon, and through a sister-exchange marriage had been traded from a distant hamlet at the other end of the Sambia Valley. Her brother Yumalo, also a fight leader, was equally important as a great shaman. He became crucial in Saku's development. Saku's mother died many years ago, when he was five. We know little of her, except that she was frail, a minor shaman herself, and well liked. Her marriage to Mon was apparently not happy. She never adjusted to living in Pundei. She bore a daughter, a son, and then Saku, all of whom are still living. From what is known,[5] all except Saku are anatomically normal. The parents fought a lot, and Saku's mother was often ill. When she became sick, she would re-

---

4. Mon and another Pundei clan brother (still living) conspired to kill Weiyu's father; Mon masterminded it. Still, Saku, whose mother was a biologic sister to Weiyu's mother, and Weiyu, are the closest of friends. Neither has much love for Mon.

5. Saku's sister is married and has children. His older brother left for the coast in 1967, while still a second-stage initiate. He has never returned to the valley, is unmarried, and has had only vague contacts through letters with Saku and others. Since I have never seen the brother, and his social development is definitely strange, he must remain another puzzle in an already strange story.

turn to Yumalo, to be treated through healing ceremonies. She died and was buried in her natal hamlet around 1958.

In early childhood, Saku had an almost nonexistent relationship with his father because of his stigma. His mother died early. We can presume his life would have been a disaster had it not been for his maternal uncle Yumalo, who stepped in at this point. Even before his mother's death, Saku spent most of his time in his uncle's household, Yumalo already functioning as a substitute father figure. After she died, Mon ignored Saku, which was apparently fine with Yumalo, who cared for him. By that time, Saku's brother, who was more interesting to Mon than Saku was, had been initiated. Age was not the only reason he had advanced and Saku had not; apparently, Mon saw Saku as an embarrassment and rejected him for years.

Saku took his mother's death very hard. He says that after her funeral her ghost came to him more than once. And something else. A few months later he was playing alone in a garden when a young boy — a spirit being — came to play with him. This spirit being, who looked to be somewhat older than Saku, befriended and talked to him and performed amazing feats. This being[6] became Saku's first and most important spirit familiar when he began to practice shamanism. Beginning as a figure in Saku's dreams as a child, he is still seen by Saku in his trance states. Next to Yumalo's spirit familiars, the child familiar (who grew in imagination as Saku grew, but who is normally masculine) has protected him through thick and thin. But Yumalo sensed that something was wrong, and when Saku told him of the child spirit's visitations, wisely told him not to pay attention. (But not to ignore him, either.) From then on, Yumalo took an even closer interest in Saku, who in effect became his adopted son.

Yumalo was a curious figure. I knew him as an old man before he died in 1977. He was a contradiction: Obviously masculine, with two wives and several children, he was both nurturant and sensitive. He was a traditionalist, yet he wore odd Western clothes, easily able to accommodate the accoutrements of both worlds. He was considerate, generous, never querulous — a fine, proud old wizard. He was feared, some say hated, by his enemies, however, because of extraordinary shamanic powers and sorcery magic that surpassed any other in the region. Though he liked women and had good marriages, he had his own hut apart from them; at the same time, he felt no stigma in planting and harvesting his own sweet potatoes (female activities). In short, Yumalo was a bundle of both feminine and masculine features, which existed within his shamanic identity.

---

6. Probably an imaginary playmate, now his symbolic double.

Saku is clear he would not have become a shaman had it not been for his uncle. True, he had all the required social ancestry to become one,[7] but that might have gone for naught without his uncle. From his earliest years, Saku had had dreams. These dreams were crucial to his calling as a shaman. Many were prophetic. Saku gives examples of dreams he claims to have had when only six or seven (before initiation) that people believed foretold the future. His uncle did more than encourage these dreams: He discussed them with Saku, taught him to interpret them, and explained that they would enable Saku to become a shaman. Yumalo did not in the slightest way disparage Saku for his hermaphrodism. And because of this tolerance and his uncle's special attention to his growing pre-shamanic skills, Saku adored him. In short, largely due to Yumalo, Saku longed to become a great shaman like his uncle, acquiring the identity/role that now is laced into his very being and that enables him, against great odds, to surmount a difficult fate.

Saku was initiated in 1964. He was older than the other boys, which probably helped him through the ordeals. But by age ten, Saku had already been toughened anyway. He had been taunted by children who said he was really a girl, not a boy, or a boy who didn't have a penis. His older brother didn't help him much, but Weiyu always stuck up for him. There were several times when Saku got into a fight and Weiyu defended him. They were friends, not just cousins. (Years later, when Weiyu was close to death from malaria, Saku sat with him, performed healing ceremonies, fed him for weeks, and nursed him back to health.) Only one thing—an odd one—stood out in Saku's first initiation: He did not bleed when the men plunged cane grasses down his nose.[8] Saku says he felt the nosebleeding was silly and not necessary for him: He would grow to be masculine quite nicely without losing any of his blood.[9] He has never bled his nose since, either.

He underwent second-stage initiation normally too, about three years later. At his first initiation, his father had begun to take more of an inter-

---

7. Saku's father, father's brother (Erujundei), and mother were all shamans, in addition to Yumalo; and their shamanic familiars had long genealogic validity. Thus, Saku is a primary shaman.
8. I doubted this story, but Weiyu and others confirm that it is true.
9. Saku told me he just did not want his nose to bleed, and it did not. His nose never has bled. Now, as a married man, it is appropriate that Saku regularly nosebleed himself, but he says that it is ridiculous and he'll have no part of it (see Herdt, 1982b). Saku says his uncle (a member of a clan with a different practice) also never nosebled himself. Saku uses that to rationalize his behavior. Perhaps the selfhood of a Sambia hermaphrodite is too fragile (his body boundaries too tenuous) to let loose anything as precious as blood. And perhaps these hermaphrodites have more femininity in core identity and do not need so clearly to mark their maleness by bloodletting.

est in him, and had even tried to persuade Saku to return to Pundei and live there. And though Saku did begin to spend more time there – his natal hamlet and clan – he continued to spend the majority of his time at his uncle's.

Meanwhile, Saku was growing, and was involved, as were the other boys, in homosexual activities. Two points should be stressed about this. First, Saku has always been known as an enthusiastic and skillful fellator, wanting to take in semen as quickly as possible. On the other hand, Saku (who had no trouble discussing it) told me that he always felt that fellatio was a little silly. (But not silly enough not to do it.) This view, as with his refusal to nosebleed himself, carried with it the sense that his body was relatively self-contained and needed no help to mature. I didn't believe him.[10] The second point to be stressed is that Saku's gender identity and erotic life are aberrant since he has never been fellated. Saku did not talk about this, because he could not discuss his hermaphrodism (not just his anatomy) with me: He could not tell me that he is terrified of others seeing his genitals. But from all indications[11] Saku was simply so ashamed that he could not be a sexual inserter. I do not know how strong Saku's sexual impulses are, but he claims to have had several wet dreams. At the same time, he continued to be a fellator well after the normal period.[12] In part, this abnormality stems from Saku having had no third-stage – puberty – initiation until 1975 (whereas his age-mate Weiyu underwent that ceremony in 1970).

The main reason Saku was not elevated in the initiation cycle was his father's (and other men's) attitude that there was no sense wasting time on him. Third-stage initiation meant that one was biologically mature and ready for marriage. "Why waste a good woman on a sterile hermaphrodite?" I have heard men say. This attitude so hurt and enraged Saku that he left the Valley and went to work on the coast around 1970. He has never forgiven his father or clansmen.

---

10. Saku felt compelled to present himself to me in this way, lying if necessary, so as to say, in essence, "I am different but still masculine and don't need the sperm other males need." Saku's other behavior belied that intellectualization: Others say he was an expert fellator. Since he was chameleonic (see below), he may have felt this so as to identify with me when alone, perhaps to prove that he was, in that sense, more masculine than other men.

11. Many initiates have said they tried to get Saku to screw them out of curiosity to see what his genitals looked like. Saku was probably wise to avoid them: Sambia initiates are inveterate gossips, not above humiliating a sexual partner. Saku is extraordinarily careful always to cover his genitals.

12. Weiyu says Saku continued to suck older males even on the coast, in the early 1970s, well after his puberty. That is aberrant. Saku confirmed this report. Further, he quit being a fellator mainly because his sexual partners no longer felt comfortable screwing such an advanced youth.

So Saku left his own land. He was in Moresby for awhile serving as cheap plantation labor. His dreams and some trance experiences continued. Then he moved near Goroka, where for three years he lived on a coffee plantation. He now became more sophisticated about the white man's world, seeing things he both liked and disliked. But after four years, disgusted with life there, he grew tired and homesick. He returned to the Sambia, but found that little had changed: He was trapped by his anatomy; others still felt him to be a freak. He worked hard, planted coffee trees, made as much money as he could (he gave most of his savings to his uncle and aunt), and eventually built a tin-roof house: *the* sign of westernization. He took up his healing practices, too, with more fervor, though he still had not gone through the shamanic initiation. A little later, in 1974, I arrived on the scene.

Saku did not stand out from the crowd in those days. He alternated between traditional garb and Western clothes (and still does). His height was normal, but his build was slight. He lacked the burly anatomy of those Sambians who look like New Guineans in racial characteristics, and his light brown skin, fair complexion, and brown frizzy hair made him look Papuan.[13] By Sambia standards, he was handsome. Closer up, though, his face was unusual.[14] I now see that it matches his personality: androgynous. His broad, intelligent forehead is faintly creased by fine horizontal worry lines. He also has creases vertical to his eyebrows, which are oddly bushy and thick on an otherwise sparsely bearded face.[15] His high cheekbones and long square nose (unusual in Sambia) give him – to me – a graceful, proud countenance. His lips are thin and grayish red, his teeth stained bright red from constant betel-nut chewing. But what strikes me most are his eyes. They are liquid, darkly beautiful, but sunken and a bit close-set. They are – I can think of no better word – chameleonic: They can seem to reflect whatever they see, and yet can seem expressive at the same time. They can be happy and sad, proud and despairing, warm and cold, dark and bright, open and mysterious. They can make him seem to be waiting, wary, suspicious, always searching for the slightest sign of disapproval or rejection. It was because of his eyes that I was more sensitive

---

13. Sambia is a racially mixed population, with both Papuan and New Guinean elements. This mixture is probably the result of migration from the Papuan Lowlands into Highland populations.

14. Why do enthnographers seldom describe the physical appearance of their informants, translators, or friends? Do we ethnographers select key informants who not only match our personalities, but (as with our friends and sometimes spouses) also resemble us physically? Would such a prototype be especially true of same-sex informants?

15. In 1974–1976, Saku had no facial hair. By 1979 he had some small growth on his upper lip, which he does not shave off. Its late appearance is abnormal for Sambia.

and careful with Saku than with other informants. I felt as if I were handling crystal.

As I got to know Saku, two aspects of his character emerged. The first I observed a hundred times. His responses are highly situation-specific: Saku becomes what he thinks others expect him to be. He reflects his environment. (Human chameleons are hard to detect and harder to study.) For instance, it took me a long time to learn that Saku makes sexual allusions or comments only in public. At first I found that, like other men, in private Saku made sexual slurs to me about women. But I felt it was contrived: There was no hostility in his slurs. (How different from the natural spontaneity with which men frequently and vigorously insult women.) When I did not respond, did not reinforce this behavior, it stopped.

The other aspect reflected a truer sense of self: "I am the shaman Saku." The shamanic identity – the trance states, dreams, identification with familiars – all were woven into himself. His core. When he was most comfortable with me, alone in my house, he showed subtle behaviors remarkable for a Sambia man. Examples: a passivity that waits for me to make a move; a quietness – quiet voice, low affect, a constant despair – with secrecy and shame behind the quietness; an embarrassed smile when he turns his head from me, more like an initiate or woman; a way of moving his whole body when speaking or looking out the window, coupled with frequent gestural use of his hands. The sum of such traits is neither wholly masculine nor feminine; and when I am with him, his presence is unobtrusive to the point that I can feel almost alone. Strange but not unpleasant.

Saku must have known he was getting nowhere with his father and clan: No woman – no masculine adult personhood – was being given, and none was in sight. His father as much as said he would not waste a woman on Saku. In 1975, this trend reached a head, and Saku disappeared. I did not know what had happened until I heard he was being initiated third-stage with distant kin of his uncle over the mountains in the Yellow River Valley. When I arrived there with friends to see their initiations, Saku stood tall in his best warrior garb. We soon heard a rumor that he had arranged a marriage and would return shortly with his new bride. Everyone was amazed. I was astonished but happy for him. Looking back, I believe Saku grew tired of being nothing. Something seemed to have snapped in him. So he swallowed his pride and went out to make a new life for himself – wife included – without his clan's help. He turned from what he could not have – a perfect male body – to what he could have.

His uncle had helped Saku again in two ways. Yumalo arranged to have his younger classificatory brother's daughter marry Saku (Saku's mother's brother's daughter, which is a marriage frowned on by Sambia). Saku asked *her* for her permission too, a mere girl who had just recently reached menarche. She agreed, knowing he was a hermaphrodite. Saku made bride wealth payment. They returned to his hamlet and took up residence. People said the marriage would never work, and they made cruel jokes about it.[16] About the same time, a collective initiation cycle was held in the Valley, and a new men's house was built in Nilangu. This was a great event. A shaman's initiation was held in the new men's house. Saku was then formally acknowledged as a shaman, with his uncle attending the ceremony. The story of that experience is told below.

Saku seemed happier. On returning in 1979, I wanted to get him to talk. We discussed many things, spent many hours on his dreams. But I could not get him to discuss his hermaphrodism, which I wished very much to learn about as another kind of "control" case for understanding the origins and dynamics of Sambia gender identity. As I struggled to allow Saku to tell me in his own way about his early experiences in relation to being a hermaphrodite, we bogged down. He was very scared when I approached the subject, nor could he tell me details of his erotic life, for that, too, impinged on his anatomy.

By the time of S.'s arrival, we had reached an impasse. Saku resisted me not by staying and being hostile – by wearing me out – but by leaving, sometimes for a day or two, or for a week. He always came back, and I never scolded him. He knew, I think, that I was a friend and that I could be trusted: He wanted to trust. But I felt he had been so traumatized for so many years that it would take something great – such as patience – to lift him out of his reluctance, pain, and fear.

What I could not know was that behind Saku's open secret – his hermaphroditic body – lay a deeper secret. When S. came and helped Saku tell me in two hours what I had tried to have him say for years, we learned of another terrible trauma, one that had inhibited him as much as his childhood. A weird white man, a European, had years before photographed Saku's body nude – in front of others – and had then, without further ado, left. Since then, a humiliated Saku had raged and despaired at what had happened that afternoon. He lived in fear that the man would return and repeat the unbearable trauma. This is where S. helped out Saku – and me.

---

16. At the time, jokes were being made that Saku's penis had finally – inexplicably – grown enough to copulate with women. The men said it would be fruitless and that the woman would spit on him. The women said his wife must be crazy or immature and that she'd soon grow bored with a man without much of a penis. What no one reckoned on was Saku's intelligence. He has arranged his life to make his wife as happy as possible. And, an important dynamic in their marriage, his wife fears Saku's shamanic powers. By 1979 the marriage was still in good order.

To conclude this introduction: Sakulambei is remarkable. His unique developmental history explains, *because* of his hermaphrodism, how a courageous person managed to survive and even prosper despite great obstacles. In creating himself, he has shown how one can, when loved enough, overcome terrible traumas and defy what fate seems to have had in mind. But Saku's fascinating story should not obscure a point more central to our undramatic thesis: Ethnographers who ignore the intimate circumstances of their work and of the people with whom they work, are dehumanized.

FIRST SESSION

H.: The context of the session was this.[17] In 1979 Sakulambei had been talking with me for several months. We had started discussing his shamanism and its relation to other aspects of his life and were working on his gender identity. Being a hermaphrodite and so identified in the community, he provided a unique chance for understanding variations and vicissitudes in the development of masculinity. Though I several times approached the subject, he had great difficulty talking about it. I was pushing him as hard as possible, aware of his shame and his anxiety that people might talk behind his back and make fun of him. I was proceeding slowly and cautiously. A few days before S. arrived, I had broached the subject again, and Saku had left. It wasn't that he had *really* left but only that he was avoiding talking about his hermaphrodism. Since I had a lot to do and was preparing for S.'s arrival, I simply let him alone during this period. But knowing S. had arrived and was important to me, Saku returned after I had sent word that S. wanted to join our conversations. We were at a crucial point. S.'s arrival put life back in our interviews.

Saku began the session by spontaneously sharing a dream with me. He related how he had actually seen S. in his dream the night before. This dream had made him very anxious; S. was a threatening figure in the dream, one who seemed to want to "kill Saku." This dream report also confirmed for Saku his special powers to see omens in his dreams, and it helped him to account for returning to talk to me after an absence. (He apologized for not contacting me earlier). Then S. asked Saku about the nature of his shamanic powers.[18] Saku went on to detail these (see below). S., sensing that Saku might reveal more about the role his hermaphrodism played in the development of his shamanic identity, suggested that Saku

---

17. Because of space limitations we summarize the transcript of this session.
18. On Sambia shamanism, see Herdt (1977).

had "secrets" to be discovered. This suggestion made Saku wary, but he seemed determined to make himself available for further talking. We closed the session after an hour, agreeing to meet the following day.

SECOND SESSION

H: Yesterday Dr. Stoller talked to you about the kind of work he does. He said he was pleased to be with you and he was very pleased with your decorations.

Sa: [Quietly] Uh-huh.

H: Yesterday he told you about his strength [*jerungdu*], which all three of us use in our work. This morning, too, you saw him use it with Nilutwo [an adult informant, a man well known to us].[19]

Sa: Uh-huh.

H: What did you think of that?

Sa: No thoughts. Whatever he says, I can follow that. That's all. [The resistance stiffens.]

H: Hm.

Sa: Yeah. Whatever he wants to talk about is all right.

H: [To S.] He says he'll do whatever you want.

S: OK. Well, let's move into this, respecting the fact that he's a good shaman. I would like his impressions of my shamanistic number with Nilutwo this morning. And I don't know if I can expect this of him, but I would like the truth rather than have him butter me up or be nervous with me. You see, my view of that performance is, "Oh, God, it didn't work." They may not see it that way, but I wouldn't want him to say, "Oh, you're a great magician," in order to make me feel good . . . I don't know how you can play that with him.

H: He wants to ask you about shamanism, his and yours. He's heard me say that you are a big shaman in this valley. He'd be pleased to learn about your shamanism and your spirit familiars. He wants to ask you first: What do you think of what he did with Nilutwo?

Sa: I guess he wanted to look inside, to see inside his liver or some-

---

19. *S:* Nilutwo is dying – transected spinal cord after falling from a tree – in terrible pain because he cannot change position, is exhausted, cannot sleep, expects his friends to steal his wife when he dies, and is enraged at fate. To relieve him, I tried, before a tense audience, to hypnotize him this morning, acting like a hotshot (UCLA) wizard and hoping, for his sake, that my sense of being a damn fool didn't show. He did not bat an eye. So, an honest failure, I finally stopped. No sooner had I left the hut, however, than he fell asleep and slept many hours.

thing. Is a bone broken inside there? He wanted to look inside of him[20] [S.'s hypnotic technique interpreted as shamanic divination for diagnosing illness].

H: What did you think of that?

Sa: It's good. It's very good. Truly good. We don't know how to do that. He was looking hard at him.

H: Yeah. He's not a bad man [S.]. He's not someone from the ghosts.[21] He's a good man.

Sa: Yeah, that's right.

H: So he knows how to do that kind of thing.

Sa: Yeah, that's really good. I was watching what he was doing to Nilutwo, and I thought, "He wants to look at all of his bones or whatever is inside of him." He looked in, and that was good.

H: [To S.] He thought what you did this morning was good. He watched you carefully and felt you wanted to get inside of Nilutwo just like a shaman divinates while in a trance. It has a magical meaning of what shamans do here.

S: So my performance is in a realm that he's familiar with.

H: Yes.

S: And I was competent, not in my results but as a performer of it in my own style. Is that what he's saying?

H: Yes. He said it was good and he was very glad that you did that.

S: All right. Now, let's move into his shamanism: What's it feel like to be a shaman? How has it changed over time? What's his sense of his power—now as compared to when he first started? Is that enough to start?

H: Yeah. Some of these questions we've already gone over.

S: Then don't spend much time on them.

H: I don't know how this can be done, but I want to ask him the question [I tried] before he ran away: his hermaphrodism.

S: OK, go to it. Maybe we're in good enough shape now.

---

20. *S:* I kept telling Nilutwo to stare into my eyes as I stared deeply into his. God knows what that act means to a Sambia man. With us it means, "You are being hypnotized. So go into a trance like you know you should."

21. *H:* Staring directly into someone else's eyes when not engaged in sexual looking or in a trance (as a shaman) is bizarre to Sambia. But because it was S.—my white-haired friend/boss, a Western doctor—it was permitted. By Saku saying S. was not a ghost, he tells us that no one but a ghost would do what S. did (e.g., in a dream), but it was okay, not bad; that's how it was sensed. In denying S. was a ghost, Saku also rejects weirder interpretations (i.e., S. is a ghostlike figure, in the "cargo cultist" sense), at least for us. But recall that he is being pressed by potential authorities for his powerless opinion.

H: Uh—I'm trying to think how to do it best. You've reinforced the part in him that's most sensitive. He's not as afraid. So I've got a good start. We were working on how he first got his powers from his maternal uncle, the man he mentioned yesterday.

S: What do you want to know that will be difficult for him to answer unless we help him respond safely?

H: What is his sex life now?

S: You might not get that so easily.

H: [Exasperated] I haven't *been* able to get it.

S: He turned you away? Or you haven't dared ask?

H: I was just preparing to move into these sensitive areas when it stopped.

S: I see. Could you—uh—

H: —If somehow I could shift some of the responsibility to you. . . .

S: That's what I was going to say—

H: —but do it differently—

S: —but do it differently—try this on: Tell him that I put my power into you. Would that make sense? Not to the extent that you are me. But that I have put it into you. Not just taught it to you, but [S. makes a noise here like an electric drill—"bzzz": The feeling is implanted in me.] put it into you so that he is safe when he talks to you about these things. [Emphasizes] "*I* will protect him because I put into *you* the capacity to protect him."

[S: By injecting my power into H., I not only let Saku know that H. now posesses my shamanic powers but I also get H. to feel it. In politer circles this is called "identification," a process we all know helps form identity—converts students to teachers or healers. It brings to life the business of education, making organic the formulating of techniques.]

H: [To Sa.] Do you want to say anything to him? If not, I have something to ask you. Is that all right?

Sa: Yeah. [Quiet and a bit depressed] You talk. I have nothing in particular to say. [Quiet. *H.:* I feel he's holding back; he's worried where we're going.]

H: All right. [To S.] To do this we need privacy, so I'm going to get rid of everyone in the house.

S: That's what he just asked you?

H: No, it's my idea. It signals him that I'm going to ask about important things.

S: Proceed, and make him know that you are *lovingly* protective. That really *is* what you're doing. Make him as comfortable as possible, and let him see you recognize how difficult this is for him.

Anything you can do to make it possible, that's what you want to do. That's what you just expressed now, in fact.

H: Yeah. [To Sa., H. summarizes S.'s message.] Now, I think that if we want to work this way we should kick everyone out. Is that all right?

Sa: That's your choice.

H: Is that all right?

Sa: [Almost inaudible] That's all right.[22]

H: I don't want anyone to hear something that belongs to you only, or to your shamanism. I want to protect you.

Sa: [Almost inaudible] Uh-huh.

[H.:   I get up. Lots of noise, people milling around. I chase them out, fasten the door, come back into the room, and talk again.]

H: He [S.] says this: He's got this strength, a power, a good power. And he wants to encircle you with protection so that inside you and I can talk about your shamanism and your experiences without your being afraid of me. [Pause. No response. Now to S.] I've said it as clearly as I can.

S: OK. Now we just have to go and see if he lets us. If he *sort* of lets us, then we can amplify.

H: You have a pretty good sense of him, his childhood, his development. But I know nothing about his sex life, and he and I have *never* discussed his hermaphrodism.

S: Well, why don't you now do it.

H: I want to ask you about your shamanism. I want to ask you some things I haven't asked you about before. About the time you felt the spirit familiars come inside of you. Those of Yumalo. In the *narangu* [shaman's initiation] of Nilangu hamlet [1975], you still didn't have any of Yumalo's familiars, right?

Sa: Uh-huh.

H: And Yumalo told you, "I must not fall sick. If you entice my familiars away from me, I might die."

Sa: Uh-huh.

H: But later his familiars came to you, and he hadn't died yet.

Sa: Yeah. . . .

H: [Pause] Now, when Yumalo's familiars came to you what did you feel?

Sa: [Confident] "This mother's brother of mine he's going to die. He's

---

22.   *S:* I felt pain for him here — and more as we proceeded. I didn't want my first great shaman to be just a kid decked out in his best feathers. He was scared-trying-to-be-brave and trying to honor his identity.

not walking around much. He just sits around his house." His familiars came to me. He wasn't visiting his gardens or anywhere else. He'd just sit around his house. And by and by he would die. He spoke out to me.

H: You mean he pointed to you [the accusing finger: Because Saku had taken his spirit familiars, it meant Yumalo had fallen sick.]

Sa: They performed a *narangu* here and he told me, "I won't come to you now. I won't be able to stroll around from now on. This soul of mine, soon I'll give it to you[23] and I'll die."

H: But when did his shamanic familiars come to you: then or later?

Sa: Later. When we performed that *narangu* —

H: — Yeah —

Sa: At this time — the shamanic familiars of Yumalo — *he* sent them. He himself said he thought his familiars were choosing to go to me. So he sent his familiars to me. But I thought, and then I said, "Don't give them to me: You will get sick and die. Don't just sit around the house." I told him that. And then he said, "Oh, that's all right. I shall just become inactive." [His aged uncle was saying it was all right if he now died.]

H: Now at this time they came inside of you in the *narangu*?

Sa: Yeah — [His voice trails off; he's reaching out to try and help H. understand.]

H: I thought that it happened but you sent them all back.

Sa: Yeah, at this time I spoke out to Yumalo, "Why don't you try them out on me? Try me." [The idiom here, "Try me out," means a "test." Shamans test each other to see how powerful and disciplined they are, and so he's suggesting that he told his uncle to test him to see if he was enough of a shaman to be able to handle his uncle's spirit familiars.]

H: "You can just take back your spirit familiars afterward?"

Sa: That's what I said. [Pause] And then he said, "That's all right. If I die, say, or if I really get a big sickness and can only sit around the house, then you must come and visit me." [Saku lives below down at the river, whereas his uncle lived in a village about an hour's walk away. He's suggesting here that his uncle was saying, "It's all right for you to take my spirit familiars now, though that will eventually make me sick. So when I get sick, since you have the healing power now, you must come and perform healing ceremonies on me."] Like that. So, when I saw him afterward, I didn't just

---

23. Metaphorically, not literally.

sit around [ignore and forget his uncle]. Instead, I went to him all
the time. I bought fish and rice and got other foods and gave them
to him. So [voice trails off] . . . at the time that he looked at me
when he was close to dying [1977], it was only then his spirit familiars came to me for good.

H: What do you feel then? [We skip here details of Saku's shamanic
trances and identifications with familiars since this material leads
us from the main course of the paper.]

Sa: I feel at those times that my mother's brother's soul hasn't gone
away, not gone away.

H: It's still around. He's still around with you. He's fastened to your
skin, huh?

Sa: Yeah, that's how I think; I think like that.

H: All right, I want to tell this part to Dr. Stoller so he understands,
all right? [To S.] At the time of his shamanic initiation in 1975, his
uncle's spirits wanted to come to him of their own volition. But
that would have killed the old man; it would have robbed him of
his soul. So Saku sent them back to him.

S: Why was his uncle willing to do it?

H: Because his uncle thought he was going to die. He was an old man.
I knew Yumalo: He was a . . . strong, kindly, masculine; a presence. In some ways he resembled—had the same habits as—Saku;
imitation [by Saku] mostly, I think. When he has trances now, he
often sees his uncle's face. [Saku trances frequently.]

S: [Interrupting] Benign?[14]

H: I haven't asked him that yet. Uh. . . .

S: Can I ask—for orientation; it has nothing to do with the present
subject but it will help me. Did he do the initiations?

H: Yes.

S: Despite the anatomical—if there is one—defect?

H: Yes, but I don't know the details yet, because we haven't worked
on that.

S: What happened when he was a bachelor?

H: We haven't done that yet.

S: But there must be someone here who was his age.

H: Oh, yeah, I know what *they* say, but I don't know what *he* says
[i.e., about screwing boys].

---

24. *H:* A question I might not have asked, at least not then. Perhaps I would have asked it
later. But it seems an important point, one that might make the interview go differently
now and save time later.

S: I see, Because he has testosterone, without question, in him. Do you understand what I mean? He's got appropriate facial hair and muscular build.

H: Yeah.

S: So his testes are intact. Now does he produce – you can't answer this – does he produce semen . . . and are they taking it from him, or . . . ?

H: Well, the closest that I know, is rough. But pretty reliable sources say he *never* did screw any boys. The boys always wanted to, because they were curious and wanted to find out . . . but he would never do it.

S: I see.

H: But he has told me that at least once, possibly twice, he had wet dreams.

S: So that as far as you know he has only had a couple of ejaculations in his life.

H: As far as I know, right.

S: Okay, you don't need me now.

H: I've figured out a way to ask about his sex. But it would be better if you asked him. . . . This may be premature, but we don't have very much time. So, if you can somehow convey the message that shamans (*kwoolukus*) are . . . if somehow it can be conveyed that strong *kwoolukus* are also masculine shamans . . . and masculine men . . . who have erections, who screw women, who produce babies. . . .

S: [Spontaneously] Tell him: me.

H: Yeah.

S: Is that the approach?

H: I'm thinking now that that's how I can do it.[25] [S. provides suggestions.] [To Sa.] Dr. Stoller wants to ask you more about your shamanism. He says, "The way of our shamans – he's talking about himself – is that a certain kind of shaman becomes a certain kind of man." [Slowly] Now this kind of man develops just like everyone: First he's a child, then he grows up. Then, he says of himself, "I found a way that I became a man." And he wonders whether it was the same for you, or of it was different for you?

Sa: This shamanism here. . . .

H: Yeah [softly, almost a whisper].

---

25. *H:* Why could I think of that at that point? S.'s presence changed something in my relationship to Saku. Perhaps S. put a friendly and supportive presence into our talking that gave *me* the space and perspective to free Saku from ambivalence.

Sa: Oh, this . . . I don't know. [Sa. is engaged here.] Before, did Yumalo do the same? I'm not sure.[26]

H: [Enthusiastic] Oh, but he isn't talking just about familiars, he's talking about his body too.

Sa: This *kwooluku?*

H: No, no – of his very body. [Spontaneously to S.] I'm going to do something that's not quite ethical, but I'm going to leave the language vague enough so that he may suspect that you are . . . you may have some hermaphroditic qualities . . . [pause].

S: Good. [I do, in the sense that I can work with hermaphroditic patients in such a way that a few thought I was a hermaphrodite. That is why I said "good" and felt that was not unethical.]

H: But I'm going to let him project it, if he can do it.

S: Fine.

H: [To Sa.] His appearance is real, but when he [S.] was born, they looked at his body and wondered: "This baby, is it another kind, or. . . . They didn't know for sure. Now, when you see him, you see that he's become the same as a man. But now he's become a shaman. And now he's a man, too. He's the same as *you* . . . but when he was born, they thought he was a different kind. And so he wants to know if it was the same with you.[27]

Sa: This . . . I don't really understand you. [Pause. Silence.] My *kwooluku* . . when, before, my mother gave birth. I don't understand well. [He understands precisely but is dodging. Still, compared to Saku's earlier sessions with H., he is not now frantic. Rather, his voice is calm; he is not frightened.]

H: Um-hm. [To S.] He says he doesn't understand.

S: What did you ask him that he doesn't understand?

H: I said, "You [S.] are now a man and a shaman; but when you were born" – and I used the neutral term for "child," not "boy" or "girl" – "they, those who first saw you when you were born – said

---

26. Fascinating that, in responding, Saku has here referred us to his beloved Yumalo. This is not only defensive. Saku modeled himself after Yumalo, using the latter in order to know what to feel and believe. Hypothesis: Saku's identity was not finished at initiation, in contrast to other males. It is still not finished. His hermaphrodism forces and allows him to pick and choose, because his aberrance has always placed him outside norms.

27. *H:* I'd forgotten I'd done this until translating the tapes in 1981–1982. It amounts to a lie: I as much as said S. was a hermaphrodite. I don't think it was harmful; the circmstances of the interview were extraordinary. I never lie with informants, but fudged in this instance. I think it helped; but readers may disagree with this tack. [*S:* One should never, in doing research, lie in order to get information. Supervision corrects such mistakes.]

you were a different kind." That's the language. But I left it so
vague –

S: That he doesn't understand it. Or –

H: He may just be resisting –

S: He chooses not to understand it.

H: Yeah.

S: Okay, skip it. You've done what you can. Ask him what he was
like when he was born. And using the same word "they" may give
him a chance to get out if it's unbearable.

H: Yeah. [To Sa.] Now, Dr. Stoller wants to ask you: "When you
were born, what kind of child were you?

Sa: At that time?

H: Yeah.

Sa: I don't know [uninvolved].

H: But, you know, what did they say . . . when you were born? What
kind [of person] were you?

Sa: My father . . . mother?

H: Yeah.

Sa: I don't know –

H: You haven't heard the news? [Meaning: What local belief is?]

Sa: Um-hm. [Straight-faced and calm.[28] Pause. Silence. *H:* Saku
cannot bear these silences. I know if I keep my mouth shut –
something I am learning to do better – he will break the silence. He
wants to please.] I heard nothing about that.

H: [Quickly] You didn't hear about it. [I feel compassion for Saku's
pain on this subject and try to comfort him, supporting his attempts to bridge the silences with communications.] [Pause] Uh
. . . . [To S.] First he said he didn't know. And then he said he
wasn't around at that time. Then he said his parents never told
him.

S: About what? I'm sure you're paraphrasing him accurately. But I
want to sharpen it up. They didn't say "what" about "what?"

H: [To Sa:] He's asking if you said, "You didn't hear well what they
said?" Is that it?

Sa: I said, "That's the choice of all mamas and papas" [plural indicates
all classificatory kin], that's what I said . . You said to me: "Is it
the same as a boy child or a girl child?"

H: Yes. [Grateful: We're finally on the same wavelength.]

---

28. Saku (like other Sambia males, who learn to lie to hide ritual secrets) is a good liar. He is
more accomplished than others becase of his shamanism (doctors don't always tell patients the truth) and probably because of his hermaphrodism.

Sa: They all said, "It's a boy child."
H: A boy child. That's what they said. [To S.] He said –
S: It's a male, boy.
H: A male boy, yeah.
S: Like every other boy?
H: [To Sa.] He asks: "The same kind of boy as all the boys around . . .?"
Sa: Yeah, the same.
H: [To S.] He says, "Yes, the same kind."
S: Now?
H: [To Sa.] He says, "Now too?"
Sa: Now, too, all the same.
H: He says, "Now too, the same." My feeling is he's a bit angry about this, but I think he's willing to talk about it.
S: Keep going –
H: Yeah. He's more willing to . . . you're dragging answers out of him. He's letting . . .
S: He's letting us –
H: Drag answers out of him.
S: Yeah. Should we give him support now and tell him that I'm glad he's talking with us?
H: Yeah.
S: And that I appreciate this . . . and he's helping me, who came from such a long distance, who wants to know about a shaman here.
H: Yeah, that's good. [Summarizes for Sa.]
Sa: That's all right. [Low; down.]
S: All right but not all right.
H: Yeah. [Pause] There is a danger that if we press him too much, he might get scared.
S: Yeah. [Quiet]
H: There is also danger that if he's willing to answer questions we don't ask him, we may never get another chance. So it's a risk either way.[29] That's *always* the risk I feel about him. And I'm willing to either way, because at this point, I will do nothing to harm him. So whatever happens, I will protect him. The research comes first, and that's OK, because I *will* protect him.

---

29.   The first, not the second risk, seemingly endangers Saku. The second risk seemingly endangers only our research, right? Wrong: If Saku wants to unburden himself of his pain and we fail to help him do that, the chances are he may bear it alone – unsupported – the rest of his life. We would be cold not to appreciate the dual risks of this sensitive juncture.

S: Try this: Shamans are . . . I'll just talk: This isn't what you should say; you and I know in reality that shamans the world over are different from everyone else.

H: Yeah.

S: He should know, and perhaps he would be interested to know, that shamans all over the world – even in my country, namely the Plains Indians, or the Southwest desert groups,[30] and the people in Siberia – all over the world, shamans are different. Nobody except someone who is different is *allowed* to be a shaman. And he should know that I come here with the information that *everywhere* shamans are different. And that's the only way they can do what they do – because they're different.

H: Yeah.

S: Start with that and then – you don't expect an answer yet – and then I want to study – and this is true when I am studying him: Is he different? And if so, instead of his being afraid of it, can you let him know that he should be proud of it because he couldn't be a shaman unless he was different? Then maybe we can approach how he is different.

H: Yeah. [To Sa.] Did you hear him? Saku? He's been giving me knowledge: I also have never heard this talk before. He's got white hair and a lot of knowledge. And so he's told me this. He said this: He wants to talk to you about this knowledge. He says he knows about shamans in all places. They aren't the same as just plain old men and women. They're another kind. [Elaborates.] Dr. Stoller is not frightening or shaming you but encouraging you to be happy about yourself. Because these powers of yours, from the *jerungdu* of your *kwooluku*, come from your being different. That different kind [of person] and your *kwoolukus* come about only from that body of yours. [Pause] When I hear him say that, I feel he is only expressing his happiness towards you. He says: "I want to help you with your own thinking about yourself." And this, too, I've never heard it before. You know, I'm just a kid; he's got white hair, he's not newborn, he's old and knowledgeable. [Pause. Long silence.] This boss of mine, he's got friends with whom he works [i.e., patients]. Now these people, are, too, a kind of shaman. They're the same body [type] as you exactly. When they were born, people looked but couldn't make sense of their [the infants'] cocks or cunts [exact translations of the Pidgin words]. And they said: "This is a male, but it's not the same as a boy, it's another kind. It's

---

30. See, for instance, Devereux (1937).

a boy, but at the same time it's a different kind." Now this boss of mine has friends, of his own, who are the same as that; they're the same, the same as you. [Lowers voice.] He's not afraid of them; he's not shamed for them. He's only happy about them. Why? Because they all have their own *kwoolukus*. And so he comes and is happy with you in the same way. And I have now told you all about that, that knowledge. Me, too, I don' know about this. Now he's come and taught me. [Pause] Now, what do you feel when you hear this? [Throughout this long monologue, Saku and S. are silent. My speech is clear and quiet. I am trying to present a point of view radically different from that of Sambia culture. I am softly impassioned in a way I seldom am in public and have been only rarely with Saku, since I dislike monologues.]

Sa: [Quickly] But this is no good. [You have to hear the tape to appreciate Saku's voice, so different from before: weary, intense, and highly strained—as if these five words resonated from within the very center of his skull, uttered through clenched teeth that shred each word as it was spoken.]

H: Do you feel it's no good because of this kind[hermaphrodites] or because of this kind of talk?

Sa: The talk. [Sullen]

H: Just the talk. Do you want me to say that to him?

Sa: That.

H: You want me to tell him? [To S.] I told him that in America you have friends who are the same kind as him. I told him they believe themselves to be males, but they're not males in the same way. They're different. And when they were born, the parents saw them and didn't understand. And that he is the same kind as them—

S: You told him, or he confirmed that—

H: I told him that he is the same kind as that. And I told him that although they're like that, you aren't afraid of them, nor do you have any feeling of shame . . . .

S: If you try something—perhaps—this is for you to say to him, but for a beginning, for me to think. Is there any way you can find out, when he came back today, what was he hoping for . . .

H: Oh, yes . . .

S: What would he like to get? And is there any way we can open that door? Does he want to ask *me* things? I'm asking him: And he's free to. It wasn't that he came here hoping to ask me questions; he probably never thought of such a thing. What did he hope for? And what does he feel now that he's hurt and it's not going the way he's hoped? He's been hanging around all this time because of something he wanted. What does he want? And can we help him with that?

H: Yeah. [To Sa.] Dr. Stoller says this: He sees you and thinks, at first you came back to work with us. He saw you and he was happy with our talking. And he thinks, at this time when you come here, do you yourself want to get some knowledge or understanding or feeling . . . . And now he's said to me: "I've sat here and asked you plenty, hammered your ear that way. Do you want to ask me anything?" He doesn't want to sit down and just ask you: not good that you think hard [worry] about him –

Sa: Ah, I'm not going to think hard about [fear] him. It's all right. [The first hopeful sign he's back with us, some warmth again in his voice.]

H: And he's thinking, "When you first came today, did you want to find out about something, or some feeling or such?" He wants to ask you about that.

Sa: Oh, yeah. That's clear. About myself yet?

H: Yeah, about yourself.

Sa: I want to say this: I'm not going to be scared or anything. And by and by I can talk to him. You know . . . here . . . they gave birth to us . . . I want to speak out to him . . .[31]

H: Um-hm.

Sa: This kind here [vague], do they [whites] all understand them all completely too . . .?

H: Yeah – [soft]

Sa: He wants to know –

H: Yeah. . .

Sa: So I'll tell him about it.

H: Yeah.

Sa: They all looked at us[32] at first – "I think it's a girl," that's what they thought. And then, later, they all looked at us and saw that we had a ball . . . they looked at us, at our ball [testes], and they all said: "I think it's a male."

H: Oh-h.

Sa: They all say that. [Pause] And, likewise we've got cocks . . . and we've got balls.

H: Um-hm.

Sa: But, our water [urine] we all lose it in the middle [extreme hypospadias: urinary meatus in female position, not at the distal end of

---

31. *H:* S.'s last comment via me turned the tide of Saku's fear and resistance. Asking Saku what he wanted acknowledged him.

32. Saku uses the plural throughout this section to refer to himself.

glans penis as in normal males]. Now, all the same, could they—would they fix it? [Voice almost cracks from strain, he sounds close to tears.] Or . . .

H: Do you want me to ask him?

Sa: Yeah . . .

H: You want me to ask him?

Sa: Yeah.

H: [To S.] Boy, that's really something. Whatever it was I said, it turned him all around.

S: What did he say?

H: I said . . . I gave almost a literal translation of what you said. And as you can see he loosened up and got less uptight . . .

S: Yeah.

H: And he said, "I want to tell him [S.]: 'I know you want to ask me about this, and you've come a long way to ask me about this, and so I'm not afraid, I'm going to tell you.' " I mean—that takes a tremendous amount of guts. So he says that the first time when they looked at him, they said he was a girl. Then they saw he had a penis and testes. And then later (he keeps using the first person plural to refer to himself) he says, "Now we have a penis." But also saying there's something wrong because the urine comes out wrong. I'm vague about that, what that means—

S: That's all right . . . It's out; he's opened it up. He finally said it.

H: Now, he wants—he asked me something which astonishes me. He wants to know if you can fix . . . him. If there is something you can do, if there's some way you can fix him.

S: The chances are in reality I can't. If I were practicing medicine, even here, the thing I would have to do, before I could answer him (I'm not telling you to tell him this), is I would have to know what more is the matter [i.e., do a proper examination to arrive at a diagnosis]. It probably is something anatomical and beyond repair; I would have to determine first what is to be fixed. Is the "fix something" to make a bigger penis, to make a more naturally male appearance, or to get an erection, or is it to ejaculate or what—you know I don't even know. But before we did any of that, I would say to him what I'd say to anyone else: Tell him he's brave to have said this.

H: Yeah.

S: Tell him I know that and appreciate it and respect him for what he just did.

H: Yeah.

S: And then we can ask him more questions . . . what is to be fixed.

H: [To Sa.] He wants to tell you about this [request]. But first, he says

that you've got a lot of strength to talk out about this. Why? Because about this something many people could be afraid. You are
brave to think and talk about this. And now he wants to talk to
you about what you asked about. "Can this something be fixed,"
you ask him that?

Sa: Um-hm, that.

H: Before he answers, he must ask you more to understand what it is
you want him to fix.

Sa: Yeah . . . Before, when we were still very small . . . . [His voice
changes: quiet anger for the first time.] Then, who came here?
Gronemann. Gronemann came. They [vague] came and looked at
us [me]. He looked at us [me] for nothing. And he didn't say anything [low, quiet voice here] . . . . They all looked inside us [me,
looked at his genitals]. But you two talked [to me] and so I am telling you.

H: Oh. [Amazed] [Around 1960 a government patrol passed through
the Sambia Valley. It was one of the early patrols, designed to assert an Australian government presence (which led several years
later to final pacification). Gronemann, a German businessman,
not a government official, accompanied this patrol. (We are not
sure why he was permitted in.) He took a sexual interest in some
Sambia initiated boys (prepubescent), which extended, in Saku's
case, to wanting to see his genitals. He photographed Saku — a
deeply humiliating experience, because Saku was ashamed of his
ambiguous genitals, because Sambia never appear nude to others,
and because the shame was compounded by others (natives?) having witnessed the photographing. Word got out about the incident, and the resulting traumatic stigma was with Saku all these
years. He was ten years old at the time.

I did not know about the photographing until this moment. I
had heard stories of Gronemann's sexual exploits with boys, but
that's all. Nor did I know until two years after this interview —
1981 — that Saku had had sex with Gronemann *before* the photographing (Saku sucked him). All in all not a nice story.

Gronemann's business interests in New Guinea enabled him to
return to the area over the years, until 1981, when he died. Saku,
aware of this, never felt free of threat.[33] See below.]

Sa: And, we [I] thought, "Later, if Gronemann comes back we [I]

---

33.   We have disguised Gronemann's identity. Though we have had to omit some, and dis-
      guise other, details about him, our presentation of Gronemann fits with Saku's experi-
      ence of him and others' reports of what happened.

want to ask him about this: 'This something here [flawed geni-
tals]—would you [Gronemann] care enough about us [me] to . . .
do something, about this [purposely vague]?' " Then . . . but . . .
[scowls[34]] Gronemann he took our [my] picture and he looked at
it, and he didn't—talk [explain why he'd done what he did: look at
and then photograph Saku's genitals] . . . . So we [I] were just
talking nothing about him helping us . . . . [In the last sentence,
Saku seems to say—in words and intonation—that he was a stupid
son of a bitch to ever imagine being made whole by Gronemann in
return for being shamelessly photographed in the nude.]

H: Ohh. [low]
S: Oh, that's sad [pain in voice on seeing Saku now] . . . .
H: [To Sa.] Do you want me to tell him?
Sa: Yeah, you can . . . no reason not to . . . .
S: Oh—he looks like he wants to cry almost. Is that right, or am I
       reading that in?
H: Yeah, that's right.[35] And that's not all. Do you know who he's
       been talking about?
S: Why?
H: I've never before gotten this [secret] part of the story. Here's what
       happened. Apparently, Gronemann was part of the first patrol
       that ever came here. Someone must have told him of Saku. And he
       must have looked at Saku and taken a picture of him. I don't know
       the details. There was some hint from Saku that he hoped Grone-
       mann could do something to change him. But then "this" was done
       to him—and I say it that way because it would have been a terribly
       humiliating experience.[36] He took the picture, and—left. So here
       are my thoughts: We are here, now, duplicating a similar situa-

---

34. Saku's present complex state—anger, fear, humiliation, confusion, hope, trust,
     distrust—has several aspects that should be underlined here. First is his puzzlement,
     now, as an adult, as to what motivated this stranger, Gronemann, then. Second is his
     still-remembered puzzlement when, as a child, he could not understand what
     Gronemann was doing. Third is his mix of fear, envy, and disorientation, the result of
     the white men's automatic sense of superiority, extending even to their seeming rights to
     invade and seize Saku's body and its secret.
35. H: Within a few moments he did silently cry, tears falling down his cheeks. I want to
     underscore that Saku is no crybaby: In all these years I've seen him cry only once in pub-
     lic, when he was deeply insulted by a clan brother. He does cry in private, I think be-
     cause he is compassionate (some Sambia men do not cry ever). But he is also tough; his
     crying here was deeply moving: a 20-year-old secret shared.
36. Sambia are prudish about exposing their genitals. They never do so, not even to bathe.
     To be stripped nude and photographed in front of Europeans or other New Guineans
     would have been, for a ten-year-old boy, terribly traumatic.

tion; he was humiliated before [at ten years old]; he's about to cry; he had this hope back then, that was pitched up and then dashed. And the guy didn't have enough . . . compassion . . . to at least say something to *calm* him, and apparently just walked off.

S: That – we're not going to do.

H: Yeah.

S: Now the question, What's wrong?, is not an anatomical dissertation . . . . At the start tell him that, we are not going to *take* anything *away* from him; we are not going to take advantage of him. He doesn't have to answer anything. I'n not going to take any pictures of that part of him. And so forth.

H: Yeah. [To Sa.] Dr. Stoller says this: He hears this story about what Gronemann did. He's never heard this story, and I haven't either. He hears this, and he feels sorry. He wants to talk with you about your asking him if we can fix this something. But first before that he wants to say this: "Now I've come here and we're talking. I'm not going to take anything from you; not at all. I'm not going to take your picture; not at all. I'm not going to take your thoughts: If you don't want to talk, or respond to me, that's okay." It would be no good if you think he'll do the same as Gronemann before: He won't do that. He hears this and he thinks: "Oh, Gronemann didn't understand; he stood and took a picture thoughtlessly, that's all."

Sa: [Quickly] And so – like this: He took our picture for no reason, and he didn't pay us for it . . . . He didn't give us good pay or anything, like clothes.

H: Yeah.

Sa: And so, I've got an angry belly about him. [Serious]

H: Yeah.

Sa: Now, if he comes and asks me again –

H: Yeah. [Thinking hard]

Sa: [Reflects] I'm talking about Gronemann, I'm not talking about you two.

H: Yeah.

Sa: And [raises voice, kinder] – you can talk to me. That's all right; there's no shame in it. [How very different is his reassurance from his mood when we began over an hour ago. He has not only revealed his secret, taken us into his confidence, and expressed his turmoil, pain, and anger, but now he says: "My anger isn't for you. Don't be afraid of the shame." He here returns S.'s earlier gift. In other words, beneath Saku's turbulence lies a warm and well-put-together man, who did not let fate burn him up.]

Sa: [Smiles] You know, the men who go round the coast . . . they [vague] see the cocks of Europeans.[37]

H: Hm. [Pause]

S: [Interrupts] I've really got to say this here: Don't say anything; let him say everything he has to say.

H: Yeah. [Quiet] Um. [To S.] He's very angry about what happened to him with Gronemann. I know that's what it [emotion] was . . . .

S: You knew — today?

H: Oh, no, I mean, right now. Before he said he was angry I could tell he was angry. And I said the right things to allow him to express his anger. He said he's very angry about what Gronemann did. He just took the picture and took off.

S: He's angry like you would be, and I would be, if someone did that to us. And he's in worse shape because he could never talk to anyone about it.

H: Yeah. [Depressed]

S: Till this morning.

H: Well, the most important message he left me with is that he's willing to talk with you. He's not ashamed to talk with you. Is there some other assurance that I can give — aside from all I have translated for you — that this isn't going to happen again? To make him comfortable —

S: There's no such thing as "I give you my word"? Or the equivalent?

H: Yeah, there is something like that.

S: First of all, I've got to know what word I give, because it's important to me to be honest to my word.

H: What I can do is say you will make a promise that you will not do so and so.

S: Well, what won't I do? I will *not* take a photograph; I will not ever humiliate him; I will not ever let anybody know about him — I might let them know about *somebody.* [And that, reader, is, in reality, all you have been told.] That is, this story that we now have, as a piece of our methodology, might be described. There's no way we can tell him that it won't make a difference. But I promise *him* that I will not — the most important thing — ever humiliate him.

H: [To Sa.] Yeah. He wants to say this to you and me. First he wants to say: He's heard this story and he feels truly sorry abut what

---

37. Not clear what Saku is referring to, but it may relate to stories men tell on returning from the coast, regarding sex with white men in coastal cities.

Gronemann did to you. Then he said to me, "You've got to tell Saku: I'm never going to shame Saku. I'm not going to give him more shame. I heard this story, and I'm really sorry. I won't shame him. You [H.] must tell him. I won't take his picture. I'm not going to shame him by telling people about him. I'm not going to make public some pictures or stories about him. All stories and knowledge of Saku belong only to him and to us, and I'm not to go talking around about this." And he says: "This is my promise."

S: Now after that is something positive: that he may feel better to have told somebody he trusts the terrible story he could never tell before. It may offer him some *relief* — of this burden — right now.

H: [Loud noise from kids screaming in the background. I drive them off.]

S: This guy's been carrying an agony around inside himself. And we've got to, if we can, free him, so that he can at least go back to the starting line of what he's got the matter with him [an incompetent penis].

H: Yeah. [To Sa.] Dr. Stoller says: He's heard this bad thing Gronemann did, and he thinks: "This shame that Gronemann made in you — is connected to your fear that came from when you were first born, when your mama and papa didn't understand about how they marked you [made sex assignment at birth] — this shame has carried to the present and is stuck in your thought, and it screws up some of your thinking."

Sa: Yeah, that's right.

H: So he wants to say: You must know that he and I won't shame you or screw up your thinking; if then you can talk about it to us, then Dr. Stoller can expel that shame. That can make it better. You can get rid of that shame, and get rid of that bad thing Gronemann did to you before. And you can live better.

Sa: Yeah. Now I can tell you about this: If I was big, like now, and he tried to do that, sorry! He wouldn't make me shamed. But, I was just a small boy. I was the same as J.[38] They had initiated me, but that's all. I had no thought. Suppose he comes back later, I've got to tell you two. If Gronemann ever came back I'd have said to him, "Before, you put a great shame on me. I'm not happy with you." [Steady voice. He's back to his normal intonation now.] Now, if he had paid me for that, paid me a lot, then I wouldn't be so angry at him. Had he done that and looked at me . . . but he didn't. He

---

38. Saku refers here to a first-stage initiate in our own village, a boy about ten years old.

did wrong. This master.[39] Me, myself, from my own strength I did things – I planted a little coffee [trees] and got a little money. Now I've built my own tin-roof house. Now I work for you and make a little money. My stomach is still hot from this [lowers voice, angry again, voice almost breaks]. I'm just sitting down now. If you want to ask me something now – that's OK, I'm not going to get shame. I can talk.

S: The only thing I would say: You've got to give him *all the space.* Ask him the right questions . . . I don't know what to tell you: You're going to have to be a good clinician. Don't take the time to tell me what he said – just let it go. Let him run.

H: Yeah. [To Sa.] Do you think I should keep talking to Stoller?

Sa: [Firm] You shouldn't worry; don't be afraid. You must tell him. It's my choice, if I want to tell him. So, you can go ahead and tell him [level-headed].

H: [To S.] He's identifying with me. He says you should talk with him: Don't be afraid or ashamed, just tell him. [To Sa.] When Gronemann first got you, you were a *choowinuku* [first-stage initiate].

Sa: Yeah.

H: You didn't see him later as an *imbutu* or *ipmangwi*?

Sa: No, I didn't. [His whole body is trembling.]

S: Is he shaking now?

H: Yes.

S: Does he want to cry? He may.

H: I thought he was about to, on the verge.

S: Does he . . . he . . . want my permission? Is it the wrong thing to do in this society?

H: It *is* the wrong thing.

S: It's all right *with me.*

H: It might be all right with you.

S: I'm telling you to tell him it's all right with me. But he doesn't *have* to. Can you tell him that?

H: [To Sa.] I was telling him [S.] this and he stopped me halfway to say that he's seeing you and he thinks that when you expressed this shame that Gronemann made in you – he sees your eyes and hands

---

39.   Note how Saku shifts back here to the Pidgin "master," where before he used "Gronemann." He has objectified Gronemann's status to be the all-powerful white man, and he implies in this projection the reality and fantasy of the endless power plays of life under a colonial regime.

	and thinks you're close to crying. You want to cry about what he did back them.
Sa:	[Quickly] Yeah.
H:	Dr. Stoller says, his own way is that if you want to cry it's all right, there's nothing wrong with that. He's told me to tell you if you want to cry, it's OK.
Sa:	It's like that. When I was still very small, I thought, "What does he want to *do* that he's taken off my grass sporran?"
H:	He himself took off your sporran?!
Sa:	Yeah. He told one of his men to do it. And at that time I thought, "He's looked at me. He wants to put nice new [Western] clothes on me." But, he didn't put them on me. Now I'm big and I think to myself, "Sorry. Before, he really rubbished me, fouled me up. He took a picture of me, and maybe he showed it around to other masters." That's what I think. So, now, I think bad of him.
S:	He's just shaking . . . shaking all over.
H:	Yeah, I know. I think it's probably reassuring for him for us to just talk –
S:	Yeah, yeah, yeah. That's what he needs [intense whisper].
H:	So he said when he was a first-stage initiate, without his permission, an older man – not one of his kinsmen – took him to the place wherever Gronemann was, which was probably in a tent or something, and they removed his grass sporran to look at his genitals. And then, it's clear if it was against his will – he was just ten years old – a picture was taken, and he's got a fantasy (I think you were right) that that picture is now being seen by others. And the meaning is that he was humiliated, because against his will they did something which is morally wrong here, they exposed his genitals and took the picture. So part of him is out there – floating in space. He said, tell him that – tell Stoller. So, this is all news to me; I never got this story before.
S:	I might do something, but I've got to know more. What's he feeling now? He's shaking from what?
H:	Well, I can feel inside of *myself – I* am shaking.
S:	Rage, humiliation, fear. What I want from him now is to get it out. Not to hold it with a shaking, but to feel free to say what the shaking is saying.
H:	[To Sa.] I told Stoller what you said. He says: "I hear this, and I am thinking about this." But he also says that he sees you and you are shaking some.
Sa:	Body-shaking [He uses the Sambia, not Pidgin, word for it.]

H: Yeah. Yet he thinks that it's not good that you hold onto this shame. You must expel it, expel it through talking. Whatever you feel — anger or what — you've got to talk it out.[40] Talk it out to him.

        . . .

S: Now what he should do is talk. To me, to you. Get it out.

H: [To Sa.] He says, "You talk, talk to us."

Sa: He looked[41] at me. I think about that, and I'm afraid of him. I'm not happy with him [low, quiet voice]. I'm not too afraid, but I am unhappy with him. He didn't — think enough of me to give me something. That's all, that's what . . . I shake for . . . [voice fades out]. I'm not happy about that. I know — before, when I was small — he looked at me, but he didn't pay me for it.

H: Um-hm.

S: [Directly to Sa.] Talk — talk to me. Is that clear?

Sa: Yeah.

H: Tell him what you must talk out about to Stoller.

Sa: [Flows] That's all, what I said to you. Before, he looked at me, and he didn't pay. So I've been afraid of him; afraid of only this Gronemann. This kind [of man] is no good, here . . . . He looks inside of their sporrans . . . at the pubic hair of *men*. That's an altogether different kind of man[42] [tiredness in voice]. So I've been afraid of him. If he had done good for me, I wouldn't think like this. Suppose he had said, "I want to do such and such, and so I'll pay you for it. And if you shake, then we can stop." If he'd said that, it would have been okay. But he looked at me and this picture he showed to all the masters: "Here's an odd kind of boy to look at." He thought that, he showed the picture to his friends. And so, I'm angry at him, heavy in my stomach at him. [To S.] I want Gilbert to understand: "Before, you [he is still referring to Gronemann] made me afraid and I didn't like it." So I didn't talk out to you [H.], but now I've told him all. [Long pause]

H: [It is important to me, and to our joint work, that Saku has acknowledged here his hiding and evasion of the subject of his her-

---

40. Talking out anger is what Sambia customarily do in moots; thus, Saku's talking is appropriate in that way too.

41. Here and above, Saku uses the term that can mean erotic looking. It is a complex thing, this looking, which here carries the sense of: "I can't shake the feeling of Gronemann and others staring at me, exposed, so cheapened."

42. Saku suggests that Gronemann got his kicks by looking at male genitals. He feels that it is not right, that it is, as we would say in these circumstances, *using* the natives, perverse.

maphrodism. This was the healthy and appropriately human thing to do. It was a way of acknowledging my struggle to get to him, and the ambivalence I felt in trying to open up this area in our work. He acknowledges, that is, the open secret we could never discuss, by telling me that the dreadful secret — of Gronemann's picture taking years ago — was a secret he could never broach. Thus, Saku has directly responded to S.'s move above — "talk to me" — while also indirectly and kindly acknowledging that I am there, and that what I had tried to do was too frightening to talk about before. Not "H. is frightening," but "this deeper secret was too frightening." This acknowledgment is for me a sign of Saku's greater trust and caring of his healthy core personality.]

S: What should I know?

H: He says most everything I've said before. Except he's added that he's never stopped being afraid of Gronemann . . . afraid that Gronemann will do the same thing. And in saying that, there's the sense that he didn't have the power to say "no" to Gronemann.

Sa: That's what I was going to say before. Now I'll say it again. [S. repeats to Sa.]

H: He said he was afraid to talk to me about this before, when I brought it up. But now he's told us both. [H. repeats S.'s words to Saku.]

Sa: I think, when I say this, I won't be afraid. If I curse him I think [lowers voice] I won't be afraid.

H: And you won't forget?

Sa: No. Now, what I said to Dr. Stoller I can't forget. [Stronger] I have to put it on the front of my face [remember it easily]: I won't forget about it; I won't forget about this. I put it on my face now and I can watch and wait. I won't forget about this. [Long pause] You know. When he came here and made us afraid that's not good. That's something truly no good. I always thought, suppose he would want to come here and take away [study] our customs or — that's all right, there's nothing wrong with that. But [almost inaudible here] when he came and did that — [pause] — *makes us afraid* in your [our] balls [sad chuckle] that's not a good thing. So when he came here and made us afraid [*pause*] that's very bad. That's what I think. You know. You masters have another kind of — a big kind of —

H: Power [despair in voice].

Sa: Yeah. A big kind of power. Yeah. But us here —

H: You don't have any.

Sa: That's right. We don't have any. [Sad undertone throughout all this talk] And when he came and shamed us, that's no good, that's something that's very bad.

S: [Cuts in] Is this unusual for him? What he's doing? [At this moment Saku is visibly shaking, his hands clasped to hold himself together. He is enraged.]

H: Yeah. Yeah, it's rare for him.

S: For him?

H: Yeah. For him.

S: And for the culture, too?

H: *Yeah. He's really tense.*

Sa: I'm really pleased with the two of you. [Saku's voice breaks at this point. Pause.]

S: [Low voice] I want to hear him think out loud. Can we get him to do that now? If we can get him to, it will help me if I can know what he's experiencing.

H: [To Sa.] He asks what are you thinking, so he can understand. It helps him to know about you later.

Sa: [Voice quickens] Oh, I am thinking he is helping me, helping me truly, I'm thinking like that. And another thing is that I'm very pleased with you. [There's a smile in Saku's voice here. This is hard to translate. His voice is low and his words vague.] And I was thinking no good about him [Gronemann]. I wasn't thinking good things ... and he came along here and did that bad thing. And another [S.] has come along here to help me. And I'm very happy about that.

H: [Repeats to S.]

S: [Quiet voice] Does he feel inside that he will be able to sleep tonight?

Sa: Well, when I go home I'll get a good sleep.

H: You'll get a good sleep, huh?

Sa: Yeah. I think bad about Gronemann; but now he [S.] has helped me and I can forget thinking about Gronemann and all these other things, and I can go home and sleep good. And I'm very pleased with him [S.]. Very pleased. And I'm very pleased with him. That's all.

H: [To S.] He says that before he was very afraid and ashamed about this and now you've helped him. And all of these feelings have gone outside of him and now he thinks that he'll be able to do and get a really good sleep.

S: That's good. If he wants to say any more, that's fine. But we don't have to have more. If he wants to do it he can tell it for *his* sake. He could — whatever the word is — deposit inside of us whatever he has to.

H: [To Sa.] Now, this is for later. Dr. Stoller says he is really pleased that you have talked to us and you have told us about this. That you have shared this with us. Now, suppose you want to finish here with this talk, that's all right, it's your choice. Or suppose later you want to say more, that, too, is your own choice.

Sa: I can come back later [lower voice] and talk.

H: Tomorrow?

Sa: Yeah. Come back later and finish with this.

S: What he tells us from now on is for his sake. We don't need more. Before, he was coming in here because Gilbert was doing research. If he wants to come in here now and talk about anything he wants, we don't need it. I don't mean "Fuck you! We don't need it." I mean he now has an opportunity to come in here and talk about *anything* he wants. He can bring it to us for his sake. And if he doesn't want to he doesn't have to.

H: [To Sa.] Dr. Stoller says: "I was working with you to get your thoughts. I, too, wanted to know about you. From now on ... We won't ask more about that. But if you, for yourself, want to come and talk, well, that's your own choice. We would be pleased to do that with you, to help you lose your fear. So that you won't be afraid or shamed of this anymore.

Sa: [Low voice, exhausted] That's all right.

S: I guess that's enough work for today. Unless you've got something else that you want to ask him.

Sa: Hm. [Long pause] Now what? Is that all? Is that all? Him, Gronemann, that master, that's all I worry about. He shamed me, and that's it. So, I've told it *all* to you now. That's it. I wanted to tell you [H.], but I forgot about it. I wanted to say that he [Gronemann] made me shamed before, but saying that scared me. I was shaking. And so, now, I'm really happy about the two of you. That's all for now.

H: That's it. Tomorrow you must dress and we'll talk again....

Sa: All right, tomorrow I'll come.

AFTERWORD

H: The next day we were to see Saku again, but he didn't show and sent no word. The day after that I saw him near his house. He said he was "very sorry" for not showing; he was drained but OK. I think he has been over-whelmed by our last session, needed a breathing spell to work through what had happened. He offered weak excuses for not showing, which I ac-cepted, but we both knew why he did not return. We said good-bye and kept in touch through occasional letters.

Looking back now, I realize I could never have foreseen what Saku was hiding all those years. I thought he was just ashamed of his hermaphro-dism. Had I known of the trauma he had suffered at the hands of Gronemann, I would have proceeded differently. But I could not know that, until S. came along. Perhaps it is a measure of how much Saku trusted me that we got as far as we did working alone. I lacked the skills to go further then. I've changed. Working with sensitive people like Saku has shown me: Never take anything for granted, understand as much as possi-ble before taking your guesses seriously, be as supportive as possible, and be very patient.

Saku's life is better now, he is not as weighed down. In 1981, I returned to the Sambia and worked more intensely than ever with him. His secre-tiveness was far less than before and in two weeks was gone completely. He told me more of his story, this time with less shame.

CONCLUSION

S: Measuring the observer's effect on the observed and realizing that the observed affects the observer as well have, in this century, changed the na-ture of all research — from fundamental particle physics to my discipline, psychoanalysis. More than any other investigators of human behavior, analysts have been concerned with the distortions introduced by these sub-jective factors. In recent years, no clinical task has interested us more than trying to discover how aspects of the analyst's personality influence the therapeutic relationship: those that we are aware of and that can be used effectively, and those, coming from unrecognized forces within us, that produce uncontrolled effects (countertransference). H. and I believe also that these issues of self are just as important in writing reports of one's findings.

H: Thus, in this clinical report we have presented a literal transcrip-tion of our talk with Sakulambei. Saku's history, the history of my rela-tionship to him, the ambience of our interviews, and descriptions of Saku's and our experience add depth and breadth to these clinical mo-ments. We have interpreted *ad hoc* some of this material, though much re-mains to be said. For instance, we have not attempted here to assess the normativeness of Saku's shamanic role performance in respect to his aber-rant hermaphroditic identity. Nor will we here examine the extent to which his childhood anxieties stemming from being a hermaphrodite, or from the trauma suffered at the hands of Gronemann, are adaptive or neurotic responses, for him and/or as he can be compared to others (e.g., shamans, hermaphrodites, anatomically normal men). These are significant problems, but they do not concern us in the present report. Rather, we wish only to underline the value of collecting such data and presenting them in a form that tells precisely what all the parties experience *vis-à-vis* doing and writing ethnography. Without such data, we believe, none of these questions can be adequately answered.

This study of Saku shows that clinically trained ethnographers can understand and interpret the feelings and fantasies of others, even in an exotic society. Bringing this material to bear on social institutions and relationships, or using it to explain culturally shared values, norms, and beliefs, is, of course, problematic. So much background material, contextualization of the discourse, and pertinent information on personality similarities and differences in a society is required to relate the single case to normative roles and symbolic and psychological configurations. But this is in the nature of the phenomenon: the interpretation of subjective experience (at all levels of awareness) in cross-cultural settings. It seems to us antiquated for anthropologists to believe they cannot collect such data; or that, if they could, the data would have no value for understanding such powerful issues as the nature of gender roles, religious activity, or identity formation. Moreover, in such a case as Saku's — no matter how precious the data are for studying such theoretical concerns — only the clinically trained have the empathy and skill to collect sensitive information, while allowing their informant to feel better for the process.

S: Years ago these issues were forcefully presented in detailed and scholarly fashion by Devereux (1967), though others have joined the debate (cf. Boyer, 1978; LeVine, 1982). It is hard to judge to what extent his ideas were ignored because the audience was upset or distracted and to what extent because the ideas were simply too new and took digesting. Whatever the reasons, Devereux's insight that research can transform anxiety into research method has caused no change in either ethnography or psychoanalysis. As an analyst, I find it especially surprising that he did not move psychoanalysis, given the above-stated concern with how the analyst's behavior changes what happens in the treatment. So it is disappointing that when analysts publish their ideas, they almost completely omit describing themselves when the treatment events published were taking place and who they are when reporting their conclusions. I am sure that analysts' and anthropologists' theory will improve and their research advance from the present rudimentary state if they acknowledge these factors. If an ethnographer and analyst work together, is it not more efficient to have them both in the same person.[43] Though we believe it would be, as in the rare cases of Róheim and Devereux, we do not believe it can easily be. Nor have LeVine's[44] ideas about cross-cultural teams generated much enthusiasm. An analyst and anthropologist from the same culture may share similar cultural blind spots, but they have advantages as a team. Whatever similarities are shared by H. and me, there must be personality differences if we are each to fit the mold of our respective professions. Ethnographers, for instance, must want to live for long stretches in an alien community, should yearn to identify with people different from themselves, and must give up the middle-class comforts out of which they are likely to have emerged (if they are to have had the educational opportunities needed for becoming an anthropologist). The desire to stay put, to have a family, or to enjoy the pleasures of one's own culture cannot be urges in the ethnographer strong enough to disrupt his capacity to stay away from home. On the other hand, analysts should be, whatever else goes on in their lives, people who not only think about analysis but practice it (cannot bear not to practice it). Since analyses take years and—to put it mildly—do not thrive on long, repeated absences by the analyst, we can expect that most analysts will prefer to stay home. Perhaps some day an analyst who likes to practice will find himself in life circumstances that allow him first to soak up a foreign culture until it is nonetheless his own and then to practice analysis there. (There was a bit of this process when European analysts, forced to flee, settled into new countries with new languages; but the cultural shifts were far less extreme than what the classical ethnographer experiences.)[45]

So, since it worked easily for us, we recommend that a team—a compatible ethnographer and analyst/psychiatrist—work together. When the ethnographer is accepted by people in the culture he is studying, the chances are good the colleague will also be. The two researchers as a team

---

43. LaBarre (1978, p. 70) lists several such teams.
44. LeVine (1982, pp. 220ff.) suggests collaboration between a behavioral scientist of the "host" culture and one from the outside.
45. There are other reasons why the two disciplines are not easily combined in one person. Most analysts, with premedical training, medical school, internship, and three years of psychiatric residency before starting their analytic training, are rather aged by the time their seven to ten years of analytic training have ended and they are certified as competent to practice. To lay on top of that the requirement of a doctorate in anthropology is close to absurd. So far, almost no one has been able to combine the two disciplines; and if one should, there is the danger, as with other professional hybrids, that fellow anthropologists will judge him a bad anthropologist but a good analyst, while fellow analysts judge him a bad analyst but a good anthropologist.

bring different personalities, life experiences, training, collections of blind spots and insights to their work. And, if personal and professional animosities (are they different?) are not present, they will enjoy—as we did—how the strength of one repairs the weaknesses of the other, and how what is background for one can be foreground for the other. The results should energize anthropology and analysis, and, perhaps, build a better dialogue between these disciplines of human experience.

BIBLIOGRAPHY

BOYER, L. B. (1978). On the Mutual Influences of Anthropology and Psychoanalysis. *J. Psychol. Anthropol.,* 1:265–296.
DEVEREUX, G. (1937). Institutionalized Homosexuality of the Mohave Indians. *Human Biology,* 9:498–527.
_____ (1967). *From Anxiety to Method in the Behavioral Sciences.* Paris: Mouton.
GEERTZ, C. (1968). *Islam Observed.* New Haven: Yale University Press.
_____ (1976). From the Native's Point of View: On the Nature of Anthropological Understanding. In *Meaning in Anthropology,* ed. K. Basso & H. Selby. Albuquerque: School for American Research & University of New Mexico Press, pp. 221–237.
HERDT, G. H. (1977). The Shaman's "Calling" among the Sambia of New Guinea. *J. Soc. Oceanistes,* 56–57:153–167.
_____ (1981). *Guardians of the Flutes: Idioms of Masculinity.* New York: McGraw-Hill.
_____ (1982a). Fetish and Fantasy in Sambia Initiation. In *Rituals of Manhood,* ed. G. H. Herdt. Berkeley: University of California Press, pp. 44–98.
_____ (1982b). Sambia Nose-Bleeding Rites and Male Proximity to Women. *Ethos,* 10:189–231.
_____ (1984). Ritualized Homosexuality in the Male Cults of Melanesia, 1862–1983: An Introduction. In *Ritualized Homosexuality in Melanesia,* ed. G. H. Herdt. Berkeley: University of California Press, pp. 1–81.
IMPERATO-McGINLEY, J., et. al. (1974). Steroid 5 a-reductase Deficiency in Man: An Inherited Form of Male Pseudo-hermaphroditism. *Science,* 186:1213–1243.
KRACKE, W. H. (1980). Amazonian Interviews: Dreams of a Bereaved Father. *The Annual of Psychoanalysis,* 8:249–267. New York: International Universities Press.
LA BARRE, W. (1978). The Clinic and the Field. In *The Making of Psychological Anthropology,* ed. G. D. Spindler. Berkeley: University of California Press, pp. 259–299.
LeVINE, R. A. (1982). *Culture, Behavior, and Personality,* 2nd ed. New York: Aldine.
LEVY, R. I. (1973). *The Tahitians: Mind and Experience in the Society Islands.* Chicago: University of Chicago Press.
STOLLER, R. J., & HERDT, G. H. (1982). The Development of Masculinity: A Cross-cultural Contribution. *J. Amer. Psychoanal. Assn.,* 30:29–59.

5

"Culture Shock" and the Inability to Mourn

HOWARD F. STEIN, Ph.D.

This paper explores the nature of the nativistic response to the phenomenon of "culture shock." "Culture shock" will be used to denote the painful disruption of the "identity of perceptions" (Freud, 1900) between the inner representational world and the external—largely externalized—world that serves as container for the contents of the inner world. The subject of culture shock is the experience of estrangement from, loss and "death" of culture *as though* it were an object or object representation. Much of cult and culture alike serves the function of a "linking object" (Volkan, 1972, 1981), that is, to deny the fact that loss has occurred.

The nativistic response to separation and loss consists of the denial of loss through the celebration of cultural immortality. A reassuring sense of continuity is achieved through revitalization. I suggest that nativism in its many guises is a group symptom of the inability to mourn. A mythic world of changelessness substitutes for the reality of change. Metapsychologically, the geographical space of cultural experience is revealed to be a metaphor or symbolic representation of intrapsychic and intergenerational space-time, one which began with the "potential space" (Winnicott, 1967) between mother and infant. A number of brief ethnographic and historical examples are provided to illustrate this argument.

Typically, culture shock comprises a disquieting if not disorganizing sense of disjunction between past and present. There is a loss of gratifying ties that occurs when one emigrates to a new land, or, if one is an anthropologist, when the anthropologist disembarks upon his field site. (That the emigrant feels he is *leaving* home, while the anthropologist often feels that he is *finding* home, is discussed later in this paper.) In culture shock,

The author gratefully acknowledges the criticism and encouragement of Vamik D. Volkan, M.D., Maurice Apprey, M.A.C.P., Simon A. Grolnick, M.D., and L. Bryce Boyer, M.D.

one is dislocated with respect to place and time after having physically moved to a new location, or when he experiences the world to have dramatically changed all about. In culture shock, the agent feels estranged from the familiar. He suffers from a sense of being out of place and is often disoriented. In culture shock, projectively, "The times are out of joint." Similarly, the would-be shamanistic culture hero who promises to quell the fears of his contemporaries, dreams his dream "to set things right."

Separation Anxiety and Uprootedness

Hippler (1974) writes that "culture contact has and usually does involve suffering for the contacted peoples. But a good deal of the long-term suffering seems to be related, at least in part, to indigenous psychocultural factors" (p. 336). La Barre (1972) emphasizes that *"it is not stress as such but the psychic style of reaction to it that is important"* (p. 282; also 1969, 1971). Moreover, "in many, if not most, cases the poor response and heightened pathologies among many members of some groups is as much a function of their own emotional organization as of contact itself, however stressful and poorly responsive that contact might be" (Hippler, 1974, p. 336).

De Vos (1974, pp. 557–560) extensively reviews the literature on culture change and mental health, challenging the romantic myth of stability, harmony, support, cohesion, and security in the aboriginal countryside: "One of the principal difficulties with theories of urban transition as stressful is not due so much to an incorrect view of city life as to a mistaken and romanticized image of what village, rural, or tribal life is typically like" (p. 558). It may well be that received dichotomies or "ideal types" such as rural/urban, *Gemeinschaft/Gesellschaft,* particularist/universalist, and traditional/modern are our own *idealistic* compartmentalizations of good and evil which we then superimpose upon the ethnographic universe. One notes that such emotion-laden "binary opposition" does not originate with contemporary social scientists. It is very much a restorationist social ideology embodying a group fantasy about human relationships, one espoused by such literary luminaries and culture heroes as Jean-Jacques Rousseau, Charles Dickens, Feodor Dostoevski, Leo Tolstoi, Isaiah Berlin, Aleksandr Solzhenitsyn, and Michael Novak. (See Srole [1980] for a refutation of the decadence theory of the city.) It is thus not exclusively into the "stimulus situation" or "psycho-physics" of change that we must inquire, but into the inner representation or meaning of change in order to understand what social change disrupts *and* activates. Volkan (1982a) writes:

... psychiatrically speaking, the adjustment demanded by migration to a new country can be likened to the process of mourning (Garza-Guerrero, 1974; Volkan, 1979): during the initial phase there is "culture shock" (Ticho, 1971) that causes the migrant to activate previously gratifying links to the environment he left behind, regardless of whether it compares favourably or unfavourably with the environment at hand. The resolution of this type of mourning process takes a long time and depends on circumstances. The migrant may become fixated in the initial stage and be unable to move toward total resolution [p. 141].

The attenuation and disruption of ties together with the ensuing reparative measures that accompany culture shock are incompletely explained without the dynamic concept of separation anxiety. Here I follow the lead of Anna Freud and Margaret Mahler rather than John Bowlby: that is, the central issue is not the physical distance itself, but the emotional perception of distance, the intrapsychic representation of personal distinctness or separateness. Mahler and Furer (1968) write:

The concept of separation, in this sense, means differentiation of the self from the symbiotic object as an *intrapsychic* process.... by "separation anxiety" we do not mean the behavioral sequelae and reactions to *physical* separation from the love object, as John Bowlby has used the term, but rather the gradual yet inevitable *intrapsychic* sensing of a danger signal anxiety on the part of a small child during the normal separation-individuation process [pp. 220–221].

In an introduction to a panel on issues of "separation" with long-term hospitalized psychiatric patients, Schultz (1981) notes that

... separation as an intrapsychic phenomenon is equivalent to representational differentiation of self from object. In the second use, we have an "extrapsychic separation" equivalent to the parting from (or loss of) the object. In the intrapsychic use of the term we are mindful of Mahler's concepts of separation-individuation which have received so much recent emphasis in the developmental approach to the understanding of psychopathology. Here, there are issues of the establishment of object constancy and self-constancy in the eventual differentiation of self-representations from object-representations. The second use of the term is separation-equivalent-to-parting ... the terms become interrelated when we remember that for those more deeply ill patients success at separation (parting) is to a large extent dependent upon developmental separation (representational differentiation) [p. 133].

I think that for immigrants experiencing culture shock success at parting from the past is largely dependent upon the (relative) achievement of representational differentiation. Moreover, that reticulated web of reciprocity that goes by the terms kinship and community is itself in part an interpersonally implemented defense against separation anxiety. Outer social structures of reciprocal obligation and mutual clinging serve as bulwarks against the experience of separateness, as theologies and cosmologies — even patently persecutory ones — prevent the sense of loss.

In a discussion of Turkish individuals uprooted by immigration from the country to the city, Özbek and Volkan (1976) note the replacement of the extended family by the "satellite-extended" family in the urban setting (p. 577). The term "satellite state" (Volkan and Corney, 1968) indicates:

... an individual's failure to complete the process of separation-individuation (Mahler, 1963; Mahler and Furer, 1963). It refers also to his establishment of a stable but malignant satellite adaptation; to his fixation on whatever object he substitutes for the central figure of his original struggle with separation-individuation — the mother. The person still not liberated from this object by successful individuation is forced by his dependency to remain near it, and forced by his fear of engulfment to keep it at a psychic distance. The satellite individual is beyond symbiosis with the object since he can distinguish the representations of his mother from those of his own self, but is not yet a free-standing individual.... The satellite individual feels that to shift out of his fixed orbit is to kill the mother — or to die himself. As a defense against aggression the satellite position becomes inevitable (Volkan and Corney, 1968), a kind of welcome doom [Özbek and Volkan, 1976, pp. 577–578].

The adaptation fashioned by "satellite" individuals is one based upon a new personal cult or a group cult of the past, in which old internal objects are externalized, projectively identified in new objects, and "the past" safely restored — while the individual has in fact achieved some distance from it. One who has not left cannot wish to return (see Stein, 1979, 1980a), hence the sentimental, nostalgic quality of nativistic responses to culture shock. There is an aching yearning to retrieve what was lost — which implies that at least the transient perception of differentiation and loss must precede the restitutional effort to undo it.

Furthermore, in culture shock the "loss of culture" which represents the catastrophic crisis of identity (Erikson, 1963, 1968) is experienced as object loss. Culture (or "group") is represented as a fantasied maternal object with which the tribalist feels himself to be inextricably tied and upon which he feels himself to be wholly dependent. Culture is similarly experienced as a Mahlerian "dual unity" whose "body" the tribalist does not distinguish from his very selfhood. It is therefore little wonder that tribalists and anthropologists alike can commit the fallacy of misplaced concreteness in their conceptualization and phenomenology of culture: For one truly experiences his group to be "superorganic," that is, transcending the self yet part of the (symbiotic) self (see Stein, 1980a, 1980b), a Kohutian "selfobject." In this formulation, the loss of culture is the fantasied loss of an object-environment that mirrors and embodies the "goodness" upon which one depends. "Culture" experienced as an entity is but one member of a class of *symbolic objects,* whose psychic function is to represent and perpetuate object relations that have been disrupted by death or other forms of loss.

NATIVISM AND THE INABILITY TO MOURN

Nativistic responses by immigrants and by indigenous peoples in the midst of culture change (e.g., those tribes in the 19th century which were to embrace the Ghost Dance ideology and ritual) in part can be explained by the denial of grief, that is, the inability to mourn. The nativist's vicious hatred for the surrounding culture or acculturation (I do not love them, they hate me) – quite apart from very real discrimination and exclusion – can be understood as a paranoid response to the seduction from tradition by the new, and an equally paranoid projection of all hostility within one's idealized nurturant group onto the so-called host culture. Empathy within is heightened and empathy toward the outgroup is withdrawn as a splitting of the object world into good and evil, us and them, structures social relationships according to narcissistic principles. Social structure begins to mirror and implement (shared, consensual) intrapsychic structure.

This process has been documented in several studies of the White Ethnic movement in the United States (Stein, 1974a, 1979; Stein and Hill, 1973, 1977a). Essentially, one mourns the past less as he accuses the surrounding environment of depriving him of it, and fervently seeks to restore symbolic links with the object-past. Immigrant and indigenous nativist both conduct revivals and renaissances to restore the past, to undo those inevitable separations and irreparable losses that are part of the life cycle. The current American nostalgia movement is certainly an example of this (Stein, 1974b, 1975, 1977a, 1977b, 1980a; Stein and Hill, 1977a, 1977b).

One might suggest, not altogether metaphorically, that what occurs is a reversal of affect: The nativist celebrates rather than mourns: Actually, he celebrates in order not to mourn. Again, more concretely than metaphorically, he seeks to resurrect rather than bury the dead so that they will bless instead of haunt him. The cultist may expect the ancestors to return from the dead (e.g., the Melanesian "cargo cults," the Amerindian Ghost Dance), or he simply may seek to exalt their memory in a more internalized, quietistic cult of the dead (or a cult of "living" tradition). One thinks of the daily Hebrew entreaty to God: *"Hadesh yamaynu Kekedem"* – "Restore our days to those of yore."

"Absence," goes the cliché, "makes the heart grow fonder." Such nostalgia has become immortalized in an idealization of the homeland from afar. It has served as the taproot of much nativistic music, from regionalism through nationalism proper. The musical history of 19th- and early 20th-century romanticism demonstrates unequivocally that some of the most characteristically and passionately nationalistic music was written by the great expatriates. One thinks of the 19th-century Russian composer Mikhail Glinka in Warsaw, the Bohemian Antonin Dvorak in the United States (his fervent ninth symphony is *"From* the New World," not "The New World Symphony"), the Hungarian Franz Liszt in Weimar, the German Richard Wagner throughout Europe, the Polish Frederic Chopin self-exiled in Paris, the Norwegian Edvard Grieg in Berlin, and the Russian Sergei Rachmaninoff in the United States. Each was more "native" when he was longing for home. One likewise thinks of the 20th-century American composer Irving Berlin, who wrote his famous song "White Christmas" after having left the East for Los Angeles and Hollywood; and of the 19th-century American songwriter Stephen Foster, a Southerner at heart, who wrote his "Old Folks at Home," a lament for the loss of the Suwannee River, while living in Pennsylvania. These latter two, of course, are strictly speaking regionalistic rather than nationalistic, but the distinction lies only in the symbolic geographic object of the nostalgia and heightened veneration.

The contemporary writer Alexander Solzhenitsyn, exiled from the Soviet Union, can be firmly located within the several-century-old Russophile, neo-Orthodox school of Russian intellectuals who despised secularization and modernization (since Peter the Great) and longed for the restoration of Holy Russia. As with Dostoevsky and Tolstoy a century ago, his religion serves as a medium for nationalist striving. The nativistic response is possible only in those who have left the tradition they now reverence from afar; it is an effort to overcome the painful separation they now feel. It is an affirmation of the link with what has been irrevocably lost. Stated differently, the link itself affirms the loss in the very attempt to deny, soften, or undo the loss (Stein, 1976).

One finds the identical phenomenon at the political level: the wish to re-store rather than painfully mourn what has been lost. Jews in the Babylo-nian captivity longed for the return to and restoration of Zion; under the leadership of the Persian king Cyrus, and the Jewish prophets Ezra and Nehemiah, the Jews did indeed return to their homeland. During and im-mediately following World War I, it was largely through the concerted po-litical action of eastern and central European immigrants *within* the United States that the Austro-Hungarian Empire was dismembered and the successor nation-states of Poland, Czecho-Slovakia, and Sub-Carpathian Ruthenia were formed. These immigrants would make restitu-tion for having abandoned the motherland by pressing from safely across the ocean for her autonomy, separation (from the "bad" parental Em-pire), integrity, and ethnic purity. At present one finds a similar form of irredentism-at-a-distance on the part of many American Jews, Armeni-ans, and Irish.

The ambivalence toward (internal) objects from whom one cannot sep-arate is managed by splitting: One's cult or culture group represents "good" internal objects, and the outer or new cultural group represents "bad" internal objects. While the mourning process would facilitate both internal and external structural integration, the abortion of mourning leads to internal and external structural "segregation." Newly *externalized symbolic objects* represent one's renewed internal object ties. Such sym-bolic objects can be understood to serve as *external representations* through which one can perpetuate and "validate" the illusion that the ob-ject relation persists and has not been lost.

LINKING OBJECTS AND SOCIAL CHANGE

The work of Volkan on "linking objects" and "linking phenomena" (Volkan, 1972, 1981; Volkan and Josephthal, 1980) further elucidates the psychodynamics of these symbolic objects: "[T]he linking object appears in relation to loss understood in the broadest sense to include psychical separation" (1972, p. 219) — to which I would only add *psychical* differen-tiation often precipitated by *physical* separation. Similarly, "the linking object [is] a tie with the deceased" (1972, p. 217). I would also add that whereas, to the survivor, the linking object is a tie based upon *having been left,* to the immigrant or internal immigrant it is based upon *having ac-tively left,* one's original objects and/or original linking objects behind.

"[T]he linking object is a 'token of triumph' over loss" (1972, p. 220), a substitute of wish for reality. One maintains a hopeful, all-is-not-lost attitude which amounts both to a freezing of time and its magical reversal.

The linking object, as does the externalizing defense behind it, "evokes both the impulse to destroy it and the impulse to preserve it" (1972, p. 217). The linking object is "an instrument for the control of expressions of anger arising from separation panic" (1972, p. 221). Successors to "transitional objects" (Winnicott, 1953), linking objects represent not an advance toward boundaries (as do transitional objects), but a retreat (regression) from representational differentiation which has already taken place. Volkan writes:

> The linking object belongs both to the deceased and to the patient himself, as if the representations of the two meet and merge in an externalized way. The ambivalence which had characterized the relationship with the dead one is invested in the process of distancing the object in a representation of psychic distancing, but at the same time keeping it available [1972, p. 217].

Finally,

> The linking object provides a means whereby object relationships with the deceased can be maintained externally. The ambivalence of the wish to annihilate the deceased and the wish to keep him alive is condensed in it, so that the painful work of mourning has an external reference and thus is not resolved [1972, p. 221].

One might say that "linking" or "symbolic" objects are metaphors of the "satellite" object relationship itself. By observing how the individual "orbits" around his substitute object, one gains insight into the original.

This perspective on social change and separation anxiety requires that we rethink such well-intentioned but dynamically inapt notions as "support groups," "networking," and "linkages" which are advocated by many of the helping professions. Perhaps many mental health professionals recommend or refer their clients to a host of potential "support groups" as a countertransference maneuver to ward off through their clients their own fear of separation or their own unresolved losses. It is not unknown to treat a patient for one's own conflicts, the remedy being one's own defenses. When the underlying problem is separation, a true, lasting therapeutic solution can hardly be the denial of separateness by prescribing links (cf. a special section on separation in the *Journal of the National Association of Private Psychiatric Hospitals,* 1981, Vol. 12, No. 4). Volkan agrees that "one does not find therapeutic solutions by 'prescribing links'

—to do so is really to join the patient in creating magic. Patients create their own linking objects, and the therapeutic solution is to analyze the magic in such objects" (personal communication, May 20, 1982).

MISPLACED PERSONS IN THE AMERICAN SUN BELT

In my five years of work as consulting behavioral scientist for a family medicine residency clinic in northwest Oklahoma (Enid, population 60,000), I have noted a dramatic increase in what I have come to call "displaced persons" or "misplaced persons" in the patient population (Stein, 1983). These are for the most part "internal migrants" within the United States, those largely from the North and Northeast seeking employment, more freedom, and better weather in the "Promised Land" of the Sun Belt. For many of these, there is a sense that while the rest of the country is in decay and decline, in the Southwest one may begin a new life. Many are also urban transplants, if not refugees, from small towns and farms within Oklahoma, where, 50 miles outside the city, one is transported back a century. The economy of northwest Oklahoma rests primarily upon wheat, cattle, and oil, and attracts people who are seeking their fortune. Like the past waves of immigrants to the United States from Europe and elsewhere, many of these first immigrants are males whose families follow later. Many, too, are offshoots of tightly knit, emotionally as well as economically interdependent families. They commonly take the form of the satellite extended families discussed above by Volkan. These families maintain ties with the "old family" by such familiar means as sending back a portion of the paycheck, frequent and lengthy telephone calls as well as letters and, when possible, visits.

For many the symptom cluster which brings them to the clinic is often a variety of somatic complaints, usually without accompanying somatic change. The depression is not masked convincingly, as the patients readily admit a feeling of being "like a fish out of water," isolated (except perhaps for spouse and children), lonely, sad, and at a loss for what to do once they have a job and housing. The husband-wife dyad becomes an encapsulated —and fragile—bulwark against the strange world around them. Almost instinctively, we inquire into their efforts to secure what mental health workers call "linkages" or a "support system" (e.g., church, work associates, clubs, etc.). Many are too frightened and feel too strange to try; others have launched into their own networking. Yet all seem equally unhappy.

Therapeutically, we are often too eager to help them to fill the void and deny the rage stemming from separation and loss, too eager to comply with their wish to find "attachments" and to "sink in their roots" by mustering social and community services in their behalf. It seems evident that this *culture*-syntonic "thing to do" is anti-therapeutic; it only delays the grief and individuation process. Thus the clinical "solution" actually contributed to the problem. The first clue was the fact that these displaced patients eagerly looked forward to their clinic visits and counseling not only to recover from their somatic maladies, but as a social occasion itself. While the therapy sessions seemed fruitful, they became profoundly difficult to terminate — whether at the end of a half hour or when many of the somatic complaints had gone into remission. Averting the pain of (delayed) emotional detachment from their cocoon-like families and neighborhoods of origin, these patients had become deeply attached to the family doctor, the consultant, and the clinic. They sometimes tearfully acknowledged that they had little else to which they could look forward.

Instead of *exploiting* or *manipulating* their "adoption" of the clinic as a transferential link in their satellite extended family, we began to *analyze* the links with them. Predictably, we learned that the idealization of the family of origin ("roots") was in direct proportion to the ambivalence about it; that the craving for a ("good") support system was a means of neutralizing internal punitive "bad" objects; that the fear of separation corresponded to an unconscious family injunction against emotional (even physical) separation; that the ostensible wish for attachment served as a defense against the wish for autonomy; that glowing memories of family and neighborhood were mustered as a formidable bulwark against overwhelming rage and guilt.

Case Summary

Chuck Jones was a 25-year-old white male who was originally seen at the Family Medicine Clinic for complaints of restlessness, insomnia, and low back pain of three-weeks duration. The initial physical examination by the family physician revealed a mildly obese, anxious-looking man whose general examination was within normal limits. Mr. Jones was treated with a prescription of Librium.

Within three months an attempt was made to use Vistaril to control Mr. Jones's continued anxiety. Relaxation methods aside from medication were discussed, and arrangements were made for him to enter a biofeedback program at the local hospital.

Mr. Jones returned to the clinic within a week, however, and expressed concern that he was not making adequate progress. He reported no problems at home or at his job as a traveling salesman. He related past episodes in which he had experienced derealization and depersonalization (e.g., appearing as an outsider looking at himself) and expressed fear that these feelings would return without the aid of Valium or Librium. He also expressed fear of becoming dependent upon medications. At this point the clinic consultant was requested to see the patient with the physician.

His history revealed that Mr. Jones had moved to Oklahoma from Chicago approximately one year earlier with his new wife Kathy. He was the second of five siblings and the eldest son. The couple expected to start a life of their own in Oklahoma removed from family pressures. However, they found they had difficulty making friends, and never felt comfortable with employees, neighbors, or church members in their new hometown.

Mr. Jones felt that his father regarded him as "a model son who would follow in his father's footsteps." Since his father remains a national figure in his field, Chuck found that even in the Sun Belt he was often appraised as "Jones's son," apart from his own merits. He resented his father's influence as well in persuading him to purchase a small, dilapidated house in Oklahoma rather than a larger, newer home.

Chuck related deep disturbance over guilt feelings about drug use (acid, psilocybin, marijuana) during his high school years. He felt that he had let his father down, and raised the specter of losing his father's love, by "experimenting with drugs in the past." His eyes became tearful while disclosing his feelings of guilt. As the couple attempted to make Oklahoma their home, and Kathy became pregnant with their first child, Chuck had difficulty "maintaining control" over his feelings about drug need and abuse.

Over time, Chuck allowed himself to clarify his idealization and his anger toward his father. Gradually, he differentiated his need to please his father from his need to be free of comparison with his father. Chuck accepted a job offer which he identified as based on his own merits. The couple felt much less "misplaced" in their chosen home, though tended to feel more "misplaced" in their homes of origin. They expressed confidence in their ability to build their future without fears of loss of control or drug dependency. The mourning process became his inner and outer liberation.

For Chuck Jones, "drugs" had marked his first break with his father, for which rebellious wish he subsequently atoned and against which atoning he rebelled. The more he was able to achieve a differentiation from the father imago, and gradually to accept the ambivalence of oedipal sonhood, the more he was able to take leave of those symbolic objects that had expressed and confirmed his inner status as "misplaced person." Treatment avoided the temptations of "occupation counseling" or advice on "how to choose a home," and explored with Chuck the meanings of work and home (etc.) so that, less driven by unconscious conflict, he could more freely choose his future. In examining the ties and affects that underlay his "transference" to cultural symbolic objects, the intent of therapy was to help Chuck to *loosen* (the exact opposite of cultural "support" and "replacement" therapy) those symbolic ties and internal representations that had given him a sense of emotional bondage (Stein, 1983).

As was true for Chuck Jones, the initial somatic symptoms, mood depression, and confusion (if not panic) of many "misplaced" patients were precipitated by a dramatic physical disengagement which had not been preceded or prepared for by the necessary emotional disengagement. The therapeutic task for those who had suffered from this "culture shock" consisted of some preparation. Only as they could mourn the loss of their past could they embark upon a future based upon something other than a panic-ridden flight into the romantically edited past.

I hasten to add that this clinical impression, together with the inadvertently anti-therapeutic response, is neither strictly regional nor medical. The sense of emotional dislocation and of the need for a kind of emotional relocation through nostalgia abounds nationally (see Stein, 1974b, 1982). The drama of uprootedness and the quest for secure "roots" (dynamically, linking objects) is staged in numerous contexts.

During a decade of national workshops and conventions on ethnic identity, family medicine, and family therapy, I have encountered what is tantamount to an absolute injunction: "It's not that 'you can't go home again,' as the psychoanalysts tried to brainwash us. You *can* go home again; in fact you *must*. You really never leave home." In my current research, I approach the family therapy and family medicine movements in the United States as crisis cults, one of whose organizing fantasies is the rescue and restoration of the "family." It appears that the struggle with such powerful and primitive fantasies as incorportion, attachment, and separation has led many family therapists and family physicians (with their theoretical frameworks) to defend themselves against the transference by denying or manipulating it. These defenses are institutionalized in therapeutic strategies (e.g., "staying out of the transference," "coaching" the patient or family, restructuring family relationships by prescribing behavior and defining roles, etc.). It could be said that the cult which is the therapy for the culture (La Barre, 1972, p. 172) seems to offer its symptom-defenses (viz., the denial of separation and mourning) as therapy.

ANTHROPOLOGY AND CULTURE SHOCK

I noted earlier that while anthropologists typically suffer culture shock when entering the world of an unfamiliar people — as I did upon discovering subtle differences between Slovak-Americans and those working-class and middle-class Americans of my own upbringing – they commonly come to feel more at home among "their" tribe than they felt in the home which they left. It is often, and ironically, observed that anthropologists suffer culture shock more often when they return from the field than when they enter it.

During fieldwork and thereafter, anthropologists tend to identify unself-critically with the natives and staunchly advocate the salvage, perpetuation, or restoration of tradition, together with resistance against modernization and secularization (Hippler, 1974, 1980). These tend to correspond to what anthropologists think the natives "should" want, and often are based upon a strictly relativistic assessment of group "emics." Anthropology has long had a tenacious strain of romanticism in its ethos.

Moreover, such a strictly "emic" view of man functions for anthropologists as a subtle but powerful professional defense against a psychodynamic view – e.g., the issues of separation-individuation that such a view would raise. The anthropologist's group or "tribe" becomes his linking object. "The people," a nearly universal self-designation among ethnocentric tribalists, becomes the anthropological preserve of "my people." Likewise, those whom anthropologists perceive (through the eyes of sentimentalization) to be adversaries of the natives become their own adversaries as well: a fairly clear oedipal rescue fantasy.

In many respects, "advocacy research" and "salvage ethnography" appear to enact oedipal rescue fantasies whereby the anthropologist attempts to protect the violated, despoiled mother (native or traditional culture) from further intrusion, contamination, and pillage by foreign male offenders (Western civilization, modernization, secularization, acculturation, etc.). (One also might discern in this compartmentalization evidence of primitive splitting.) This is recognizable to be a common nativist and ethno-nationalist fantasy as well (see Koenigsberg, 1975; Stein, 1979).

Only at the outset of fieldwork do anthropologists generally feel that they have indeed left, if not abandoned, home. The "culture shock" wherein anthropologists first experience the natives as bizarre or exotic gives way to a sense of the native way of life as uncanny: *Heimlich, Heimisch,* and *Unheimlisch* at once, that is, secretly familiar (Freud, 1919). Among anthropologists, the *unfamiliar* (bizarre, exotic) is the acceptable (to the superego) form or disguise for the displaced *familiar* (uncanny). In leaving behind a frequently intensely disliked homeland, one discovers that in working with the natives he is "going home" or "coming home." The Rousseauan quest for the primitive is the pilgrimage homeward. Concomitantly, the departure from the field is experienced as a profound loss. Anthropologists would not need to pronounce a solemn taboo upon "going native" were the wish to live out the family romance not powerful.

The anthropologist Bronislaw Malinowski was more the exception than the rule. Following his penchant for reading European novels and bellowing Wagnerian tunes, Malinowski instituted his own private nativistic cult to deal with the culture shock involved in living for several years with the Trobriand Islanders, whereas most anthropologists idealize the culture they find rather than the culture they left. This occurs whether or not considerable geographic distance exists between the native culture and their own (e.g., travel from the continental United States to Micronesia, versus travel from the university to the local ethnic enclave). In either case, what matters is the observer's psychogeography, which is to say, the emotional distance he maintains. In discovering one's "tribe" or "people" among the natives, one retrieves the past and its relationships as he wishes they had been, attempting not only to undo the actual familial past, but to restage it, doing better this time. One is active rather than passive. One hopes that many of the traumas and disappointments in one's family of origin and culture of origin will be assuaged by one's adopted culture. Of course, the native culture is experienced as much "through a glass countertransferentially" as one experiences his aboriginal culture.

I have come to discover that some of the ethnic families to whom I have become deeply attached served precisely this function: a home away from home, a surrogate "good" family, a way of demonstrating to myself that not all ethnics are viciously or subtly anti-Semitic (contrary to the certainty of many in my upbringing that persecution was always imminent), etc. For a period, they had become my own idealized satellite extended families, conveniently displaced from my own family of origin. Now, we frequently send young anthropological graduate students to the field with the injunction: "Know thy biases and preconceptions," as though one could consciously, willfully, do so. It is, however, the essence of transference phenomena that one is unconscious of those biases and preconceptions that affectively count! Therefore throughout my fieldwork, in my medical supervision/research in the present as in my ethnic research in the past, I have felt increasingly compelled to inquire into why I am noticing what I am noticing, whether I might be emphasizing one thing too much while minimizing another, and so on.

If ethnography is a species of autobiography (La Barre, 1978), then ethnographic fieldwork can in part be understood dynamically as a restitutional and reparative phenomenon: setting up a "good" home in order not to have to separate from the past or to mourn it. The culture shock that occurs among anthropologists upon their return home from the field consists of the abrupt separation from that idealized "good" family or tribe, and the conflict attendant upon becoming anew a member of the deidealized "bad" family or tribe.

CONCLUSION

I have argued that for immigrants, indigenous peoples, and anthropologists alike, "culture shock" refers to the rekindling of unresolved attachments, separations, and losses, and leads to nativistic attempts to deny (if not reverse) painful losses by setting up symbolic objects which will repair the broken symbiosis by halting (or reversing) developmental and intergenerational time.

BIBLIOGRAPHY

DeVOS, G. (1974). Cross-Cultural Studies of Mental Disorder: An Anthropological Perspective. In: *Child and Adolescent Psychiatry, Sociocultural and Community Psychiatry,* Vol. 2, ed. G. Caplan. [*American Handbook of Psychiatry* ed. S. Arieti.] New York: Basic Books.
ERIKSON, E. (1963). *Childhood and Society,* rev. ed. New York: Norton.
_____ (1968). *Identity, Youth and Crisis.* New York: Norton.
FREUD, S. (1900). The Interpretation of Dreams. *Standard Edition,* 4&5. London: Hogarth Press, 1953.
_____ (1919). The "Uncanny." *Standard Edition,* 17:219–256. London: Hogarth Press, 1955.
GARZA-GUERRERO, A. (1974). Culture Shock: Its Mourning and Vicissitudes of Identity. *J. Amer. Psychoanal. Assn.,* 22:428–429.
HIPPLER, A. (1974). Some Alternative Viewpoints of the Negative Results of Euro-American Contact with Non-Western Groups. *Amer. Anthropologist,* 76:334–337.
_____ (1980). Review of *The Politics of Anthropology: From Colonialism and Sexism Toward a View from Below,* edited by Gerrit Huizer and Bruce Manneim. *J. Psychol. Anthropol.* 3:219–221.
KOENIGSBERG, R. (1975). *Hitler's Ideology: A Study in Psychoanalytic Sociology.* New York: Library of Social Science.
LA BARRE, W. (1969). *They Shall Take Up Serpents: Psychology of the Southern Snake-Handling Cult.* New York: Schocken.
_____ (1971). Materials for a History of Studies of Crisis Cults: A Bibliographic Essay. *Current Anthropology,* 12:3–44.
_____ (1972). *The Ghost Dance: The Origins of Religion.* New York: Dell.
_____ (1978). The Clinic and the Field. In: *The Making of Psychological Anthropology,* ed. G. D. Spindler. Los Angeles: University of California Press, pp. 259–299.
MAHLER, M. (1963). Thoughts about Development and Individuation. *The Psychoanalytic Study of the Child,* 18:307. New York: International Universities Press.
_____ & FURER, M. (1963). Certain Aspects of the Separation-Individuation Phase. *Psychoanal. Quart.,* 32:1.
_____ & _____ (1968). *On Human Symbiosis and the Vicissitudes of Individuation.* New York: International Universities Press.
ÖZBEK, A., & VOLKAN, V. (1976). Psychiatric Problems within the Satellite-Extended Families of Turkey. *Amer. J. Psychother.,* 30:576–582.
SCHULTZ, C. (1981). The Value of Working Through: An Introduction to the Subject of Separation. *J. Nat. Assn. Priv. Psychiat. Hosp.,* 12:132–133.

SROLE, L. (1980). Mental Health in New York: A Revisionist View. *The Sciences*, 20:16–20, 29.

STEIN, H. (1974a). Confirmation of the White Ethnic Stereotype. *University of Chicago School Review*, 82:437–454.

_____ (1974b). Where Seldom Is Heard a Discouraging Word: American Nostalgia. *The Columbia Forum*, 3:20–23.

_____ (1975). Ethnicity, Identity, and Ideology. *University of Chicago School Review*, 83:273–300.

_____ (1976). Russian Nationalism and the Divided Soul of the Westernizers and Slavophiles. *Ethos*, 4:403–438.

_____ (1977a). Identity and Transcendence. *University of Chicago School Review*, 85: 349–375.

_____ (1977b). In Search of "Roots": An Epic of Origins and Destiny. *J. Pop. Culture*, 13:11–17.

_____ (1979). The White Ethnic Movement, Pan-ism, and the Restoration of Early Symbiosis: The Psychohistory of a Group-Fantasy. *J. Psychohistory*, 6:319–359.

_____ (1980a). Culture and Ethnicity as Group-Fantasies: A Psychohistoric Paradigm of Group Identity. *J. Psychohistory*, 8:21–51.

_____ (1980b). Bowen "Family Systems Theory" — The Problem of Cultural Persistence, and the Differentiation of Self in One's Culture. *The Family*, 8:3–12.

_____ (1982). "Health" and "Wellness" as Euphemism: The Cultural Context of Insidious Draconian Health Policy. *Continuing Education for the Family Physician*, 16:33–44.

_____ (1983). "Misplaced Persons" — The Crisis of Emotional Separation in Geographical Mobility and Uprootedness: A Contemporary Grapes of Wrath in the American Sun-Belt. Presented at The Third Annual Conference of the High Plains Regional Section, Society for Applied Anthropology, February 18–20, Denver.

_____ & HILL, R. (1973). The New Ethnicity and the White Ethnic in the United States: An Exploration in the Psycho-Cultural Genesis of Ethnic Irredentism. *The Canadian Review of Studies in Nationalism*, 1:81–105.

_____ & _____ (1977a). *The Ethnic Imperative: Examining the New White Ethnic Movement*. University Park: The Pennsylvania State University Press.

_____ & _____ (1977b). The Limits of Ethnicity. *The American Scholar*, Spring: 181–189.

TICHO, G. (1971). Cultural Aspects of Transference and Countertransference. *Bull. Menn. Clin.*, 35:313:–314.

VOLKAN, V. (1972). The Linking Objects of Pathological Mourners. *Arch. Gen. Psychiat.* 27:215–221.

_____ (1979). *Cyprus — War and Adaptation*. Charlottesville: University Press of Virginia.

_____ (1981). *Linking Objects and Linking Phenomena: A Study of the Forms, Symptoms, Metapsychology, and Therapy of Complicated Mourning*. New York: International Universities Press.

_____ (1982a). Abstract of "Psychological Problems of Turkish Migrants in West Germany," by P. Suzuki. *Transcultural Psychiatric Research Review*, 19:140–141.

_____ & CORNEY, R. (1968). Some Considerations of Satellite States and Satellite Dreams. *Brit. J. Med. Psychol.*, 41:283.

_____ & JOSEPHTHAL, D. (1980). The Treatment of Established Pathological Mourners. In: *Specialized Techniques in Individual Psychotherapy*, ed. T. Karasu & L. Bellak. New York: Brunner/Mazel, pp. 118–142.

WINNICOTT, D. (1953). Transitional Objects and Transitional Phenomena. *Internat. J. Psycho-Anal.*, 34:89–97.

_____ (1967). The Location of Cultural Experience. *Internat. J. Psycho-Anal.*, 48:368–372.

6
The Charismatically Led Group: The Mental Processes of Its Members

LEON BALTER, M.D.

This paper addresses the question of what mental processes make and effect an individual's membership in a group led by a charismatic leader. Social scientists have tended to ignore the question of the psychology of group formation. They have neither the psychological concepts needed nor the technique required for investigation. But psychologists have done relatively little in this realm as well, probably because interpersonal transactions are so obviously important in group formation as to inhibit a purely intrapsychic approach. Even more important, the individuals participating in a group frequently undergo wide fluctuations from the mental states that characterize their functioning as unaffiliated individuals. As group members, they show relatively little self-awareness, and so cannot offer much to explain their altered mental state in the group.

A more radical difficulty also obtains. The direct psychoanalytic investigation of unconscious mental processes is difficult in group situations because absolute privacy and confidentiality are not present. Conversely, in all its properties, the psychoanalytic situation *interferes* with group participation. Indirect, retrospective investigation of group participation therefore seems to be more feasible.

Probably the most difficult obstacle in the path of psychological investigation of group membership and group formation is purely conceptual. The social sciences — sociology, anthropology, political science, economics, etc. — are autonomous disciplines. They have their own traditions and modes of investigation. They formulate their own basic concepts, develop and test their own theories. To explain group formation and associated group membership on the basis of psychological processes is to approach a reductionism inimical to the autonomy of social scientific disciplines. Such autonomy is not surrendered lightly. This reluctance does not derive only from natural self-aggrandizement inherent in any purposive endeavor, scientific or otherwise. More importantly, it stems from the fact that a discipline – just *because* it is a discipline – structures and constrains the thinking of those who compose it. Basic concepts of the social scientific disciplines are challenged by even more basic psychological concepts. Reductionism – or even what looks like it – is disruptive and thus eschewed.

But multi-individual phenomena have their own intrinsic aspects and forms which cannot be elucidated by intrapsychic investigation. And even though the psychological investigation of group formation is attended by all sorts of difficulties, the effort nevertheless recommends itself. The addition of the psychological perspective to social research may be of some worth – and it has already been effected to some degree by social scientists themselves, albeit hesitantly. The psychoanalytic value judgment "It is better to know than not to know" applies to the other scientific disciplines as well. Whatever contribution psychoanalysis may ultimately make in this direction can only be salutary. It is in this spirit that the present study is offered.

This investigation will address the problem of the psychology of group membership and group formation in the context of an extremely circumscribed domain. The charismatically led group is only one of a great variety of group types. In manifest structure (morphology), it is made up of a cohesive collection of invididuals who are all subordinate in the same way to an idealized leader who is not one of them. With regard to them, the leader is exceptional – that is, *extra*ordinary. He is not like his followers in some crucial way. For this reason, Weber's (1958) term "charismatic" has been adopted here to describe this sort of leader. As will be seen below, the present investigation will, of necessity, expand and elaborate on Weber's use of the term. The reason for this is simple. The psychological investigation of charismatic leadership from the point of view of the followers and the impetus to group formation will make equivalent on the *psychological* level phenomena previously seen as dissimilar on the *sociological* level. The essential underlying psychological identity of seemingly different group formations necessitates that the term "charismatic" either be discarded or extended. Here, the latter option was chosen in an effort to bridge the gap, too long maintained, between the psychological and the social scientific disciplines.

Also, in the examples of charismatically led group formation investigated psychologically below, it will become obvious that the sorts of leader described do not have the glory, glamour, high historical importance, revolutionary dynamism, or God-given majesty commonly associated with charismatic leaders. Rather, the leaders described below have only one quality which they share with the more eminent exemplars: the attribute accorded them by their followers of being exceptional and extraordinary in a manner that is critically important to the followers. This same quality seems to be essential to the more conventional uses of the term.

It will also be seen that, like their more illustrious fellows, the charismatic leaders studied here are not objects for identification by their followers. The radical differentiation of leader from followers-members is extremely important. It separates charismatically led groups from all other group-types with leaders. In the latter, identification with the leader, as a group-formative process, takes place in some variable degree. The absence of such identification is, in fact, the essential meaning of the charismatically led group's morphological quality: the leader is extraordinary in comparison with the members.

Most of the psychoanalytic interest in this sort of group has concerned itself with the psychology of the charismatic *leader*. The present study will determine the psychic properties of the leader's *followers,* the *members* of this type of group. As will be seen below, the psychoanalytic approach to charismatically led group membership will require several different investigative strategies, all mutually supportive, all converging. Freud's (1921) *general* theory of group formation will be the basis of this *special* theory of charismatically led groups.

EXAMPLES

The Youth Group

The charismatically led youth group has been seen in different eras of human history and is quite widespread in any given era. It has a membership composed of postpubertal youngsters, and has an adored leader who is either youngish or actually only slightly older than they. Most typically, the membership is composed of one sex and the leader is also of that sex. As will be seen below, this is not accidental; the socialization functions of this type of group will be accomplished most effectively when it has these particular characteristics. In modern times the youth group is frequently seen in summer camps, boarding schools, and scout troops. There, youngsters are characteristically separated according to sex and come to have collective "crushes" on youngish counselors.

An example of the youth group was given by Redl (1942) in his important paper on leadership and group emotion. Redl made his observations in a school for disturbed children where psychotherapeutic and educative activities occurred simultaneously, though in different contexts. Because of this, social and psychological phenomena could be studied in the most suitable settings without mutual interference.

This group of boys are between fifteen and seventeen years of age. Most of them are far beyond their preadolescence — at the verge of transition from earlier adolescence into later adolescence. The teacher in charge of them is, or has the appearance of being, very young. He has an attractive exterior. He is somewhat juvenile but not too unpleasantly so in his views and behavior. He also stands for "work and discipline," and gets his youngsters to comply without much outward pressure. . . . the basis on which he gets them to accept his authority is. . . . mainly . . . that he strongly sympathizes with the drives of the children. They are clearly aware of it. He plays a dual role in his teaching. In his own super-ego, he is identified with the order and the demands of the school which he represents; but he is keenly aware of the instinctual demands of the youngsters. In order to combine both he has to display considerable technical skill. If he succeeds, he makes his class feel secure and happy; if he fails, they are frightened either of him or of their own drives. The children adore him, but they also accept what he stands for without much question. The boy who misbehaves is not the greatest danger to the emotional equilibrium of the group. He elicits moral pity rather than indignation from the others. The danger is the boy who tries to get a more intensive emotional counter response from the teacher than the others, while less ready to pay for it by conscientious output of work. He is hated and despised by them. A single youngster in that group, feeling negatively viewed by the teacher, is unhappy rather than frightened. Undesirable thoughts and actions still remain confessable. To be "understood" — accepted — is the minimum requirement of group happiness in this class [p. 577].

By early and middle adolescence, with the physiological maturation of the individual, the instinctual drives have already become intensified and are capable of being gratified in adult fashion. At the same time, however, the psychological developmental process at this stage involves the still-continuing shift away from the parents as the primary focus of those drives to extrafamilial objects of the adolescent's own generation. Attitudes toward the drives themselves must be changed. Correspondingly, there must also occur a modification of the youth's morality and ideal standards. He begins adolescence with values characteristic of latency. They are rigid, categorical, literal, and harsh. In order to make the transition to extrafamilial objects and an instinctually satisfactory life, his morality and ideals must become more flexible, conditional, and moderate. There is a characteristic acute conflict in early and middle adolesence between drives and moral-ideal standards. Adolescents accomplish the integration of the two more or less successfully using a variety of techniques. Of interest here is the role which the youth group plays in this process. In this particular example, the youth group occurred in a school situation.

Redl pointed out that the teacher of these adolescent boys embodies in himself the reconciliation of youthful instincts and adult morality in a particularly dramatic fashion. On the one hand, he "stands for 'work and discipline.' " On the other hand, he "is, or has the appearance of being, very young. . . . is somewhat juvenile. . . . strongly sympathizes with the drives of the children. . . . is keenly aware of the instinctual demands of the youngsters." And, "they are clearly aware of it." He has achieved *in himself* the conflict resolution integrating youthful instinctual impulsions and established morality — a resolution which the boys subjectively experience in themselves as precarious and tenuous at best and which is objectively impossible for them at this stage of their development. The teacher thus becomes for the boys an exceptional and extraordinary person — "The children adore him. . . ." He has the charisma of instinctual and moral integrity. As such, he is the externalized embodiment of an ideal: pleasure in the instincts without moral conflict, and moral rectitude without instinctual frustration. He also takes over, in this context, the conscience function of the superego: "He . . . stands for 'work and discpline,' and gets his youngsters to comply without much outward pressure. . . . they also accept what he stands for without much question."

The youngsters idealize, "adore," their teacher. He becomes their leader. His orientation becomes theirs — but not through identification with him. They do not become like him — that is, morally and instinctually integrated *within themselves*. Rather, they ascribe authority over themselves to their teacher and submissively follow his directions. Through his authority, he steers them through the precarious passage between instinctual gratification and moral rectitude. In effect, he is their director, their conductor for achieving the goals of adulthood (a firm sexual identity alongside a firm social morality) before they can do it by themselves. What would be an internal intrapsychic conflict *within* each of the boys is now negotiated in the sphere of the interactions *between* the teacher and the boys. In his functional position as their externalized conscience, he is in danger of undermining their view of him as an ideal of instinctual ease. In his capacity as the latter, he runs the risk of disillusioning them as the embodiment of their morality. If he is able to maintain both positions, he will be able to bring the boys to *where they can be both moral and instinctual with no overt conflict*. That is, he will have resolved their conflict. This is what Redl meant when he wrote: "He plays a dual role in his teaching. . . . In order to combine both he has to display considerable technical skill. If he succeeds, he makes his class feel secure and happy; if he fails, they are frightened either of him or of their own drives."

The fact that each boy puts the teacher in this particular conflict-resolving position does not, in itself, lead to the formation of a group among the students. Redl did, however, indicate where to look for the motive for group formation. He said that the group becomes emotionally disequilibrated and, by implication, disrupted when a boy wants "to get . . . intensive emotional counter response from the teacher . . . while less ready to pay for it by conscientious output of work." This perspicacious observation permits an inference about the unconscious dynamic in this group formation: The formation of the group may be seen as an effort to keep just this occurrence from happening— not solely with regard to this particular boy or that one, but with regard to all of them. More specifically, each boy would like to obtain emotional-instinctual gratification from the teacher in a manner that would escape "the order and the demands of the school," as personified in the teacher. Each boy, therefore, not only looks to the teacher as a means of resolving his general adolescent moral-instinctual conflict, but also brings that same conflict into his personal relationship to the teacher. Each boy wants to circumvent the conditions of conflict by getting from the teacher emotional-instinctual gratifications without taking into account moral principles. Moreover, he wants to obtain his ends with the leader's participation and, thus, his implicit or explicit forgiveness. Such inveiglement of the teacher, who functions as an externalized conscience, would be a resolution of the boy's adolescent conflict around the person of the teacher on the *individual level*— that is, without the participation of the other boys. However, any success on the part of any *individual* boy would necessarily result in the disillusionment of *all* the boys (including the one gratified) as to the teacher's embodying both their conscience and their ideal. The teacher's authority would disappear and with it his conflict-resolving direction of all the boys. They would thus all be left on their own, each with his own adolescent conflict to resolve by himself.

Accordingly, each youngster resolves his adolescent conflict *as expressed in relation to the person of the teacher* by policing himself and all the others into a conformistic uniformity. That is, all the boys adopt a particular common quality by partially identifying with one another. In this situation, that quality is the rigorous, submissive adherence by them all to the teacher and his ethos of balanced gratification and discipline—not only generally, but more importantly, in their respective personal relations to the teacher-leader. This ensures the inviolability of the teacher's authority as externalized conscience and ideal. In their idealization of their leader, the boys submissively follow his directives, balancing instinctual satisfaction and social morality. In their mutual partial identification, they apply that balance to their personal relations with their leader. In so doing, they make their respective relations with the leader uniform and equal.

What creates the group is not the common idealization of the leader but the conflict resolution that results from the boys' equalizing partial identification with each other. This resolution takes place only indirectly on the leader's initiative. After all, he does serve as a director for them all, equally and uniformly. Most immediately, however, the group forms on the initiative of the members themselves.

It should be noted that any deviation from this regimented behavior on the part of any boy brings down upon him the intense aggression of all the others: "He is hated and despised by them." This reaction bespeaks the fact that the boys have mobilized a directly antithetical attitude toward such a disequilibrating example. That is, each boy has established a reaction formation in himself which, with repression, keeps unconscious the desire for special gratification through and with the leader.

It may now be seen why the socialization process facilitated by the youth group is most effective when it is not coeducational, but restricted to one sex, and when the leader is of that same sex. The leader is considered exceptional and extraordinary (charismatic and authoritative) in a manner that is of critical importance to *the followers,* in their particular age-specific and sex-specific developmental predicament.

This charismatically led mode of resolution of adolescent conflicts has not escaped the notice of psychoanalysts. Indeed, Anna Freud (1958, pp. 269–270), in her classic paper on adolescence, noted it as one of the defenses against infantile object ties.

The Timmes of West Africa and the Betrayed Wife of Vienna

In the youth group, the leader was considered exceptional because of his own personal accomplishment of integrating social morality and the drives of youth; this qualified him to serve as a director for his followers in carrying out that same developmental task of conflict resolution. In this section, another reason for the elevation of a leader to charismatic status will be discussed, namely, the conflictual hostility directed toward him by his followers.

In *Totem and Taboo,* Freud (1913) told of certain ceremonials of veneration which some primitive people visit upon their charismatic rulers. These ceremonial obeisances inflict much suffering upon these personages:

The dignity of their position ceased to be an enviable thing, and those who were offered it often took every possible means of escaping it. . . . Among the natives of Sierra Leone the objection to accepting the honor of kingship became so great that most tribes were obliged to choose foreigners as their kings [pp. 45–47].

These charismatic rulers were alleged to be truly exceptional by virtue of their magical omnipotence, and their followers externalized upon them the ego-ideal function and/or conscience. Freud discerned in the anxious and exaggerated solicitude of the followers of these leaders the same qualities seen in obsessional neurotics, in whom repression and reaction formation keep out of consciousness and overt behavior the underlying aggression toward the loved object:

If we now apply this to the case of privileged persons, we shall realize that alongside of the veneration, and indeed idolization, felt towards them, there is in the unconscious an opposing current of intense hostility [p. 49].

Freud then went on to describe the social customs of certain tribes in West Africa which express this more obviously. Of particular relevance to the present investigation is that charismatically led group formation may take place through the raising up of a charismatic leader *in order to get rid of him,* even by killing him outright:

Indeed, owing to the variety of outcomes of a conflict of this kind which are reached among different peoples, we are not at a loss for examples in which the existence of this hostility is still more obviously shown. 'The savage Timmes of Sierra Leone,' we learn from Frazer, 'who elect their king, reserve to themselves the right of beating him on the eve of his coronation; and they avail themselves of this constitutional privilege with such hearty goodwill that sometimes the unhappy monarch does not long survive his elevation to the throne. *Hence when the leading chiefs have a spite at a man and wish to rid themselves of him, they elect him king.'* Even in glaring instances like this, however, the hostility is not admitted as such, but masquerades as a ceremonial [p. 49; my italics].

As is well known, among tribal peoples the taking of a man's life (especially that of a member of the same tribe) is treated with much greater gravity than is such murder in the streets of the modern cosmopolis. To take life may bring down upon the head of the murderer the curses of the dead man's spirit, the vengeance of his relatives, and the wrath and punishment of the whole tribe. Accordingly, severe conflict occurs within anyone who is mobilized to rid himself of a hated fellow tribesman. The conflict resolution found among the Timmes of Sierra Leone is to elect him king. Once invested with temporal and magical powers, he is even more formidable. But the ceremonials — with their sadism covered by sanctity and tradition — provide the way. Indeed, the murderers may not even experience their murderous feelings or intent. These latter attitudes, through the reaction formation of veneration, are kept repressed. The brutal ceremonials are thus compromise formations which have the idealization of the charismatic ruler as their manifest content. Submissive, self-negating, masochistic grovelling before the leader hides from all parties the ultimate, murderous motive.

This was Freud's analysis of the ceremonials directed toward royalty, even when the sadism of the practices is attenuated and made more subtle. In that situation, the defensive use of repression and reaction formation still bespeaks a conflict between hostility and fear of retribution:

> These ceremonials unmistakably reveal their double meaning and their derivation from ambivalent impulses, as soon as we are ready to allow that the results which they bring about were intended from the first. The taboo does not only pick out the king and exalt him above all common mortals, it also makes his existence a torment and an intolerable burden and reduces him to a bondage far worse than that of his subjects. Here, then, we have an exact counterpart of the obsessional act in the neurosis, in which the suppressed impulse and the impulse that suppresses it find simultaneous and common satisfaction. The obsessional act is *ostensibly* a protection against the prohibited act; but *actually,* in our view, it is a repetition of it. The 'ostensibly' applies to the *conscious* part of the mind, and the 'actually' to the *unconscious* part. In exactly the same way, the ceremonial taboo of kings is *ostensibly* the highest honour and protection for them, while *actually* it is a punishment for their exhaltation, a revenge taken on them by their subjects. The experiences of Sancho Panza (as described by Cervantes) when he was Governor of his island convinced him that this view of court ceremonial was the only one that met the case. If we could hear the views of modern kings and rulers on the subject, we might find that there were many others who agreed with him [pp. 50–51].

While elevating the leader resolves conflict about the hostility directed toward him, it is not immediately clear why a *group* should be created by the

activity. However, the data supplied by Freud (from Frazer) give some indication why it becomes a collective phenomenon. Where the hostility is
apparent, the leader is reluctant to be elevated and idolized; and even
where the aggression is muted, the wary candidate for greatness may still
be quite unwilling to assume such high honors. In fact, his opposition may
extend to dangerous extremes:

> Thus in Cambodia, where there are kingships of Fire and Water, it is
> often necessary to force successors into accepting these distinctions.
> On Niué or Savage Island, a coral island in the South Pacific, the
> monarchy actually came to an end because no one could be induced
> to take over the responsible and dangerous office. 'In some parts of
> West Africa, when the king dies, a family council is secretly held to
> determine his successor. He on whom the choice falls is suddenly
> seized, bound, and thrown into the fetish-house, where he is kept in
> durance till he consents to accept the crown. Sometimes the heir
> finds means of evading the honor which it is thought to thrust upon
> him; a ferocious chief has been known to go about constantly
> armed, resolute to resist by force any attempt to set him on the
> throne' [p. 47].

A collective multitude of individuals is necessary to ensure that their respective conflict-resolving idealizations will be effected. Their very num-
bers, cohesion, uniformity of purpose and action, and equality of subordinate status are the guarantors of their common idealizing conflict
resolution. Seen another way, *as individuals acting alone,* each may experience the anxiety evoked by the resistance and retaliation of the man chosen for leadership. Thus, the resolution of conflict through idealization
evokes another conflict about the person of the leader. The unified power
of the members—that is, their group formation around the unwilling
charismatic leader—resolves this second conflict. Through mutual partial
identification the members establish their shared idealization of the
leader. The content of that mutual partial identification utilizes the same
repression and reaction formation which is expressed in their disparate
idealizations. But it also establishes the strength of their purpose, which
makes their common enterprise of choosing a charismatic leader safe.

The tribal peoples of Sierra Leone showed a dynamic of charismatically
led group formation which is not confined to the jungles of West Africa. It
may, in fact, be found in the most civilized places. Modern business cor-
porations often collectively rid themselves of their chief officer by promoting him, with pomp and circumstance, to an honorific office created
especially for the purpose. This is genially called "kicking him upstairs."

Religious congregations and institutions of higher learning get rid of their elderly supreme leaders (pastoral or professorial) by solemnly promoting them to *emeritus* status. Nor is this group-formative dynamic restricted to what are conventionally called "groups." As will now be demonstrated, it may occur within a marital drama and may even be investigated by psychoanalysis.

In 1930, Deutsch described the psychoanalysis of a Viennese housewife in which the patient's pre-neurotic behavior bore a remarkable resemblance to the grimly idealizing ceremonials of the Timmes of Sierra Loene. Because the main intention of the analyst was to treat a neurosis, that transient, pre-neurotic stage was not fully investigated — or, at any rate, not fully reported — as a group phenomenon at all. Nevertheless, the state of mind in question approximated, and perhaps was identical with, that of membership in a charismatically led group-of-two. Accordingly, it will be discussed here from that point of view.

The attempt to form a group took place as a possible alternative to the neurosis which eventuated. When the patient's orientation of group membership could not be maintained, the neurosis ensued.

A patient began her analysis with the statement that there was nothing wrong with her and that she only came to me because her husband, whom she considered "nervous," had insisted on it. I had, however, already learned from her husband that an actual conflict had evoked neurotic difficulties in the patient, and this was substantiated in the analysis. After fifteen years of marriage, the husband had fallen passionately in love with a niece who had just married into the family. In an evident desire to get rid of his guilt, and with regard to the platonic nature of his love, he had initiated his wife into the secret [p. 8].

Deutsch emphasized that this situation put the betrayed wife in a situation of intrapsychic conflict regarding not only her unfaithful husband but also the niece, her rival in love:

The normal mode of reaction would have been: either to renounce the [male] object and find a new one after a period of mourning, or else to enter into a struggle with her rival. But the first of these solutions the patient could not adopt, because, as the analysis showed, certain infantile attitudes, which she had continued to preserve, had the effect of binding the patient more strongly to the loved object in proportion as it withdrew from her. And the second possibility remained closed to her, because her aggressive vindictive tendencies were so intense that they had to be rejected and repressed [p. 9].

It was to resolve this pre-neurotic state of conflict that the betrayed wife tried to form a charismatically led group-of-two consisting of herself and her husband. The hated rival, the niece, was put in the position of the charismatic, idealized leader:

> [T]he patient . . . entered into the role of her husband's "best friend," . . . suppressed every reaction in any way hostile, and tried by every means in her power to establish a friendly relationship with her new relative. The young woman seemed to her to be the most wonderful creature in the world, entirely occupied her yearning fantasies, and it was only when the lack of response on her part frustrated our patient's attempts at friendship that she encountered neurotic difficulties [p. 8].

In other words, the chosen leader, like the cautious candidates for leadership in tribal West Africa, refused to accept such an honor (though probably for quite different reasons). And, *un*like the case of the Timmes, the designated leader could not be forced to cooperate. So the betrayed wife's attempt at group formation broke down.

Now this interesting behavior on the part of the betrayed wife was a derivative of her infantile Oedipus complex and of the particular resolution of the oedipal conflicts she had used at that time:

> [T]he analysis revealed that she had been in similar conflicts several times before in her life, which she had always solved in the same way, by means of a compromise. . . . This compromise was: to renounce the heterosexual love object, but to force heself between the man and the woman and destroy the bond by taking homosexual possession of the woman. Thus had she tried to separate her parents in childhood, an action which masked itself in an excessive love for the mother. And this childhood situation was the source of . . . masculine tendencies which she had later sacrificed to her husband [p. 10].

As can be seen, the betrayed wife's idealization of the niece was a compromise formation, a conflict resolution. Deutsch made clear the nature of her conflict over the niece: "[H]er aggressive vindictive tendencies were so intense that they had to be rejected and repressed." Using the defenses of reaction formation and repression, she turned her rivalrous hostility toward this mother-figure into worship of "the most wonderful creature in the world." Structurally stated: She externalized the ideal function of the superego onto her rival. This unsublimated homosexual attachment expressed also the underlying hatred toward her oedipal rival. For by elevating the niece to the position of "the most wonderful creature in the world," that creature was excluded from the comradely solidarity which the betrayed wife and her husband might have formed. The West African Timmes killed their leader; the Viennese housewife isolated hers. As in her oedipal phase, the betrayed wife resolved her conflict over her rival by "taking homosexual possession of the woman" (or trying to). In the current situation, the idealization was also a masochistic acquiescence to her rival's triumph over her in the realm of love.

It is of interest to note the subsequent neurotic development of her hatred toward her oedipal rival in the guise of the niece. Since the betrayed wife could not use the idealization of the niece as a way of resolving her conflict over her aggression, she expressed that aggression later in a neurotic fashion by persecuting her servant girls but being unable to fire them. Still later, in the transference neurosis, she again tried the same idealizing defensive ploy of winning her rival's love—this time in the person of the female analyst (Deutsch, 1930, p. 9).

But if, as we have seen, the betrayed wife (temporarily) resolved her conflict about her rival through idealization, why was it necessary for her to enter into the role of her husband's "best friend?" And what exactly did this role mean? Remember that the betrayed wife was also in conflict regarding her relationship to her husband. That conflict concerned the person of the niece. The husband, loving the niece passionately, withdrew his love from the betrayed wife. The latter reacted most directly to her husband's love for the niece with an intense hatred toward him. This alienating feeling, however, was not the only attitude she had toward her unfaithful husband. Deutsch pointed out that although the betrayed wife was alienated from her husband, she could not renounce him and deal with her positive feelings by mourning his loss. This was because "certain infantile attitudes, which she had continued to preserve, had the effect of binding the patient more strongly to the loved object in proportion as it withdrew from her."

This conflictual orientation, like that toward her rival, may be elucidated by its origin in the infantile Oedipus complex. Part of her resolution of the oedipal conflicts was to "renounce the heterosexual love object" (her father). Now there seems to be a contradiction between this infantile attitude toward her father (renunciation) and its adult derivative (binding herself more strongly, the role of "best friend"). Actually, the paradox is explained by the assumption that the betrayed wife transformed her heterosexual love for her father and husband *by identifying herself with them.* In that way, she both renounced them as love objects and also bound herself more strongly to them. This then is the meaning of taking on the role of her husband's "best friend." This also is the origin of the masculine tendencies which played an important part in her neurosis. Regarding her father and her husband, she partially identified with their masculiine attitudes and established a cohesive relationship based on masculine uniformity. In the adult instance (regarding the husband) — and probably in the infantile one also (regarding her father) — this partial identification defended her against the conflictual anger and hatred she felt toward the heterosexual object. The partial identification that made her her husband's "best friend" utilized the defenses of repression and reaction formation, which kept her hostility toward her husband unconscious and not expressed.

Further, establishing the nonfeminine role of her husband's "best friend" is an expression of the submissive, masochistic relationship to the charismatic niece who triumphed over her in the realm of love. For, in joining her husband equally (through partial identification with him) in his masculine infatuation with her rival, she in effect, was saying to him: "Yes, I agree with you. She *is* the most wonderful creature in the world! You *should* love her more than you do me! You see, *I* love her the same way." And this masculinizing partial identification with the husband (and probably with the father) provided the idealization of the niece with an additional instinctual (homosexual) force. In other words, the partial identification with the husband supported and reinforced the betrayed wife's conflict-resolving idealization of the niece, her rival.

The analysis made here of the betrayed wife's pre-neurotic behavior, which follows Deutsch's very closely, allows one to see parallels between this marital drama and the previous examples of charismatically led group formation, provided that the "group formation" is viewed from the subjective point of view of the betrayed wife. The betrayed wife constituted a unit of such a group insofar as she subjectively experienced her husband to have attitudes similar to her own and this corresponded to a sense of cohesion with him. As in the other instances of group formation, there were two conflicts here. One was resolved by idealization of an exceptional person, the "leader." That idealization externalized the ideal function of the group member's superego onto the leader and established a submissive, masochistic relationship to her. The second conflict (hatred of a father-figure and fear of his loss) revolved around the person of the leader. It was resolved by the partial identification of one "group member" with another (subjectively perceived as mutual). The content of that partial identification *manifestly* showed submission to the leader. *Latently,* the identification effected repression and reaction formation of conflictual hatred. It constituted a group-formative conflict resolution. It also established equality and uniformity among the "members" in their respective relations to the leader. And finally, as in the previous examples, the group-formative conflict resolution served to preserve and maintain the conflict-resolving idealization of the leader.

This analysis validates Freud's (1921, pp. 119–221) thesis that the solidarity of (charismatically led) group members is based on reaction formation. However, it invalidates Freud's view that the reaction formation is always against the rivalrous feelings among the group members. Indeed, rivalry was central here, but it concerned the *leader*. And there *was* latent hostility toward the fellow member, but it was not concerned with rivalry for the exclusive love of the revered leader, as Freud suggested; rather, it was a consequence of betrayed love.

This example shows that the leader of a charismatically led group may not necessarily try to influence the members of the group. And, indeed, the leader may be oblivious to the group's very existence — let alone know whether he or she *is* a leader of others. More important, this example shows the possibility that membership in a group may be a figment of a person's imagination. Nevertheless, for all of that, such a fantasy — taken for reality — may resolve conflict.

The Grade-School Class

This example is a composite picture of a typical sort of preadolescent grade-school class. Redl (1942, pp. 576–577) described it, as he did the youth group above, from separate sorts of observation (social and psychological).

> This group is composed of approximately ten-year-old children, most of whom are just at the point in their development where they most fully represent the end states of "childhood" immediately before the outbreak of pre-adolescent symptoms [pp. 576–577].

Redl was here describing a classroom situation made up of late latency children (just becoming preadolescent) and a teacher. The children form the group. While Redl's description of the children is in terms of average-expectable psychopathology, for the present purposes it would be useful to emphasize the average-expectable intrapsychic conflict situation typical of late latency, preadolescent children. At that stage of development, the child has all the mental structures that adults have, but those structures are not as well consolidated. Instinct control and superego regulation are rigid and brittle. Superego functioning may, at times, be ineffectual as a motivating force against impulsive discharge. When superego functioning is effective, it is harsh and categorical, simple and concrete. Accordingly, preadolescent children have inherently unreliable drive regulation. They are in constant danger of impulsive outbursts and guilt. This becomes even more acute in schoolroom situations, like the one under discussion here, where children must control themselves for long periods of time.

Blos (1962) has described the transition point between late latency and preadolescence in boys in these terms.

> Only with reference to the boy is it correct to say that the quantitative increase of the instinctual drive during pre-adolescence leads to an indiscriminate cathexis of pregenitality. In fact, the resurgence of pregenitality marks the termination of latency for the male. At this time boys show an increase in diffuse motility (restlessness, fidgetiness), and in oral greediness, sadistic activities, anal activities (expressed in coprophilic pleasures, "dirty" language, a disregard for cleanliness, a fascination with odors, the skillful production of onomatopoetic noises), and phallic, exhibitionistic games [p. 61].

Blos's description of boys at this developmental phase is pertinent here because just these tendencies would be conflictual in a classroom situation. While preadolescent girls typically have a different emotional-instinctual orientation, theirs is nevertheless characterized by its active, assertive thrust—a posture which would also be conflictual in a classroom situation. Blos stated his general agreement

> with the subdivisions elaborated by Helene Deutsch with reference to the girl. She refers to the opening of adolescence as pre-puberty (ages ten to twelve) which is the "prerevolutionary" era when the girl experiences the "greatest freedom from infantile sexuality." At this stage the girl shows a decisive "turn toward reality" and an "intensive process of adaptation to reality" which is characterized by a "thrust of activity." "Playacting" and "tomboyishness" testify to her "renunciation of infantile phantasy"; her "interest shifts from anatomical differences to physiological processes."

> This formulation fits well into the model which I have described; however, I suspect that the girls' "thrust of activity" which precedes the increase of passivity constitutes an attempt to master actively what she has experienced passively while in the care of the nurturing mother; instead of taking the preoedipal mother as love object, the girl identifies temporarily with her active phallic image. *The girl's transient phallic illusion gives this period an exalted vital tenor* which does not lack a danger of fixation [p. 70; my italics].

Thus, preadolescent children, whether boys or girls, experience an instinctual spurt of potentially unruly impulses. Their rigid and harsh morality makes this developmental change conflictual. The classroom situation only actualizes the conflict.

Equally important to understanding this instance of group formation is the leader — the teacher of this class of late latency, preadolescent children. Redl described him as being the perfect externalized embodiment of the conscience function of the superegos of these children. He and his moral attitudes are correspondingly strict, categorical, and simple:

In charge of them is a teacher who fits the following description: "He is an elderly gentleman of stern but not unfriendly exterior, decided, but fundamentally mild in his manner. He stands for 'order and discipline' but they are values so deeply ingrained in him that he hardly thinks of them explicitly, nor does it occur to anyone to doubt them in his prescence. He believes in good and thorough work, knows very clearly what he expects and leaves no doubt about it in the minds of his students" [p. 577].

As can be seen, then, the submission of these children to this teacher — an incarnation of strict morality — constitutes for them a strategy of conflict resolution. Their own inherently shaky moral regulation is taken over by this impressively moral teacher. That is, their conscience is externalized onto him. This occurs in precisely the circumstances where they need such external moral props the most — in his class:

The atmosphere of the classroom may be easily described. The children accept his values without question. . . . As long as they behave according to his code they feel happily secure — sheltered. Thoughts and imaginations which do not comply with his code are suppressed in his presence [p. 577].

From the point of view of these children, this teacher, full of consistent moral integrity, is truly extraordinary. The strength and constancy of his moral rectitude supply them, through submission to him, with the moral strength and constancy each of them needs to control his own late latency, preadolescent impulsions. Because this teacher is so central to their efforts to avoid guilt, they prize him very much. As Redl showed, the children idolize him; they idealize him. Of special interest here, *they also fear him*. It is fair to say that he intimidates them — not through his coercive power over them as a teacher, but through the moral authority he has over them by virtue of his taking over the conscience function of the superego in each of them:

> Their emotions about him are a mixture of love and adoration, with an element of anxiety in all those instances in which they are not quite sure of his approval. . . . When questioned or doubted by this teacher, tears come more easily than words; behind the happy security felt in his presence there is a nagging fear of its loss which streams into awareness every once in a while without apparent cause [p. 577].

It should be stressed that the intimidation which this teacher-leader exerts over his students-followers is not based upon his own initiative. To be sure, he is "elderly," "stern," "decided," "knows very clearly what he expects." But he is also of "not unfriendly exterior," "fundamentally mild in his manner." The intimidation is based upon the subjective perceptions of the children themselves. He has taken over the critical function of the superego and the children fear his criticism. The children's fear would correspond to guilt when superego functioning is fully autonomous. And even when the conscience function of the superego is not fully autonomous, as in this case, the teacher and his moral attitudes have intrapsychic effects which correspond to those of a fully internalized conscience: repression of morally condemnable thoughts:

> They all love their teacher and trust him infinitely, but certain thoughts must never enter their minds in his presence [p. 577].

Further, there is even a hint that he also takes over the function of judgment or reality testing. For Redl stated: "The jokes he makes, or acknowledges, are funny" (p. 577).

As with the youth group above, Redl did not indicate directly why the children should form a *group* around this teacher-leader; that is, why they should set up cohesive mutual relations among themselves. But, as with the youth group, Redl did describe how the mutual harmony among the children becomes disrupted, and in the conditions of group disruption, the underlying group-formative dynamic may be exposed and revealed:

> If one youngster is not quite so ready as the others to concentrate his filial adoration upon this type of a teacher, makes unfitting remarks, unruly gestures, or shows a lack of submission, the others will experience a deep feeling of moral indignation — even though they may

have enjoyed this youngster's jokes a few minutes previously during the recreation period [p. 577].

What Redl described was not only the investment which each child has in his own submission to the leader, but also the investment which each child has in *the others'* submission to the leader. There is a pressure for conformity to the teacher's code of "order and discipline" and "good and thorough work." That conformity is policed by the aggression — "moral indignation" — aroused in the children against any deviant from their uniform and equal submission to the leader and adherence to his code.

But Redl's description tells more. It indicates what deviation is all about. First and foremost, it is rebellion against the teacher himself who, Redl implied, is in a parental relation: "If one youngster is not quite so ready as the others to concentrate his *filial* adoration upon this type of teacher . . . or shows a lack of submission. . . ." But a youngster may also make "unfitting remarks, unruly gestures . . . jokes. . . ." In other words, insubordination to the teacher also means that the children are giving in to the age-specific impulses with which they are struggling, in general. The children are expressing the same conflict *in relation to the person of the teacher* that they resolved by subordinating themselves to him. This applies to all the children of the class. Each one of them is a potential deviant.

The very expression of those impulsions by any *one* student in direct defiance of the teacher and his moral code will be dangerous for *all the other* students. For even though the teacher is "stern" and "decided," he is also "not unfriendly" and "fundamentally mild." In other words, there is danger that the teacher, when crossed by an unruly pupil, will *not* evoke punitive sanctions against the offender. This would correspond to a hypothetical intrapsychic condition in which the conscience determines what is moral and immoral but does not induce the feeling of guilt. The intimidating power of this stern teacher rests in the authority which his students ascribe to him. But they also make sure that this authority will never be challenged, except under threat of *their* own punitive aggression (moral indignation). If their leader's moral authority were to be *freely* challenged, he could no longer embody their conscience. He could no longer serve his conflict-resolving function for them. Accordingly, each and every one of them polices each and every other one of them in an effort to enforce conformity.

Each child becomes emotionally interested in assuring that the teacher's code be adhered to by all the others, in addition to himself. An implicit pact of equality and uniformity is set up whereby each helps all the others to conform (and thus be safe from their dangerous impulses), while all the others help each to do the same. Thus, the children have submitted to the teacher so that they may feel safe from their instincts; they have also submitted to their mutual conformistic pressure (establishing uniformity, equality, and cohesion) for the same reason. The mutual adherence to the conformistic pressure utilizes in each child repression and reaction formation against the conflictual impulsions of preadolescence. That mutual adherence—the children's mutual partial identification—also forms a group out of the several disparate children.

This example shows how charismatically led group formation is typically used in the pedagogy of young children. The condition described makes for a less anxious, less impulse-ridden learning atmosphere. But it does much more. The charismatic authority invested in the teacher (in *this* instance, on a moral basis) leads to intense suggestibility in these latency children. That is, the teacher secondarily takes over their reality-testing function. For the teacher induces them to believe as true what their senses deny: the spherical shape of the earth, the heliocentric planetary system, the atomic structure of matter, the nature of gases, the theory of evolution, etc. What has taken man many centuries and much emotional pain to discover and to believe, these children accept at one stroke on the word of their charismatic teacher *simply because he wants them to believe it.* This influence very frequently extends to the realm of values, i.e., to the ideal function. Through the educational process, the children may thus easily come to see the superiority of the prevailing culture, political system, and/or religion. And they may just as easily see the flaws and faults in others. Both in the fundamental matter of respect for the teacher, and in these derivative matters of socialization and education, *any* nonconformism is typically met by latency children with hostility and scorn. The conflict-resolving nature of the teacher's authority makes it too important to be brooked.

The Forced Group and the Marching Chemist

The previous example of charismatically led group formation analyzed groups composed of late latency, preadolescent children—about ten years of age. The present group is also of this sort. While for the grade-school class, as a type, the element of intimidation (on a moral basis) was only slightly involved in the group-formative process, in the present example intimidation by coercive force is of central importance in the formation of the group. Again, the material comes from the sensitive and perceptive descriptions of Redl (1942).

This is a class of children approximately ten years old, near the verge of preadolescence. In charge of them is an elderly, or middle-aged teacher, among whose motives for teaching were one or both of the following: He is compulsively bound to repeat a certain pattern of "discipline" against the children because this is the only way he can prove late obedience to some of the demands of his own parents; or, his most intensive drive satisfactions lie in the direction of sadism, and he has to use the children as objects for that purpose. This teacher will not "stand for" anything, but has to "impose" some kind of capricious "order" or "discipline" all the time. Nor will he be satisfied to do so quietly. He will require a noisy machinery of special tricks, rules, and revenge techniques. His concept of discipline, too, will be of the most compulsive, unrealistic sort; the way he works it out is as "unchild-minded" as possible. In short, there is a "regular tyrant" in charge of this class [pp. 577–578].

Redl thus emphasized that this teacher performs no obvious emotional function for the grade-school children. He does not "stand for" any abstract principle, morality, or ideal that they may discern. He presents his personal will as the unpredictable measure of all things. And because his concept of discipline is "compulsive," "unrealistic," and "unchild-minded," it is impossible for the children to actually measure up to his demands. Consequently, all that *is* predictable is his criticism and displeasure. Further, he imposes his will in a ruthless, compulsive, and/or sadistic manner, systematically terrorizing his ten-year-old students, and all this in the context of a schoolroom situation, where the students are expected to behave and perform in ways that are supposedly standardized and gradable.

What is important about Redl's observation is that, contrary to common sense expectations, a group forms under the subordinating leadership of this "tyrant."

Everyday psychology might tempt one to expect children to hate the teacher and fight him as much as they dared. Indeed, this does happen in a few examples. . . . The entirely different reaction from the youngsters is surprising. These children submit easily. They rebel against the silly pedantry of this tyrant less vehemently than other groups do against the reasonable demands of their beloved teacher [p. 578].

Unfortunately, Redl did not adequately explain why the youngsters submit so easily. Redl did state that the children "identified" with the teacher. But it must be realized that Redl used the term identification in a much wider sense than that used here and generally. In any case, it clearly did *not* happen that the children became like their teacher in any obvious way.

Further, it is important to emphasize that the manifest submission of the children to this cruel teacher was not merely a prudent, pragmatic acquiescence to *force majeure*. Redl was quite firm in asserting that the children were expressing sincere inner attitudes in their collective submission. As in the other examples from Redl reviewed here, penetrating insights into the group phenomena are obtained when the group's uniformity is disrupted:

> Nor do they submit only temporarily. . . . this is illustrated by the youngster who does dare to rebel in such a class. He has a difficult time. He has everyone against him, the teacher, the other youngsters, and himself. The others show intensive signs of moral indignation, eventually becoming afraid of the child [p. 578].

The presence of a rebel in the class allows the observation, which might otherwise have been impossible, that the children are in some important way sympathetic to the teacher, agree with his tyranny, and will attack anyone who violates it. Indeed, Redl suggested that the rebel himself participates in this attitude, albeit incompletely. One knows the attitude has a moral quality because "the others show intensive signs of *moral* indignation" at the rebel. And its defensive nature is indicated by the fact that the others collectively become afraid of the deviant.

Redl's further observations on the "forced group" indicate against what the defense is mobilized. It is against the hostility the children unconsciously bear. But it is not clear toward whom the hostility is directed — toward the teacher or toward one another:

> The emotional relations these youngsters develop among themselves seem less intensive than in the other illustrations. Children of such classes develop little "comradeship". . . . and they seem to be afraid of each other, and distrustful. They seem to fear that too much intimacy might endanger the successful repression of their hostility and might force them to realize what cowards they are [p. 578].

As a tentative explanation of the formation of the forced group, the following is suggested: In his own menacing and sinister way the tyrannical teacher is, an "exceptional person" to these children. He is certainly different from them in a very crucial way. But he infuriates them too, primarily because of his manifest unfairness — his demands for "order" and "discipline" which, in their capriciousness, allow no order or discipline. Their very hostility which he so provocatively generates in them toward himself, is itself, conflictual. For any manifestation of it in any pupil would bring down upon his head a greater than usual amount of the tyrant's aggression through his "revenge techniques." In other words, the classroom situation is designed to provoke, around the person of the teacher, conflict between rebellious anger and anxiety over intense counteraggression. One way to resolve this conflict is to take on the values of the teacher, especially the only one he expresses with any consistency: collective submission to his personal authority. This resolution entails ceding to the teacher critical judgment and values in the realm of ideals and morals – that is, adopting for oneself the teacher's will as the measure of all things. The students externalize superego function, conscience and ideals, onto him. The externalized functions may also include reality testing. Further, each pupil considers that the teacher's injunctions are valid not only regarding his own behavior, *but also regarding the behavior of all the other pupils.* The teacher's uniform and equal intimidation of the pupils *as a collective* has two effects: It forces them to identify with one another in their common submission to the teacher, and it makes them view their uniformity and collectivity as a positive value.

This is what produces the group. It also explains the pupils' righteous indignation at – and eventual fear of – a rebel who transgresses their value of collective uniformity: His submissive cooperation is necessary in order for each and every other pupil to attain the collectivizing ideal. Each must continually affirm the collective uniformity because it keeps at bay the frightening hostility which each pupil bears toward the teacher. This also explains Redl's observations that little "comradeship" is developed in these circumstances: The pupils come to regard each other as mere instruments by which each can defend himself against realistic anxiety about the teacher's (counter) aggression. Their value to each other is not based upon love or sympathy, but rather upon defensive need. It may thus be seen that their common, group-formative submission to the arbitrary will of their teacher-leader utilizes the defenses of repression and reaction formation, which keep in check their conflictual rebellious hostility toward him.

The foregoing explanation of the group-formative dynamic in the forced group is different, in certain respects, from those of the other examples. In the other examples, there was a clear distinction between (1) the conflict-resolving motivation that led to idealization (externalization of superego functioning onto an extraordinary person), and (2) the conflict-resolving motivation to form a group around the leadership of that person. Instances did occur in which the conflict that was resolved through group formation was a more specific version of the conflict that was resolved by idealization of the leader. That is, the group-formative conflict was the same kind of conflict as that which formed idealization, only the former pivoted around the person of the leader and the latter was more general in its scope. In the instance of the forced group, the two conflict-resolving motives collapse into one. There is no general version; the conflict is specifically about the leader. The conflict resolved by the externalization of superego functioning onto the leader pivots directly around his person and establishes uniform and equal relations with him among the followers, and mutual relations among themselves. The conflict resolved by group formation has as its essential group-specific uniformity the submissive superego-externalizing relation to the leader.

This explanation of the forced group may be validated with clinical data from another source. Whereas Redl concentrated on the group phenomena of this sort of group formation, the following clinical vignette will give the complementary view from within the mind of a member of a comparable forced group.

During a prolonged, inconclusive, and extremely unpopular war, a former graduate student in chemistry was drafted into the Army. During his basic training, he was ordered to drill, along with other inductees. The drill officer was clearly from a lower social background than the recruit and much less educated. The officer was both watchful and insistent that the new soldiers march in straight ranks and files, in step to his cadence. The chemist obeyed. He heard his immediate neighbors around him muttering about "Army stupidity" and "playing soldier." He shared these sentiments. He, and they, felt humiliated, infantile, and impotent. He observed his own contempt for the pointless activity and his loathing for the surrender of will to a stranger for whom he had no respect. He then realized that, in fact, he *did* have respect for the drill officer who scrutinized their marching so critically. It seemed to him that behind the drill officer was the might of the Army and, behind that, of the state itself. Disobedience toward the drill officer could entail punitive retaliation of formidable proportions. That was why he obeyed the orders so resignedly. Suddenly the obese man in front of him lurched to one side, almost losing his balance. The resigned chemist observed the misstep and, to his amazement, a sharp and intense anger flashed in him against the hapless man. *"He's not doing this right! He's ruining it!"* The angry reaction was especially surprising to him because never before in his life had he valued such marching; and further, he had always known himself to be sympathetic and helpful to others in difficulty.

One may see here, from the point of view of an individual, some of the same phenomena noted in the forced group described by Redl. There is one person (the leader) who intimidates a collection of others (members) *as a collection.* The tendency of the intimidated members is to submit to the arbitrary directives of the leader, but the intimidation provokes anger toward the leader. The expression of anger against the leader would be construed as a rebellion against his directives and would evoke the counteraggression of the leader. There is therefore an *ad hoc* change of values (the ideal and/or conscience function of the superego) in the member(s). The new values affirm and validate the forced collective condition of the members. There is no conscious anger toward the leader (repression). The uniform collective behavior of the members is diametrically opposite to the expression of anger toward the leader (reaction formation).

Several years later, the incident came up in analysis and could thus be studied in retrospect. Analysis showed that the drill situation had aroused in the chemist a strong unconscious defiant and rebellious attitude. It was associated with a series of childhood events in which he had been forced bodily into constrained and painful situations — all relating to a fractured leg and its complicated course of repair and healing. There had been multiple operations and hospitalizations. He had experienced the events as humiliating, for he had taken great pride in his physical agility and talent in sports, which he saw as masculine. The childhood surgical experiences had become a paradigm for danger situations evoked by multiple sexual and aggressive wishes. Accordingly, in situations of academic rivalry or intimate closeness he would never allow himself to be "boxed in," "pinned down," to "take it lying down," "be vulnerable." In the analysis, when rivalrous impulses or passive wishes toward the analyst arose, every chance circumstance was used as pretext to stay away from the consulting room. This would occur periodically and his unconscious fears had to be interpreted repeatedly. The analytic work would ultimately show that his experience of the childhood fracture and, more pointedly, his operations and hospitalizations were seen in light of yet earlier intrauterine fantasies mobilized around a miscarriage of his mother's, about which he felt murderous responsibility. The operations and confinements were the talion punishment he unconsciously knew he deserved and from which he spent much of his life trying to escape.

Of importance here, the drill situation evoked in the chemist the humiliating experience of being pinned down, injured, and confined. Had all of this been conscious, he would have felt the anguish and outrage corresponding to the childhood events and their fantastical elaboration. But instead of this, something else occurred. He preconsciously saw things from the drill officer's point of view, took on the values the officer was obviously presenting. "It is good to drill, and to drill well." Analogous phenomena had occurred during his various hospitalizations. Like the drill situation, his confinements in the hospital had been situations of no recourse. He could not express the rebellious protest inside him. Just as governmental prosecution was the threat behind the drill officer's commands, so in the hospital the surgeon's knife, paralyzing anesthesia, and more operations were the threats associated with uncooperative behavior. The little patient became a "real trooper." He assiduously took his medicines, conscientiously guarded his leg cast, diligently did his exercises — and generally became a model patient. At night, he would frequently awaken with anxiety from dreams he could not remember.

The process described may be seen as ceding some of what had previously been the superego's regulatory functioning to the intimidating "exceptional person" as a form of conflict resolution. In both forced groups, the intimidating person provoked anger and also ensured that the anger would be conflictual. The submission to his regulation — taking on his values — kept in check the problematic anger and assuaged the anxiety about an external danger. This formulation thus makes a distinction between (1) compliance to irresistible external force where there is no conflict and no allegiance to the intimidator, and (2) submission to external intimidation where conflict is provoked and then resolved through allegiance. In both forced groups, the intimidator's values, which were assumed by the members, pertained to the collectivity itself. Allegiance to the intimidator implied, therefore, that a positive value was put upon *the collective submission of all to the leader*. Thus, the mutual partial identification of the members in their shared submission to the leader also entailed that each and every member value the submission of all the other members. In this very important respect, the process of adopting the intimidator as leader (externalizing superego functioning onto him) is expressed by the process of group formation (the mutual partial identification of the members). As noted above, in all the other groups analyzed in this paper, these two processes could be differentiated more clearly in terms of the conflict-resolving motives involved.

THE RELATION TO THE LEADER: IDEALIZATION

Generalizations

The six instances discussed above permit certain generalizations about the relationship which the member of a charismatically led group has to the leader of that group: (1) The member views the leader as exceptional, extraordinary in comparison with himself. That is, the leader is radically different from the member in some crucially important manner. (The nature of that crucially important manner will be stated shortly.) In psychoanalytic terminology, which stresses only the *positive* feelings involved, the member's view of the leader has been called "overestimation," "overvaluation," or more generally, "idealization." As will be seen below, the fact that members also have negative feelings extends and modifies the concept of "idealization." In sociological terms, the member views the leader as possessing "charisma." (2) The member has externalized onto the leader at least one of his superego functions, possibly together with the ego function of reality testing. The six examples indicate that the two superego functions most likely to be externalized and most fundamental to the process of idealization are the ideal function and conscience. The externalization of the function of reality testing is a secondary phenomenon, dependent upon the externalization of one of the other two. (3) The member views the leader as an authority over himself. (4) The member adopts a submissive, masochistic attitude toward the leader. (5) The relationship with the leader resolves conflict for the member. (6) Any kind of conflict may be resolved in this way.

These generalizations clarify the way in which the leader must be extraordinary or exceptional in comparison with the member and the importance of that comparison for the member. *The leader must be different from the member in a way that resolves conflict for the member.* Hence, because the nature of the conflict may vary from one charismatically led group to the next, the manner in which the leader is exceptional will vary correspondingly. Thus, charisma can only be defined on the basis of the follower's reaction to it. The present study has indicated what that defining reaction must be.

Ambivalence

Reich (1940, 1953) and Greenacre (1966) have studied the phenomenon of idealization from two complementary points of view. Reich studied it in the object relations of extremely submissive women; Greenacre, in the transference. Both authors showed that submissive attitudes are an essential part of idealization and also that there is an intense infantile ambivalent orientation toward the idealized object. Intense conscious admiration and veneration defends against an intense unconscious hatred. Interestingly, Greenacre also demonstrated that idealization of the analyst and of analysis is associated with a strong *affiliative* impetus, causing the analysand to want to become a member of the "world of psychoanalysis." Reich and Greenacre further showed that idealization was a compromise formation, a resolution of conflict. When the conflict-resolving function could not be maintained (i.e., when disillusionment took place), the underlying negative/destructive feelings became manifest.

The present study shows that leaders who are considered by their followers to be exceptional and extraordinary may be feared, in addition to or instead of being admired. This suggests that the concept of idealization may profitably be extended to include views of the object as fearsome and awesome. Under this latter condition, the negative aspects of the leader may be more prominent and conscious to the follower, while the positive aspects may be less prominent and conscious. This is, in fact, the case in paranoia where the persecuting object is always exceptional and extraordinary and where the positive passive, masochistic (libidinal) attitudes are kept unconscious (Bak, 1946; Freud, 1911).

Seen from the vantage point of this study, the concept of idealization may then refer to an inherently ambivalent, submissive conflict-resolving attitude toward an object who is viewed as exceptional and extraordinary compared to the subject, in which adoration and fear of the object may be conscious in any degree of admixture and in which the complementary admixture is repressed. This definition of idealization has heuristic value in ordering and categorizing clinical phenomena.

To summarize so far, the preceding discussion describes the member's relationship to the charismatic leader from various metapsychological points of view. From the *structural* point of view, the leader takes over to some degree the functioning of the member's superego and possibly also the ego function of reality testing. From the *dynamic* point of view, the relationship to the leader constitutes a resolution of intrapsychic conflict within the member. From the *adaptive* point of view, the member cedes authority (regulatory power) to the leader. From the *economic* point of view, the member cathects the leader with inherently ambivalent masochistic instinctual trends, as indicated by a motivation (a wish) to submit to him. The *genetic* point of view remains to be discussed.

The Oedipus Complex

The externalization of superego functioning may, on theoretical grounds, be inferred to comprise a regressive process re-evoking the infantile Oedipus complex in post-oedipal mental life, but, in fact, such externalization may not *necessarily* entail a regression in sexual orientation. For instance, the externalization of superego functioning onto others takes place in leaderless groups *without* an accompanying phallic-oedipal investment of those others (Balter, 1978). This latter phenomenon is an example of what Wixen (1970) termed "object-specific superego responses" —where superego regression takes place in terms of object relations but not in terms of sexual zone or sexual organization. However, there *is* some evidence that the attribution of charisma entails a superego regression not only in object relations but in sexual zone as well.

The examples provide some hints of this. The betrayed wife's attitudes toward her idealized rival were clinically shown to derive directly from a mode of resolving rivalry conflicts that was characteristic of her oedipal phase. In the grade-school class, Redl described the adoring attitudes of the pupils toward their stern teacher as "filial." Other sorts of evidence leading to a conclusion of regression to the Oedipus complex are commonly known. There is the manifestly *erotic* aura which the charismatic leader very often possesses for his followers, even though the charisma may not be based on sexual attractiveness, as such. To followers of the opposite sex, this phenomenon usually takes the form of wishful sexual fantasies. To those of the same sex, there are fantasies of the leader's prodigious sexual feats.

These data, as well as theoretical considerations concerning the loss of superego autonomy, suggest the following inference: From the *genetic* point of view, becoming a follower of a charismatic leader entails *a circumscribed regression in superego functioning, such that the leader takes on the emotional-instinctual position of the oedipal parent.*

Masochism

The regressed oedipal emotional-instinctual position of the leader may be more precisely specified. To do this, reference must be made to Brenner's (1982) very recent reformulations of superego formation and functioning. According to Brenner, the superego forms as a particular cluster of compromise formations which resolve conflicts principally of the phallic-oedipal period. These compromise formations, therefore, of necessity embody the motive to avoid punishment by the parent(s) (various defenses) and the wish for sexual union with the parent(s). Of importance to the present discussion, Brenner demonstrated that the instinctual trends inherent in these compromise formations are not only aggressive, as Freud (1923) argued, but also libidinal (or more accurately, libidinal and aggressive *mixed*). In particular, Brenner showed that *masochistic* trends directed toward the parental objects are always present to some degree. Accordingly, these masochistic trends must be expressed in superego functioning. This phenomenon is present *a potiori* in moral masochism. Now, the present investigation suggests that *the regression of superego func-*

tioning entailed in following a charismatic leader takes place in those parts of the superego that derive from the masochistic instinctual trends of the phallic-oedipal period.

This conclusion is compatible with the fact that superego regression in the follower is only partial. Further, as Brenner (1982) pointed out: "[T]he degree to which a masochistic element participates in superego formation and functioning may be presumed to vary from one person to another, depending both on constitutional endowment and on the vicissitudes of childhood development" (p. 511). The present formulation takes one step in the direction of solving the problem of "choice of group type"— analogous to the thorny psychoanalytic problem of "choice of symptom." For the greater the degree of masochism fostered in childrearing, the greater the degree to which masochistic trends are absorbed into superego functioning—*and therefore,* the greater the susceptibility to becoming a follower of a charismatic leader. This complements the findings of Adorno et al. (1950), who proposed to explain the tendency to follow authoritarian (charismatic) leaders on the basis of certain qualities of the family. The present formulation makes more specific the psychological mechanisms by which those qualities of the familial environment produce those political tendencies.

The present study demonstrates a wide spectrum of conscious attitudes toward the leader—all of them submissive but by no means all adoring. Various admixtures of fear occur along with veneration. In the most extreme case, the forced group shows that pure fear may bring about the same psychological and group-formative relationship to the leader that adoration produces. The existence of a continuum between fear and adoration means that the term "charismatic"—like the term "idealization"— has to be either dropped or extended to include more manifestly ambivalent and frightening attributes of the leader.

The view of the charismatic leader as an ambivalently regarded figure was not explicit in Weber's (1958, pp. 249–250) description of him. Weber used quasi-religious terms. The leader's followers feel toward him "faithful devotion." His power is viewed as "divine." "Genuine charismatic domination . . . emanates concretely from the highly personal experience of heavenly grace and from the god-like strength of the hero." But it was Otto (1917) who put this attitude toward "the holy"—which, like the idealizing transference, has its own affiliative impetus—in proper psychological terms. He formulated his idea of the holy in the phrase: *mysterium tremendum et fascinans.* By this he meant: the "wholly other" which inspires fascination and dread, terror and ecstasy. This is the view that the follower of the charismatic leader has of him and also the view that the oedipal child has of his parents.

The Heterogeneity of Collective Idealization

The study of the group member's relationship to the leader demonstrates that in these examples idealization (1) comes about through the externalization of different superego functions, (2) refers to different exceptional, extraordinary qualities of the leader, and (3) resolves different sorts of conflict in the members. These findings are very important. They lead to a conclusion which could not be derived from any one example by itself. The adoption of a passive-masochistic, submissive (i.e., idealizing) relation to the charismatic leader is not dependent on which superego function of the member is externalized onto him, which quality of the leader is viewed as extraordinary by the member, or which conflict in the member is resolved through his relation to the leader. Therefore, in principle, one could find *in any given charismatically led group* different members, all of whom submissively follow the same leader, who nevertheless externalize different superego functions onto him, consider different qualities of the leader exceptional, or resolve different conflicts through their relation to the leader. Accordingly, since all the examples studied here do not determine the intrapsychic processes of all the individual members by direct psychoanalytic means, the conclusions drawn must be seen only as *first approximations* to understanding the members' collective emotional-instinctual relations to the leader. Each example highlights particular prominent facets of that relationship. Clearly, then, there may be *among* the members a mixture of motives and meanings they effect regarding their leader. And further, *within* any individual member, there may be the same sort of mixture. The fact that the leader may be different things to different people within the same group was a point rightly emphasized by Redl (1942, p. 585). This insight may now be stated as pertaining to the common, uniform, collective subordination to the charismatic leader.

Attenuated Charismatic Leadership in Other Led Group-Types

The idealization of the leader takes place to some degree in other group-types which have leaders. Thus, in this particular respect, charismatically led groups are not *qualitatively* different from other led groups. In a future communication on the general theory of group formation, a broader perspective than the one presented here will be proposed. It will attempt to demonstrate that, generally, in groups with leaders *both* idealization of the leader *and* identification with the leader obtain as group-formative mental processes which define the members' relation to the leader and that these two mental processes are *quantitatively* in reciprocal relation to each other. Hence, to the degree that a leader is idealized, to that degree his followers do not identify with him; to the degree his followers identify with him, to that degree they do not idealize him. Intrapsychically, this reciprocity would reflect the paradoxical tension within the superego between the two parental injunctions:

"You *ought to be* like this (like your father)" and "You *may not be* like this (like your father) — that is, you may not do all that he does; some things are his prerogative" [Freud, 1923, p. 24; italics in original].

This formulation would thus make the charismatically led group a limiting and very special case among all led group-types where *only* idealization of the leader obtains and where *no* identification with him takes place — or is allowed. The charismatically led group exemplifies in pure form a relation to the leader which other led group-types have in attenuated and adulterated form.

GROUP FORMATION: MUTUAL PARTIAL IDENTIFICATION

Generalizations

The examples illustrate that the members of a charismatically led group have common, shared qualities which characterize their membership. This occurs because they partially identify with each other, and corresponds to their being led by the same commonly idealized leader. The group-specific partial identification (i.e., the modification in ego functioning that takes place by virtue of being a member of a specific group) may be in any sphere whatever: emotional, behavioral, conceptual, ideological, attitudinal, etc. The shared quality is to be distinguished from each member's idealization of the leader. Nevertheless, it always expresses the member's idealizing, submissive (passive-masochistic) attitude toward the leader. But also, *through its commonality,* the shared quality expresses the equality and uniformity of the members' respective relationships to the leader.

It is important to emphasize that the most immediate intrapsychic vehicle of group formation is *not* the common idealization of the leader, but rather the mutual partial identification of the members. The members' common idealization of the charismatic leader *defines the kind* of group they form; but their mutual partial identification *effects* their group formation.

The choice of the group-specific common quality may derive either from the leader's or the group members' initiative. As Freud (1921, p. 107) noted, identification may express *any* sort of instinctual or emotional attitude toward the identificatory object. So also in charismatically led groups, the common quality of the members may bespeak different attitudes toward each other in each different context. They may love, fear, or hate one another. A corollary of this statement is that no member necessarily expresses through that common quality the same attitude toward the others as any other member.

The examples illustrate that the formation of the group through the mutual partial identification of the members constitutes a particular mode of intrapsychic conflict resolution for each member. This group-formative conflict within each member occurs around the person of the commonly idealized leader. That is, each group member has conflictual attitudes toward the charismatic leader; and that conflict is resolved through the member's partial identification with all the other members. A corollary of this statement is that the disruption of the group formation has one of two results: (1) the dysphoric affects (*viz.*, anxiety and/or depressive affect) which have been kept latent by the membership become manifest in the members; or (2) those dysphoric affects are kept latent by other, newly appearing conflict-resolving means (e.g., neurosis, as in the case of the betrayed wife).

One may derive another inference. The relative intensity of a group member's involvement with the group, the degree of relative importance the group has for him, the relative strength of a member's membership, will be commensurate with the relative intensity of the conflict resolved. It is then clear that members of the same group do not necessarily have memberships of (quantitatively) uniform intensity, even though their shared group-specific characteristics are (qualitatively) uniform. This may easily be verified empirically.

The Two Conflicts

It is further important to stress that both mental processes — the idealization of the leader and the mutual partial identification of the members — constitute, in principle, separate and distinct conflict resolutions. The examples show that (1) the two conflicts may be quite different in content (e.g., the Timmes of West Africa, the betrayed wife), (2) may be of the same sort (e.g., the youth group, the grade-school class), or (3) may even be identical (e.g., the forced group).

A definite link must exist between the conflict resolved by idealization and that resolved by mutual partial identification. However, that link cannot be defined *a priori*. It arises out of the interpersonal and psychological situations of the group formation. Nevertheless, a generalization may be made about the relation of the two conflicts to each other. The conflict resolved by idealization of the leader has what Waelder (1930, p. 54) called "ontological primacy" over the conflict resolved by mutual partial identification of the members. That is, the group-formative conflict resolved by mutual partial identification would not exist without the conflict resolved by idealization. The following may then be inferred: if the idealization of the leader is disrupted — if disillusionment with or destruction of the leader occurs — the group will necessarily fall apart; but if the mutual partial identification becomes disrupted, the idealization of the leader will not necessarily be affected. This is in fact what happened with regard to the betrayed wife. When she could not effect the idealizing homosexual attachment to her rival — that is, when she could not "take possession" of her — her whole effort at forming a group-of-two with her husband broke down. She then became subject to the neurotic resolutions of conflict about her hostility toward both parental figures.

The Content of the Group-Formative Conflict

The examples also show that there is no specificity to the *kind* of intrapsychic conflict resolved by formation of a charismatically led group through mutual partial identification. The only consistencies are the person about whom the conflict occurs (the charismatic leader) and the mode of conflict resolution (mutual partial identification of the members). Freud (1921) also held that conflict about the person of the leader causes the members to identify partially with each other and, in so doing, to equalize their respective relationships with the leader — and so to become a group. However, Freud saw the intrapsychic conflict about the leader as highly specific. According to him, all the leader's followers want exclusive gratification from him. There is, then, a conflict between each member's rivalrous aggression toward the others and his anxiety over the leader's disapproval of and punishment for that aggression. The very wide range of group-formative conflicts around the person of the charismatic leader, as demonstrated by the examples studied, indicates that Freud's formulation was too narrow in its scope. The members of any given charismatically led group may resolve different conflicts through their memberships, and, moreover, it is possible for several sorts of conflict to coexist in any individual and to be resolved through his membership. What is necessary for group formation is that each member resolve his own idiosyncratic conflict about the commonly idealized leader in the same manner as the other members — i.e., through identification with the other group members. This requirement necessarily imposes limitations on the individual regarding possible membership in any particular charismatically led group. Obviously, some uniformity in the kinds of conflict resolved will facilitate group formation and make it more probable.

The examples also illustrate another consistency regarding the group-formative conflict. The conflict not only revolves around the person of the leader but is concerned with each member's own tendency to disrupt the leader's conflict-resolving function. Stated in other terms, the group forms around the charismatic leader in order to preserve, bolster, and maintain the leader's conflict-resolving function for each member of the group. It would seem that the idealizing mode of conflict resolution (i.e., the regressive mobilization of the ambivalent, masochistic trends of the Oedipus complex in relation to the leader) has a tendency to engender conflict. Actually, this phenomenon is homologous to one observed by Brenner (1982). He noted that the superego not only originates out of conflict but also participates in (i.e., engenders) conflict thereafter. It is also well known clinically that a conflict resolution which engenders further conflict will tend to be unstable. Either the relatively inconclusive conflict resolution will come undone and re-evoke the original conflict, or the second conflict will be resolved also and by other means. This latter situation obtains in charismatically led group formation. The fact that the content of the members' mutual partial identification always manifests submission to the leader may thus be seen as the collectivized support for the inherently unstable idealizing conflict resolution of the individual.

This formulation—that the group-formative conflict resolution supports and maintains the idealizing conflict resolution—recommends itself heuristically. It explains why the idealizing transference (Greenacre, 1966) and the "idea of the holy" (Otto, 1917) should both possess an affiliative thrust, as noted above (pp. 199 and 202). They both entail an idealizing conflict resolution which itself inherently provokes conflict around the idealized object. The wish of the idealizing analysand to become a member of the "world of psychoanalysis" and the wish of the faithful adherent of "the holy" to be a member of a like-minded congregation both bespeak the same thing: the need to maintain collectively the shaky idealization established individually. This same explanation may be applied to the general tendency for a cohesive assemblage of followers to crystallize around a person perceived by them all as extraordinary.

The Two Defense Mechanisms

The examples also show that the group-formative conflict is always resolved through the two defense mechanisms repression and reaction formation. These two defense mechanisms are always utilized in the content of the mutual partial identification of the members. They counter each member's tendency to disrupt the leader's conflict-resolving function and serve as a sort of morality for the group. The fact of the two defenses being used correlates well with another finding obtained by entirely different means, namely that persons strongly disposed to follow authoritarian (charismatic) leaders tend to manifest repression and reaction formation as predominant aspects of their personalities (Adorno et al., 1950). The use of these two defenses indicates that some aspect of the group-formative conflict about the leader will always be unconscious to the member, and that some aspect of his manifest group participation – signifying his submission to the leader – will always be diametrically opposed to a latent and conflictual attitude about the leader.

Pathways to Group Formation

The examples investigated show that the transition from being a non-affiliated individual to being a member of a charismatically led group may take place in more than one way. Most obvious in the examples is the distinction between purely external, deliberate collectivizing intimidation (the forced group) and purely internal, spontaneous, unconscious election (the betrayed wife). The other examples may be seen as falling in between those two to form a "complemental series" (Freud, 1917). In that series, the external collectivizing intimidating factors in the production of conflict and in its resolution complement the internally determined tendency to cohere. It would seem that the greater the role played by intimidation, the more heterogeneous the group members may be. Conversely, the smaller the role played by intimidation, and hence the more spontaneous and internally determined the pathway to group membership, the more homogeneous the individuals must be.

Freud (1921, p. 93) discussed heterogeneity of groups and the factor of their being held together by external intimidation. (He termed groups having this latter attribute "artificial," and spontaneous groups "natural.") He vaguely implied that homogeneous groups were spontaneous, whereas heterogeneous ones needed external force. Freud seemed more concerned, however, with the durability and stability of different types of groups. He explicitly stated: "In groups, the attributes 'stable' and 'artificial' seem to coincide or at least to be intimately connected" (p. 93). The present study, which determines the *psychological* conditions for (charismatically led) group formation, may make a more precise statement about group stability. The group will be stable so long as the members use idealization of the same leader to resolve idiosyncratic conflicts and so long as their individual conflicts around the person of the leader are resolved by their all assuming the same quality (denoting common submission to the leader). This formulation leaves the *specific* role of external force, or its absence, out of consideration.

One may further infer that in any given charismatically led group the various members do not necessarily have to arrive at their respective individual resolutions of group-formative conflict by the same route. Conceivably, each of the members may contain within himself his own idiosyncratic ratio of external and internal determinants: The reasons for idealization of the leader may be different for each member of the same group, and the group-formative conflict may be different in detail from member to member. Nevertheless, the individual group member cannot possibly be oblivious to the other members if there is to be *mutual* relatedness among members. Obviously, the choice of the same charismatic leader and mutual partial identification bespeak the individual's awareness of other people as possible vehicles by which to resolve his highly personal conflicts.

Aggression against Deviance

All the examples (except the Timmes and the betrayed wife) indicate a tendency for aggression to be directed against members who break the group-specific uniformity. In the latter exceptional example, the other "member," the patient's husband, did not deviate from the shared adoration of the niece-leader. The aggression against deviance may come from the leader (as in the forced group) or from the other members (as in the remaining examples, including the marching chemist and the forced group). In any case, aggression against deviance is part of the psychology of charismatically led groups. It seems that if the leader does not initiate such a reaction, the members themselves will do so. This behavior contrasts with that of leaderless groups, in which aggressive reaction to deviance is either absent or relatively muted (Balter, 1978).

The explanation for this reactive aggression should come from the clinical investigation of *individuals*. However, owing to the absence of an adequate psychoanalytic theory of aggression, there is no consensus on this point. Clinically based hypotheses formulated so far explain the aggressive reaction to nonconformity on two different bases: (1) a reaction to the psychic pain resulting from the disruption of a conflict resolution (Brenner, 1975); and (2) a reaction to the disruption of narcissism referring to the sense of self as embodied in the mutual partial identification with the other group members (Kohut, 1972; Rochlin, 1973).

Group Psychology and Group Morphology

The above generalizations indicate the relationship between the *mental* and the *social* levels of conceptualization for charismatically led groups. The group formation around the *oedipal* figure of the charismatic leader, *resolving conflict* about him, maintaining his *authority* through the use of *repression* and *reaction formation,* effecting this through *identification* with each other's group-specific "morality," and enforced by *aggression* — all this suggests that membership in a charismatically led group may be seen as *a circumscribed regressive transformation of the superego* from an internal, idiosyncratic and personal regulatory agency to an external, stereotyped, and social regulatory agency. One may see aspects and elements of superego functioning and structure rearranged and redistributed in an essentially different configuration which replaces autonomous superego functioning with integration into a supra-individual entity, a charismatically led group.

This may be seen from another point of view. The two group-formative mental processes (idealization of the leader and identification with each of the other members) constitute the minimal defining psychological characteristics of a group member, the modular unit of the multi-unit social organization. In conjunction with its psychological replicas, this individual unit coheres with those other units to form a supra-individual entity, a charismatically led group.

Certain general objective properties of this social phenomenon are direct correlates of general psychological processes within the members. The common idealized leader is the group's *sole organizing principle.* The manifest, equalizing common quality of the members (the content of their mutual partial identification) establishes their *mutual relatedness* and their *unity.* In this way, the common quality in each and every member defines the group's *boundaries.* The intensity of conflict about the leader resolved in each member is the quantitative factor determining his individual contribution to the group's *cohesion.* The aggressive reaction to nonconformism is a negative-feedback mechanism enhancing the group's *stability.*

Charismatically led groups are, thus, phenomena with well-defined morphological and psychological characteristics; each set of characteristics is reflective of the other. Certain constraints should then exist between these two sets of characteristics. For instance, the morphology of this sort of group dictates that the leader be exceptional and extraordinary in the group context. That is, the leader must be different from the way in which the group members are similar to each other. The psychology of this sort of group dictates that the leader be admired and/or feared as something which the members, in their uniformity, are not. Accordingly, it is impossible to have a group in which the objective morphology corresponds to the charismatically led variety but in which the subjective attitude of the members toward the leader is not idealization. For the same reason, it is impossible for the leader to be constrained to conform to the members' group-specific uniformity.

The Group Task

The various examples studied show that a charismatically led group may have any sort of practical task whatever. Indeed, one example, the betrayed wife, had no manifest task at all. Even though the group's manifest morphological structure and its inherent psychological structure are highly specific, there is no necessary correlation between its morphological and psychological structures, on the one hand, and the practical purpose to which its members are consciously and collectively devoted, on the other. However, it is clear that the manifest purpose of the group task must not be in conflict with the latent purpose — i.e., the conflict-resolving function — of the members' mutual partial identification.

It follows from the relative lack of constraints imposed upon the formation of charismatically led groups that they may be formed in the most diverse circumstances and mobilize quite diverse people to act in concert. This sort of group formation is, in fact, the kind most easily effected when unified and uniform collective action is most urgently needed — that is, in emergency situations. In this respect, charismatically led groups contrast strikingly with leaderless groups (Balter, 1978), in which group formation takes place in highly specific contexts and requires a great deal of psychological uniformity among the members to effect the group formation.

IMPLICATIONS

Fantasy and Reality

The fact that the relationship to the leader and the mutual relationships of the members in a charismatically led group both resolve conflict has some pertinence to whether reality testing is brought to bear regarding the nature of the leader and of the other members. According to Waelder's (1930) principle of multiple function, the relation to reality is only one of several aspects of a conflict resolution, and it may not be the most determinative. The claims of other aspects of conflict may be more intense, so that the epistemological or adaptive aspects of the relation to reality may be compromised. Indeed, to some extent, this must always be so. In this very radical and important sense, every resolution of conflict is a "compromise."

Seen in this way, it is not surprising that the member's perception of the leader may not be congruent with the latter's actual nature. In fact, the view held of the idealized object *must* be divorced to some extent from the factual reality of that object. This is implied in the term "overestimation." In general, it is what the member fantasizes about the leader that is relevant. And, just as important, it is the taking of that fantasy *as reality* which makes the fantasy psychologically effective in resolving conflict. The defensive, conflict-resolving functions performed by idealization have been well discussed clinically by Reich (1940, 1953) and by Arlow (1963). The interests of conflict resolution may then motivate essentially imaginary and fallacious views of the charismatic leader on the part of his followers, views about which reality testing is neither desired nor accepted. To take this process to its limiting case, inner need and not actual fact can determine belief in the very existence of the charismatic leader.

The same considerations about conflict apply to the nature of the members. Their supposedly common attributes may be imaginary. And even their very existence may be fantasized, somewhat like the imaginary companions so prevalent in childhood. In the examples of charismatically led group formation presented above, the instances of the marching chemist and the betrayed wife involved other "members" whose existence *as fellow members* was only assumed and not actually demonstrated to the member.

Shifting the definition of group membership from an *actual social* process to a set of well-defined *intrapsychic* processes allows for the possibility of conceptualizing fantasied leaders and fantasied fellow members, for the mental processes involved may just as well take place with regard to fantasied objects — believed to be real — as with regard to ones concretely demonstrated to be real. This is well known in symptom formation and is subsumed under the concept of *psychic reality*. The concept of psychic reality may now be applied to group formation.

Sublimation

Most of the examples studied above bore out Freud's (1921) view that both the relationship of the group member to his leader and his relationship to his fellow members are sublimated (aim-inhibited, neutralized). The one exception was the betrayed wife's unsublimated attitude toward her idealized rival. Both sorts of tie in the other charismatically led groups, while expressing instinctual trends, were not manifestly, directly instinctual. Freud thought that manifest, direct instinctual involvement between leader and members or among members exacerbates the supposedly universal rivalry conflict resolved through group formation. The instinctual preference of the leader for a member or of one member for another undoes the conflict-resolving equality. Hence, group formation and sublimated object relations are supposedly inextricably bound together. Freud (1921, p. 142) went so far as to suggest that (charismatically led) group membership has a psychotherapeutic effect on members through the sublimation of otherwise psychopathogenically unruly impulses.

It is important here to note one very peculiar case: that of the charismatic leader who is sexually intimate with followers while the latter still remain members of the group and the group remains intact. This happens only when the equality in the relation to the leader is *not* broken — that is, when the leader has sexual intimacy with all the members equally or where all the members have such intimacy with each other as a form of common submission to the leader. Freud (1921, p. 140), in fact, took this issue up in a short discussion of orgies but did not greatly clarify it. He was too wedded to the idea of an inherent opposition between unsublimated impulsions and (charismatically led) group formation. However, Sperling (1956) did take up the issue more directly in his investigation of group perversions. One of his examples (pp. 58–60) was of a woman whose husband was in the position of charismatic leader to her and another couple. He induced his three followers to have "sexual intercourse in a group, and finally with an exchange of partners" (p. 59). This situation *approximated in actuality* the condition of all members being in equal unsublimated, sexual relationship to the leader; and that condition was very probably *reached in fantasy*. Certainly, sexual activity itself was a shared submissive act in regard to the leader.

The extreme instances of orgies and group perversions — that is, charismatically led groups in which unsublimated sexual gratification is the group task — indicate *that sublimation is not an essential factor in group formation but that equality is*. But if sublimation is not essential, it must certainly be very conducive to charismatically led group formation. As Freud (1921, p. 140) pointed out, it helps to tone down rivalry, jealousy, and possessiveness among members. It also maintains the idealization of the leader, for it protects his image from the intimate familiarity that promotes reality testing and breeds contempt.

SUMMARY

The various charismatically led groups studied here allow for certain generalizations about this group-type. Membership is effected through two mental processes: idealization of the leader and mutual partial identification of the members. Idealization is a form of conflict resolution which entails the ceding of superego autonomy (authority) to the leader or (what is the same thing) adopting toward him a regressed, ambivalent relationship entailing the mobilization of the passive, masochistic trends of the oedipal phase and manifested by adoration and/or fear. There is no specificity to the kind of conflict so resolved.

The member's partial identification with all the other members is a resolution of conflict about the leader which effects the group formation and causes the members to share a common quality that establishes uniformity among themselves and equality in their respective relationships with the leader. That common quality may be in any sphere of ego functioning whatever and may represent any sort of relationship among the members. The group-formative conflict, too, may be various; however, it is always engendered by the members' tendency to disrupt the idealizing conflict resolution—that is, to be in some way insubordinate to the leader. Accordingly, the shared quality of the members will always express their common submission to the leader and utilize the defenses of repression and reaction formation. Deviation from the group-specific uniformity mobilizes aggression toward the deviant from the other members, if not from the leader.

Charismatically led group formation may be effected (1) spontaneously by the members, (2) through intimidation by the leader himself, or (3) by a complementary combination of the two. There is no specific correlation between the conflict-resolving dynamic of the group's formation and the manifest group task. The nature of the leader and/or the other members may, in actuality, be purely imaginary; all that is necessary for the two defining mental processes to occur is that the member believe in the reality of the conflict-resolving nature of the leader and that of the other members. Sublimation of the relationship with the leader and/or with the other members is not essential to group formation. Equality of the members' relationship to the leader is essential, regardless whether that relationship is sublimated.

BIBLIOGRAPHY

ADORNO, T., et al. (1950). *The Authoritarian Personality*. New York: Harper.
ARLOW, J. A. (1963). Conflict, Regression and Symptom Formation. *Internat. J. Psycho-Anal.*, 44:12–22.
BAK, R. (1946). Masochism in Paranoia. *Psychoanal. Quart.*, 15:285–301.
BALTER, L. (1978). Leaderless Groups. *Internat. Rev. Psycho-Anal.*, 5:331–350.
BLOS, P. (1962). *On Adolescence: A Psychoanalytic Interpretation*. New York: Free Press.

BRENNER, C. (1975). Affects and Psychic Conflict. *Psychoanal. Quart.*, 44:5–28.
_____ (1982). The Concept of the Superego: A Reformulation. *Psychoanal. Quart.*, 51:501–525.
DEUTSCH, H. (1930). The Part of the Actual Conflict in the Formation of Neurosis. In *Neuroses and Character Types.* New York: International Universities Press, 1965, pp. 3–13.
FREUD, A. (1958). Adolescence. *The Psychoanalytic Study of the Child,* 13:255–278. New York: International Universities Press.
FREUD, S. (1911). Psycho-Analytic Notes on an Autobiographical Account of a Case of Paranoia (Dementia Paranoides). *Standard Edition,* 12:3–84. London: Hogarth Press, 1958.
_____ (1913). Totem and Taboo. *Standard Edition,* 13:1–164. London: Hogarth Press, 1953.
_____ (1917). Introductory Lectures on Psycho-Analysis. Part III. *Standard Edition,* 16:243–296. London: Hogarth Press, 1963.
_____ (1921). Group Psychology and the Analysis of the Ego. *Standard Edition,* 18:69–143. London: Hogarth Press, 1955.
_____ (1923). The Ego and the Id. *Standard Edition,* 19:3–66. London: Hogarth Press, 1961.
GREENACRE, P. (1966). Problems of Overidealization of the Analyst and of Analysis: Their Manifestations in the Transference and Countertransference Relationship. *The Psychoanalytic Study of the Child,* 21:193–212. New York: International Universities Press.
KOHUT, H. (1972). Thoughts on Narcissism and Narcissistic Rage. *The Psychoanalytic Study of the Child,* 27:360–400. New York: International Universities Press.
OTTO, R. (1917). *The Idea of the Holy.* New York: Oxford University Press, 1977.
REDL, F. (1942). Group Emotion and Leadership. *Psychiatry,* 5:573–596.
REICH, A. (1940). A Contribution to the Psychoanalysis of Extreme Submissiveness in Women. *Psychoanal. Quart.,* 9:470–480.
_____ (1953). Narcissistic Object Choice in Women. *J. Amer. Psychoanal. Assn.,* 1:22–44.
ROCHLIN, G. (1973). *Man's Aggression.* New York: Dell.
SPERLING, O. (1956). Psychodynamics of Group Perversions. *Psychoanal. Quart.,* 25:56–65.
WAELDER, R. (1930). The Principle of Multiple Function. *Psychoanal. Quart.,* 5:45–62, 1936.
WEBER, M. (1958). *Max Weber: Essays in Sociology,* ed. & trans. H. H. Gerth & C. W. Mills. New York: Oxford University Press.
WIXEN, B. (1970). Object-Specific Superego Responses. *J. Amer. Psychoanal. Assn.,* 18:831–840.

7

On Telephoning, Compulsive Telephoning, and Perverse Telephoning: Psychoanalytic and Social Aspects

RENATO J. ALMANSI, M.D.

Telephoning is so essential to everyday communication and so deeply woven into the fabric of our business and social lives that we could reasonably expect that it would have invited extensive analytic attention. In fact, few analytic papers deal specifically with the subject and very few incidental remarks are to be found elsewhere in the literature. This is even more surprising when we recall that perverse and obscene telephoning is so widespread a pathological behavior as almost to constitute a social ill: We know of few people who have not at some time or other been the object of this always disagreeable and, in many cases, anxiety-provoking kind of attention.

In this paper I shall examine some of the general psychological aspects of telephoning, including the magical character that the telephone may assume in certain cases and its relationship to the search for mastery; the role that aggression may play in telephoning; the bearing of object relations on telephoning in general and compulsive telephoning in particular; and the way in which telephone behavior may relate to the Oedipus complex and the formation of superego structures. I shall also present data from the analysis of a patient who used the telephone extensively in the service of a voyeuristic perversion. Finally, I shall discuss the psychological factors involved in the use of the phone as an adjuvant in therapy and in the operation of hotline social services.

Among the means of communication, the telephone occupies a niche all its own. Radio and television impart general information in an impersonal way, the phone establishes real personal contact between two people. Letters and telegrams lack entirely the dialogic quality of the phone conversation and, of course, are not as quick or immediate forms of communication; it is of no small importance that one or the other party's answer has to be delayed. Moreover, the written word lacks to a greater or lesser degree the highly personal, individual characteristics imparted by the human voice, with its infinite subtle nuances and possibilities for emotional impact.

The easy and instant contact with distant people which the phone permits and the very private and personal nature of telephone conversation have important implications in the field of object relations and make it a valuable adjuvant in therapy and in a number of important social projects, among them crisis intervention centers, suicide prevention, supportive therapy of old, lonely people, hotlines for teenage mothers, drug users and others.

Another important characteristic is that it permits one to speak easily and anonymously to perfect strangers, allowing it to be used for perverse and criminal purposes.

If we observe, in different cases and circumstances, the various psychological mechanisms at work in telephoning, we come upon a number of dynamic factors that condition a broad spectrum of normal and abnormal behavioral manifestations. Some of these factors proceed from such universal human needs as the maintenance of object relations and the achievement of control over one's environment, and are related to such normal psychological themes as the Oedipus complex or legitimate self-assertion. But these same psychological factors may be distorted by neurotic mechanisms such as we find in compulsive telephoning and telephone behavior dominated by gross, unsublimated aggressive needs. They may also become involved in perverse uses. Needless to say, the multiplicity of psychic motivations and the complex interrelationships between the various psychic institutions may result in complicated clinical pictures in which the boundaries between the schematic subdivisions presented above may become blurred and even disappear—a kind of continuum between the normal and the pathological and between the various types of pathological behavior. This makes it all the more important to spotlight those psychological factors and recurrent themes which seem to be of particular importance in understanding the psychology of telephoning.

TELEPHONE, MAGIC, AND THE SEARCH FOR MASTERY

The frequent connection between telephoning and the wish to obtain magically, often by way of identification, mastery over one's environment needs to be traced to its genetic roots. We may be able better to understand the magical aspects of telephoning if we consider that a very young child, who constantly sees people talking to one another, is talked to by others and talks or tries to talk back to them, must be fascinated when he first sees someone speaking on the telephone with an invisible auditor; there is something magical about this in and of itself. This fascination is enhanced when he is first placed at the phone and begins to hear and recognize the voice of a well-known person. It is a voice that has somewhat strange new characteristics and yet it is unmistakably the voice of *that* person who, oddly, is not to be seen. He can in turn answer and be recognized and understood, yet how the communication takes place is not at all clear to him. Anyone who has observed a child on the phone for the first time can see, portrayed on his face, puzzlement and surprise, and in the effort to handle a new and strange situation his tentative and cautious way of answering. It is a surprising and altogether new way of communicating with people whom the child has known and with whom he had been accustomed to communicate directly.

Thus, in the child's unconscious the phone may become an uncanny, magical object:[1] From this early fascination it is only a relatively short step to that belief in the existence of special and unusual powers that is the essence of magical thinking.

The interest thus aroused is likely to be only transient and leave no significant psychic traces. If, however, such primitive experiences become too bound up with the child's early object relations, his conflicts therein may impart to them the cathexis necessary for their becoming fixated and a basis for symptom formation.[2] This is precisely what happens in the case of compulsive telephoning, and what happened in the case of the perverse

---

1. This feeling of uncanniness is also, perhaps, a carry-over from the feeling experienced by the infant at the time when the human voice becomes a percept different from all other auditory percepts and, subsequently, when words begin to acquire specific meanings. I have documented this transition clinically in a detailed study (1958) of a hypnagogic phenomenon that involved auditory components which unquestionably harked back to experiences that had occurred approximately between the sixth and eighth months of life. Fascination with the human voice may, in some cases, be the basis of audiophilic interests: It may be the reason why Thomas A. Edison appreciated the phonograph above all his other inventions. Was he perhaps searching in his effort to reproduce sounds — and in his profound deafness — not only the everyday aural connections with his environment but also for some much more distant voice deeply buried in his past and well beyond any possibility of recollection? We cannot know for sure. But his extremely close relationship to his sweet mother-teacher (Miller, 1931) is certainly consistent with this possibility.

2. The same process, of course, may develop in the case of eye-catching objects. In a case that cannot be related here in detail, a small musical carousel given to a two-year-old by a very beloved surrogate mother spawned a fascination with rotating mechanisms and, eventually, obsessive ruminations on and schemes about rotating perpetual-motion machines. Here, too, the role of object relations was essential.

patient I shall discuss in this paper as well as in the cases described by
Silverman (1982a) and Shengold (1982).

In this way, the early fascination with the telephone may become involved in the libidinal, aggressive, and defensive operations of the psyche,
and give way to neurotic or perverse developments. At times, in connection with other conflictual components, mainly derived from the Oedipus
complex and from primal scene experiences, the phone may become a
powerful stimulant to the development of scientific interests.

Often, the interest in the phone and the magical quality attached to it
may find expression in the need to gain mastery over the environment not
only through thought but through action, which is very important to a
small child who longs for the marvelous powers of the adults who sur-
round him. How far back this mechanism may go is illustrated by an anec-
dote related to me with considerable excitement, broad smiles, and a triumphant gleam in the eye by an exceptionally intelligent adult, a scientist
with a special interest in mechanical research. He was under a year old
when his overanxious mother became greatly alarmed by what seemed to
her to be a frequently recurring, extremely odd behavior of his. Several
times a day he would suddenly make a fist of his right hand, bring it to his
right ear, and make noises with his mouth. The persistence of this pattern
of action so alarmed her that she called the pediatrician to the house.
While examining the child the odd behavior recurred but the pediatrician
noticed something that had escaped the mother. Just before the child
started the routine, a telephone had been ringing in the next apartment.
Obviously, this precocious child had been highly impressed by the strange
and magical aspects of his parents talking on the telephone and was trying
to do the same whenever he was reminded of it. This was a clear instance
of mastery through identification, in an attempt to emulate the adults'
ability to talk not only in the normal way but also in their other mysterious
fashion.

The same need for mastery appears to have been operative in the nine-
year-old patient described by Silverman (1982a), whose positive and negative oedipal conflicts expressed themselves in castrating wishes toward the
analyst-father and, in turn, in the wish to be castrated and loved as a
woman. In a period when his father had undergone a herniorrhaphy which
greatly magnified his castration anxiety, he seized compulsively upon the
phone as a way of expressing his active and passive libidinal strivings and
his aggression, and, at the same time, of relating from a safe distance to
the people who excited him, especially to one of his sisters towards whom
he felt much sexual excitement and whose muscular boyfriends he greatly
admired and envied. His telephoning was closely connected associatively
to the frequent telephoning of his sisters and to his listening in on their

conversations with their boyfriends. It enabled him to identify at the same time both with his sisters and their men friends, to express his sexual fantasies about both and to ward off his anxieties by distancing himself from their sources and from an extremely strong anxiety-provoking transference. Thus the telephone served the purpose of expressing his libidinal strivings and at the same time his defenses. It became the means of symbolically[3] gaining control over a very threatening situation and, most outstandingly, a magical instrument that enabled him to express his multiple omnipotent fantasies, take control of the analyst's phone and chair, enter the forbidden, desirable private space of women, assert that he was not castrated, make macho displays of fearlessness, attack people with impunity, and impersonate a young man who a girl thought was calling her.

It is of interest that, in order to exteriorize his conflicts and express them symbolically, this patient chose an object that he could *actually* use, consistent with his tendency to act out, his high level of motor activity, and the extreme pressure of his urges. I believe this consideration applies in general to all those cases in which the phone is used for the purposes of acting out instinctual impulses and masturbatory needs.

Shengold's (1982) patient's intense need for control and mastery expressed itself both in his symptomatology and in an absorbing interest in Nazi history and memorabilia. His basic pathology revolved around his powerful anal impulses and homosexual conflicts. His compulsive telephone flirtations, which involved a female identification and were equated in his mind with the compulsive masturbation of his adolescence, were directed to the mastery of his anxiety through the "fucking" of women, which made him feel "like the conquering male." He thus tried to stabilize his identity as a male and distance himself from his identification with the phallic mother.

He also tried, at the same time, to keep close to her. The woman on the other end of the line certainly stood for the mother. The particular importance that the phone assumed in the patient's pathology was intimately connected with his relationship to his mother and with the extensive anal stimulation she had given him in childhood through anal cleaning prac-

---

3. The symbolic aspects of the telephone will not be discussed in detail here since they have been dealt with in the papers by Silverman (1982a) and Shengold (1982), both of which emphasize its bisexual and masturbatory connotations and review the scanty literature on the subject. Shengold also points out how the telephone may stand symbolically for an enema, a connection by tube. In one of my patients (see the following section on object relations), it stood for a connection, a tie to the object, and literally an umbilical cord between him and his mother, and was related to intrauterine fantasies. In my perverse patient the tie had a particularly strong oral connotation.

tices and overstimulating enemas. In this way he was able to keep with her a "connection by tube."

As will be seen later, the pathology of my perverse patient was in several important respects reminiscent of Shengold's case.

The Role Of Aggression

As I suggested earlier, the normal manifestation of the aggressive instinct in, for example, the search for a reasonable degree of control over one's environment and the need for legitimate self-assertion may often give way, when the aggressive drive is particularly strong, the defenses against it inadequate, and the superego insufficiently developed, to various types of pathological manifestations. Aggression, indeed, plays a central role in neurotic and perverse telephoning. This certainly applies to Silverman's (1982a) patient, whose repetitive, provocative, and aggressive behavior in life, in analysis, and on the phone was so intimately intertwined with his libidinal urges and defensive needs. Similar aggressive mechanisms were also certainly present in Shengold's (1982) patient, who started to talk of his "telephone masturbation" during a session in which he was angry at the analyst about his bill, and after he had spoken of his anger following a quarrel with his employer. His aggression expressed itself not only in his interest in Nazism but also in his contemptuous attitude towards his sexual partners and in his compulsive and joyless sexual activity. To quote Shengold, "in his compulsively assumed identity as a Don Juan, he was preoccupied with submitting to, becoming enraged with and then conquering phallic women." The anxiety he was trying to distance with his telephone activities was motivated to a considerable extent by his highly destructive fantasies, the strongly repressed aggressive component of his powerful anal impulses.

My perverse patient, whose extreme aggressive anal impulses had been well documented by a Rorschach test, would occasionally, after having been mistakenly recognized on the phone by a woman as her lover, drop the pretense and come out with a very aggressive coarse remark to make her realize she was talking to a stranger. In this way he achieved his sadomasochistic goals of shocking the woman and causing himself feelings of tremendous guilt.

On one occasion, in a period when he was angry about the necessity of paying my bill, he began a session complaining of severe abdominal distress, constipation, bloated feeling, and flatulence. Then, after a long silence, he said, "Just now, I don't know why, I am thinking of a joke I heard some time ago. A psychoanalyst moved to Arizona and his first patient was an Indian chief who lived in an extremely isolated place, a great distance away. It was decided that the only practical way to conduct the analysis was by the use of smoke signals. The next morning at the appointed time the analyst was on top of his hill, looking in the direction where the smoke signals were to come from. Just at that moment, at the Atomic Proving Grounds, an atom bomb was exploded. He was overcome with shock and surprise, covered his eyes in terror, and said, 'Oh my God. If I had only known that he had a problem like that, I would never have taken him as a patient!' " My interpretation, to the effect that he was angry at me and would have very much liked to destroy me utterly with an "atomic" blast of his intestinal gases, was met with uproarious laughter.

The needs to impersonate, to deceive or seduce, or to shock or attack or dominate the invisible auditor to be found in all instances of obscene or perverse telephoning are certainly expressions of the aggressive nature of these patients and their very strong urge for mastery.

The importance of keeping in mind the aggressive motivations behind perverse telephoning was proven to me on one occasion when I found myself on the receiving end of an obscene telephone call. I was awakened at six in the morning by the voice of a man who seemed to have a slight speech difficulty and who asked me a brief, very silly, aggressively obscene question about my wife. I understood him perfectly, but to gain a little time to find a proper answer, I acted as if I had not. With the utmost politeness I apologized for not having understood him and asked him to repeat his question. When he did, I replied in the friendly and booming voice of a person who has been most pleasantly surprised: "Ooohh! You are a _____" (a most unflattering and obscene characterization). Obviously disappointed at having been deceived at the beginning by my tone of voice, of having been made fun of and violently attacked, the caller immediately hung up.

Object Relations And The Compulsion To Telephone

The relationship between compulsive and perverse telephoning and the origins and structure of object relations deserves particular attention. This relationship is rooted in the fact that telephoning is of course a form of social communication and is bound, therefore, to reflect facets and nuances of the speaker's ties to his early objects: The middle-aged son or daughter who every day calls his or her mother on the phone "just for a chat," the anxious person who calls a trusted friend for a little conversation or advice even in matters of minimal importance, the lonely person who spends hours on the phone in interminable conversation with a number of acquaintances, all represent instances that can best be understood in the general context of the vicissitudes of early object relations.

In the case of my perverse patient, to be discussed in detail later, telephoning represented one of the most obvious expressions of his orality and of his very severe separation anxiety, which had originated in a nearly fatal intestinal illness between the ninth and 15–18th months of his life. The telephoning had begun one day while his wife was hospitalized for an appendectomy and he was in bed with a cold and an upset stomach. He was extremely anxious and afraid that she might die. Subsequently, a feeling of loneliness and abandonment regularly precipitated his bouts of perverse telephoning. On a genital level, this represented an attempt to keep contact with and conquer the oedipal mother.

As we have seen, the need to retain contact with the object was also present in the patients described by Silverman (1982a) and Shengold (1982). On the other hand, telephoning can serve the purpose of protecting the object against the full impact of the caller's aggression, a motive that was clearly indicated in my perverse patient and in the patient described by Silverman (1982a).

Since telephoning involves aural contact, it is necessary to underline the importance of the auditory aspects of the relationship to the object. When a loss is threatened, a regressive revival of the first contacts with the object may take place; in this setting, the voice is of primary importance, not only in terms of the meaning of words but also the tone of the voice, both of which may play a particularly significant role.[4] Under such circumstances, a compulsion to hear a friendly human voice may develop.

This type of problem appeared very clearly in another of my patients, a highly intelligent man who entered analysis out of fear that his extramarital activities might lead to the breakup of his marriage and the loss of his five-year-old child, to whom he was greatly attached. He had been married before and had broken up the marriage for no apparent reason, just as with very little logical reason he had become angry at and detached from his present wife, a beautiful, intelligent, and sensitive woman. He had established two simultaneous long-running affairs, and juggled the three women with increasing discomfort. He often tried to break off the

---

4. The importance of the percept of the human voice in the formation of object relations and in the very early period of life in which this influence makes itself felt have been discussed by me in other papers (1958, 1983). The influence of the tone of the voice was studied experimentally by Eissler (1952) in acute schizophrenics. Eissler found that the patients clearly reacted to his affects and emotions and especially to variations in the timbre of his voice.

extramarital affairs but as soon as he took some positive steps was overtaken by anxiety and did the impossible to resume the relationships. This recurred several times and was aggravated by the fact that his two lovers finally attempted a break by establishing other relationships.

This patient had to use the telephone a great deal in his work. As he himself noted, however, he tended to overuse it to an inordinate degree. At times he saw his hand reaching for the telephone and then realized he had no need to make a call. During a temporary separation from his wife he found himself alone almost every night in the small apartment to which he had moved. He would call, one after the other, his mistresses, former girlfriends, and other women he knew till late in the night, after which he would watch television until he fell asleep. On one occasion, while on a business trip, he called one of his mistresses long distance and from her response had the impression that she might be with another man. In spite of her denials, he called her again in a frenzy, to be reassured. That night he dreamed of himself in a telephone booth frantically reaching for the dial with one hand while searching for change with the other.

Associations to this dream led to a recollection which he had mentioned previously several times. He was the first-born child, three years and three months old when his younger brother was born. His mother had been in the hospital for eight days, during which time he had stayed at someone else's home. One day he was brought to the hospital. All he remembered of the visit was that he had been placed "on a black telephone box" overlooking the nursery window so that he might see his brother. He did not remember seeing his brother or his mother. There are several aspects of this story which are most probably not factual; it is obviously a screen memory that has been heavily re-elaborated. One point, however, is sure: The birth of the brother had in some mysterious way been connected in the patient's mind with a telephone. We may speculate that we are dealing in this with a displaced recollection of an actual call, possibly from the hospital announcing the brother's birth.

The associations which followed related to his constant rivalry with his brother, which continued despite the fact that the patient was by far more successful professionally and financially. He then spoke of a business situation (that cannot be described here) which clearly related to competition with another man and which embodied intrauterine fantasies. This led him to speak of one of his mistresses holding him in her arms, then of his childhood fights with his brother whom, as an infant, he had once kicked violently. He still remembered his mother yelling, "He has killed my baby." His relationship to his mother, however, had always been extremely close. He had been the apple of her eye and could do no wrong.

In this case, then, among other meanings, the telephone clearly stood for a connection, a tie, and literally an umbilical cord between the patient and his mother.

The counterpart to this is the distance that the telephone interposes between the speakers, which serves both the purpose of defense and the dilution, as it were, of object relations. In this respect, Shengold (1982) points out how in psychotic or borderline patients "the telephone can maintain some object ties at a bearable distance, providing separation without loss and contact without fusion."

Finally, the telephone often makes it easier to counterfeit genuine object ties: Since the speaker is invisible, hypocritical words will not be betrayed by the expression on his face. This is just one way in which modern technology influences human contacts. At times it may substitute for them. Modern life brings modern problems: The telephone, like such other modern contrivances as the radio or the television, is often used to substitute for human contacts, something of which we are often aware in the productions of our patients.

THE OTHER'S VOICE — THE OEDIPAL TRIANGLE AND THE SUPEREGO

The case just described leaves no doubt as to whose voice the patient was searching for in his compulsive telephoning: the soothing, warm, loving voice of the preoedipal mother which could give him reassurance that she would be always with him. In other patients, oedipal motives may be preeminent, as in those described by Harris (1957), all of whom were strongly attached to their aggressive and seductive mothers and extremely antagonistic to their fathers. The triangular oedipal situation was clearly displaced onto their telephoning. One of these patients was afraid of using the phone lest the man on the other end "cut him off." Another felt that his phone conversations with his money-grubbing alcoholic father were among his most traumatic experiences; he equated them with castration. A third patient was afraid to use the phone when his father was within hearing. My perverse patient, in his compulsive telephoning, as well as in many other life situations, searched desperately for both the oedipal and the preoedipal mother; but here, too, the depreciated mental image of his alcoholic and ineffectual but highly feared father was intense. If a man answered the phone he felt terrorized. He feared to an almost unimaginable degree that the call might be intercepted by the police, that he might be caught in the act, thrown into jail, disgraced, and that he might thus lose his job and his family. Behind such fears lay a very harsh superego which made him view himself as a thoroughly contemptible person who deserved nothing but unhappiness and ruin.

In a patient described by Silverman (1982b), the superego's disapproval was manifested in anxiety dreams in which the patient, during a period in which he was afraid of losing his mother, heard on the phone an unfamiliar and coldly menacing voice or a threatening buzzing sound instead of the friendly parental voice for which he yearned. This patient, like another patient described in the same paper, felt safe as long as he received vocal assurances that his behavior was acceptable enough for him to be loved and protected from harm. But hostile voices or loud and harsh noises signified that punishment for his misdeeds, actual or fantasied, was imminent. Silverman's findings are obviously highly pertinent to the cases mentioned by Harris (1957) and to the perverse patient described by me: The "other" on the phone may not only be the positively experienced maternal object but may also be, at the same time, the aggressively perceived, threatening paternal one. The oedipal triangle is completed in this synthesis: Out of the oedipal conflict the superego functions develop and are expressed in the form of a "voice of conscience."

On The Pathogenesis Of A Case Of Perverse Telephoning

My patient was a businessman in his mid-thirties who came into analysis principally because of anxiety connected with his multiple voyeuristic activities, severe hypochondriacal complaints, and work and marital difficulties. Since his history and the course of his long analysis have been presented in detail in a previous paper (1981), and the relationship of his scoptophilia to his fear of object loss examined in detail in another (1979), I shall limit myself here to a few essential facts concerning his pathology and to a discussion of those factors which relate to the origins and the psychological significance of his telephone perversion.

His voyeuristic behaviors included frequent use of pornography, peeping through windows for hours at a time accompanied by masturbation, compulsion to look at women's breasts, and drawing scenes of polymorphous perverse sexual activities involving fellatio, cunnilingus, and lesbianism between big-breasted, hard-looking, high-heeled females (at times he added a penis to a female genital in his drawings). He also wrote stories with polymorphous perverse content revolving around similar themes, including the sexual enslavement through cunnilingus of a young innocent girl by an older lesbian. His scoptophilia was closely connected to the enormous impact of his repeated observations of the primal scene between his parents between the ages of two and three and a half, to his consciously remembered curiosity about his parents' sex life and sexual activities in general, to his absorbing interest in women's genitals and breasts throughout his youth, and to his fantasies of lesbian relations between his mother and sister. The most prominent expression of his voyeurism came in his activities on the phone, which I shall discuss in a moment.

My patient's presenting symptoms also included such severe hypochrondriacal concerns as fear of the future, fear of death, the fear of cancer of the stomach, rectum, and penis, and fear of the possible consequences of his masturbation, which had been a problem since early youth. There were also multiple, lifelong intestinal disturbances (bloated feeling, belching, indigestion, pains in the stomach), pains in the back and chest, constipation, and occasional diarrhea. His marital life was marred by continuous struggles with his intelligent but aggressive, frigid, and penis-envying wife. His business life was characterized by extreme lack of productivity, fear of inadequacy, and a strained relationship with his boss in which unconscious homosexual leanings were easily detectable. Frequent overeating and overdrinking usually aggravated his abdominal complaints. At times there were bouts of depression. Dishonesties which could have resulted in very serious consequences were occasionally a problem; they were followed by deep feelings of embarrassment and guilt.

Let me summarize the findings of his long analysis. The patient's main difficulties involved severe fear of object loss, which was genetically connected to his intense oral cravings and to an almost fatal and extremely debilitating intestinal illness he had suffered between the ages of nine and 15–18 months; this fear of object loss was at the root of his scoptophilia, in that it had brought about an increased need to maintain visual contact with the object and to incorporate it visually. There was also intense castration anxiety (chiefly on the basis of his outstanding oedipal problems, greatly enhanced by his mother's grossly seductive behavior), a basic confusion of sexual identity, much latent homosexuality in conjunction with passive feminine fantasies, marked anality, and deep anal-receptive longings. Masochistic trends were prominent and there were many indications of his wish to identify with a strong father along with deep resentment of, coupled with attraction to, his mother, who appeared to him as a threatening, phallic woman. Reversals of sadistic and masochistic roles, oscillations between activity and passivity and between heterosexuality and homosexuality were frequent, and were aggravated by his basic confusion of the sexes and by the highly composite nature of his sexual object. There was also a strong tendency to magical thinking and a constant need to deny passivity and homosexual feelings.

As stated in the section on object relations, the telephoning had begun while his wife was hospitalized for a surgical intervention, which caused him considerable anxiety—he was afraid that she might die. He was at home in bed, alone, sick with a cold and a upset stomach. Depressed, anxious, bored, not knowing what to do, he made his first calls. This setting became a pattern; subsequently he often was overtaken by the wish to telephone if he was alone, sick, or idle. He mostly called up women picked at random from the phone book; due to his fear of discovery, only in a very few cases did he dare to call the wives of distant acquaintances. In the course of these conversations he muffled his voice (he pretended to have a cold) and tried to be recognized as an acquaintance. He found great delight in the game of trying to figure out what sort of person she was and the supposed relationship between her and the person she thought he was. He derived a great feeling of power from the fact that he deceived his interlocutor. He called this game "a way of looking into the woman's mind." He hoped he might be acknowledged as a previous sexual partner, but even if he was just thought to be an acquaintance, he skillfully tried to turn the conversation to sexual matters by the use of various artifices. Usually he complained of not feeling well, and when asked about this, he hinted at marital difficulties. Having thus stimulated the woman's curiosity, he complained, seemingly with great reluctance, about his wife's hunger for "unnatural sexual practices" and of her "insatiable sexual demands." He thus tried to engage the woman in talking of her own sexual activities, his main purpose being that of getting her reaction to cunnilingus and "big penises." He tried to drag the conversation out while slowly masturbating, holding the ejaculation back as long as possible. When possible he used obscene words. If he succeeded in getting a descriptive reaction from the woman, he became extremely excited and ejaculated. On some occasions, in the course of such calls, he dropped the pretense of being an acquaintance and blurted out an obscene remark which shocked the woman, and immediately hung up. On one such occasion he had the impression that the woman had fainted; he felt like a "murderer." At times, he was mistakenly taken for the woman's lover, and after a very exciting conversation, was invited to the woman's apartment. He never went, although he felt greatly tempted; he remained in a state of extreme tension and impotent anger.

These calls were made from his home, his office, and frequently, for the sake of prudence, from public phone booths. He estimated that in the course of a year they numbered in the thousands. Of these, only a very small percentage were "successful." His perverse phoning was attended by an overwhelming sense of guilt and the fear of discovery.

The assessment of the origins and structure of this perversion must begin from the fact that the use of the phone was a constant and indispensable part of this patient's business life.[5] His livelihood depended almost entirely on the contacts he made on the phone and for this reason each of them was fraught with tremendous fear that he might fail. This was compounded by his feeling of inferiority, his keen awareness of his generally poor business performance, and his chronic financial difficulties. For him, the telephone was literally a lifeline to his sustenance in every sense. It was, therefore, intimately connected unconsciously to his pregenital attachment to his mother and to the impact left by the intestinal illness of his childhood.

This oral connotation was clearly indicated in his associations when he first spoke of his interest in cunnilingus, and then shifted to talk of the devices he used to bring about a "successful" conversation with a woman. He went on to describe an instance in which he was mistaken on the phone for the young lover of an old and experienced woman. This made him so excited that he ejaculated twice. This excitement was connected to fantasies of which he spoke often of having an older woman as a mistress, which had not only an oedipal connotation but also a definite nurturing oral one.

On another occasion, after mentioning this fantasy again, he went on to say that the previous day in a restaurant he had seen the breasts of a waitress who had bent over to serve him. He felt the need to phone: He wanted to talk about "tits." He then spoke of an old friend of his mother into whose bed he had occasionally crawled as a child; he had been fascinated by her white skin, her silky underthings, and her perfume; then he said that recently he had seen a man at the beach clutching is girlfriend's breasts. This intermingling of genital and pregenital themes was a prominent feature of his analysis.

As is clear from this material, telephoning served one of his most essential needs, that of keeping contact with the orally experienced object. This need also expressed itself in the easy and chummy way in which he made contact with people in bars and, most outstandingly, in his strong, depressive, and angry reactions on the occasion of any interruption in the analysis.

Another factor which had a decisive influence in fixating his interest on the phone, giving it a frank sexual aim, was the fact that in his youth he had often seen his mother listening in on party line conversations. On

---

5. The patient I described in the section on object relations also had to do a great deal of telephoning in the course of his professional work. We may reasonably wonder to what extent the daily extensive use of the phone and these patients' dependence on it for their livelihoods, in conjunction, of course, with other, deeper mechanisms, may have contributed to its compulsive use. This would be an example of a perfectly normal, habitual action facilitating the choice of a compulsive and perverse symptom.

some of these occasions he had seen her masturbating at the same time, from which he had gathered that a salacious conversation was going on. (Interestingly enough, on one occasion the patient told me that in his own phone conversations he was very keen to learn whether the woman was interested in sexual matters.) It is a measure of the degree of repression to which this recollection had been subjected that the information that the mother had masturbated on those occasions emerged more than two and a half years after he had told me that she used to listen in on the party line.

The mother's activities on the phone played a central role in the structure of the perversion. On one side the patient identified with her in his attempts to discover women's innermost secrets. (Throughout the analysis, his tendency to identify with her emerged on many occasions, playing a large role in his feminine identification and homosexual leanings). On the other hand, he identified with her interlocutor in the same attempt to discover her secrets. Curiosity, he stated, had always been for him "an incurable disease." Thus, in his telephoning there was a strong element of oedipal seduction and an attempt to gain mastery within the oedipal conflict.

At the same time, the telephoning was a way of degrading women, a reflection of the extent to which he viewed his mother unconsciously as a lewd woman and of his extreme ambivalence toward women in general. All of these reactions — his tendency to identify with mother, his need to discover the most intimate details of her sexual responses, his wish to seduce her, and his fantasy of her as a prostitute — were genetically connected to his primal scene observations.

At the same time that it expressed the patient's instinctual demands, telephoning also served the defensive purpose of exciting women from a safe distance, thus fending off actual sexual contact and castration anxiety. Similarly, his interest in cunnilingus involved exciting a woman without the use of his penis. His ambivalence was most obvious in his relationships to his wife and his boss, both of which were characterized by attraction and a simultaneous defensive need to avoid contact and distance himself from his libidinal and aggressive urges.

In parallel fashion he used telephoning to express aggression while, at the same time, protecting the object against its full impact. Aggression was an outstanding part of his character structure and manifested itself not only in some of his telephone activities, as described before, but in his marital and business life as well. This was confirmed by a Rorschach test administered before the analysis, and found expression, together with the defense against it, in the transference: On one occasion, he confessed with great embarrassment that he had felt sorely tempted the previous day to call me up to tell me to fuck myself.

This review of the various genetic factors which participated in the formation of the perversion would be incomplete if it did not mention that one of its most important roots was the need to appear fearless in order to offset his omnipresent fear of being a "hick" and an inferior and insignificant being (in fact, the weak, powerless little child of the primal scene and of the intestinal illness). Telephoning made him feel invincible: It was a dare which gave him a huge thrill — he compared it to "putting his head in the lion's mouth" (associations connected this expression to his interest in cunnilingus). Even more important, it enabled him to deny passivity, homosexual feelings, and his enormous feeling of intellectual and sexual inadequacy. It buttressed his self-image and was a way of rebelling against society and of finding compensation to which he felt entitled for his losses and for the wrongs which he felt had been inflicted upon him. His dishonesties stemmed from the same psychological motivations.

In sum, this patient's telephoning served a very broad spectrum of instinctual needs both in the libidinal and the aggressive realms. His other considerable symptomatic behaviors included an obsessive and unfulfilled search for sexual outlets, excessive drinking, overdependency, rages, an insatiable need for material and emotional supplies, and antisocial acts. All these symptoms were closely related to the same genetic factors which underlay his telephone activities.

ON THE USE OF THE TELEPHONE AS AN ADJUVANT IN THERAPY

The use of the telephone as an adjuvant in dynamic psychotherapy and psychoanalysis is, to the best of my knowledge, very common but seldom mentioned in the literature: It may be felt by some that it represents a departure from an absolutely "pure" technique and therefore a technical error. It is, of course, perfectly correct that under average therapeutic conditions direct contact between therapist and patient represents the only technically correct procedure. Yet in certain seriously ill patients the phone may have to be used in case of emergency or to overcome otherwise insuperable resistances.

Saul (1951) describes a highly disturbed female patient who, because of her intense transference, could not talk directly to him in times of special distress. The telephone diluted the transference to intensities that she could endure. For about one year phone conversations were alternated with office visits until she was able to discuss her problems entirely in personal interviews. The outcome of the treatment was highly successful. The fact that the overcoming of the resistances took place in the way chosen by the patient herself, Saul points out, had important implications for the ego. Long-term telephone contacts between therapist and patient also occurred in 14 cases mentioned by Rosenbaum (1977) in which treatment had to be interrupted because of a change of residence of the analyst or the patient.

Although I have never had to carry out long-term telephone contacts like those described in the papers by Saul and Rosenbaum, and believe that their use is probably relatively rare, I have, as every therapist has, been obliged fairly often to handle emergency calls from severely ill, suicidal patients in situations of grave crisis and stress. When the patient was already well known, it was possible to give suitable interpretations consistent with the patient's specific needs and pathology. Supportive help as well is almost always indispensable in these cases.

The special, immediate line of communication afforded by the telephone has proven of enormous importance in saving not only many treatments but many patients' lives as well. Indeed, in such cases, it would be a grave technical error not to use any means at one's disposal that could avert the dangers faced by the patient and allow the continuation of the treatment. These points have also been emphasized by Harris (1957).

As to the psychodynamics involved in such cases, it must be borne in mind that these telephone contacts are bound to stimulate deep-going reactions at all levels of psychic functioning. With regard to their implications for the ego, Dickes (1967) points out that in such cases the analyst presents himself to the patient as a real person—as a representative of reality—thus strengthening the therapeutic alliance. It must also be emphasized, however, that there are important unconscious transference implications: The therapist's willingness to break a rule for the patient, the closer contact thus brought about and the supportive role he assumes, so close to that of a nurturing parental figure, will of necessity make it easier for the patient to transfer onto the therapist the feelings he formerly experienced toward his early objects. The characteristics of the therapist's voice and the many subtle nuances of the spoken word may assume particular importance on these occasions. Indeed, the transference phenomena taking place under these circumstances may easily impart to the therapist's voice the superego connotations discussed in a previous section, greatly enhancing the therapeutic effectiveness of the telephone contact.

PSYCHODYNAMICS IN HOTLINE THERAPEUTIC SOCIAL SERVICES

Since 1953, when the Telephone Samaritans, a religiously inspired suicide prevention center, was founded in London, many other crisis intervention centers based on the use of the telephone have been established in

Europe and the United States, where they have made significant contributions to the welfare of society. Besides suicide prevention centers, which are the best known, these include centers for the support of the elderly, the lonely, or the visually impaired, hotlines for teenage mothers, centers for rape victims, drug hotlines, poison control centers, centers for the follow-up therapy of alcoholics, and telephone counseling for hypertensive patients. The selective granting of telephone privileges to prison inmates also serves a therapeutic purpose.

It seems reasonable to assume that some of the psychodynamics operative in these situations do not differ basically from those we have already discussed. The "umbilical cord" character of the phone line, so important to the patient described in the earlier section on object relations, and the oral connotation of the phone as a lifeline, so crucial to my perverse patient, should explain the place the telephone may occupy in the unconscious minds of poor, lonely, and depressed people isolated from the world by the neglect of others and their own feebleness or visual impairment. For them, as for the suicidally depressed patient, the desperate pregnant teenager, the rape victim, and the panicky drug user, the phone can be the carrier of hope, of a friendly and empathic voice, and can bring about a much-needed revival of positive experiences with original objects. What we have mentioned in the section on object relations regarding the importance of the characteristics of the voice in the context of object relations is highly pertinent in this connection.

Moreover, the structure of the telephone apparatus itself tends to enhance the emotional value of the voice. Miller (1973) points out that "the speaker's lips are, in a sense, only inches away from the listener's ear. This leads to an unusual kind of intimacy" (p. 16).

The fact that the caller and the therapist do not know each other and that the caller remains anonymous differentiates very significantly hotline conversations from other therapeutic telephone contacts and may make them even more advantageous. Evans, Werkhoven, and Fox (1982) speak of the protective sense of distance and privacy and of the feeling of control experienced by anonymous subjects in these settings. Grumet (1979) points out that in such situations the ambivalent patient can achieve closeness at a safe distance, just as did the patients described by Silverman (1982a) and Shengold (1982). Also, the fact that the therapist is not visually present may greatly facilitate the discussion of embarrassing material. Nor should one minimize the significance to these patients of the magical aspects of telephoning: The hope for quick relief, greatly heightened by intense anxiety and the need to master it in every way possible, the absence of the view of the therapist, which facilitates fantasy production, and the process of transference to the voice and the unknown center from which it emanates, all contribute to maximize magical mechanisms and expectations.

In conclusion, I would emphasize that considering the multiplicity, the variations and the intertwining of the dynamic factors which may participate in the formation of telephone behavior, the material presented here can be only a small sample of the many possible clinical constellations.

It is my hope that this paper may stimulate further studies in this field, which is of considerable interest both to the psychoanalyst and to the social scientist.

BIBLIOGRAPHY

ALMANSI, R. (1958). A Hypnagogic Phenomenon. *Psychoanal. Quart.,* 27:539–546.
―――― (1979). Scopophilia and Object Loss. *Psychoanal. Quart.,* 48:601–619.
―――― (1981). Scopophilia and Separation Anxiety (with Notes on a Case of Voyeuristic Perversion). In *Downstate Psychoanalytic Institute 25th Anniversary Series,* Vol. 3, ed. S. Orgel & B. Fine. New York: Aronson, pp. 23–43.
―――― (1983). On the Persistence of Very Early Memory Traces in Psychoanalysis, Myth and Religion. *J. Amer. Psychoanal. Assn.,* 31:391–421.
DICKES, R. (1967). Severe Regressive Disruption of the Therapeutic Alliance. *J. Amer. Psychoanal. Assn.,* 15:508–533.
EISSLER, K. (1952). Remarks on the Psychoanalysis of Schizophrenics. In *Psychoanalysis with Schizophrenics,* ed. E. Brody & F. Redlich. New York: International Universities Press, pp. 130–167.
EVANS, R. L., WERKHOVEN, W., & FOX, H. R. (1982). Treatment of Social Isolation and Loneliness in a Sample of Visually Impaired Elderly Persons. *Psychol. Reports,* 51:103–108.
GRUMET, G. W. (1979). Telephone Therapy: A Review and Case Report. *Amer. J. Orthopsychiat.,* 49:574–584.
HARRIS, H. (1957). Telephone Anxiety. *J. Amer. Psychoanal. Assn.,* 5:342–347.
MILLER, F. T. (1931). *Edison-Benefactor of Mankind.* Philadelphia: John C. Winston & Co.
MILLER, N. (1973). The Telephone in Outpatient Psychotherapy. *Amer. J. Psychother.,* 27:15–26.
ROSENBAUM, M. (1977). Premature Interruption of Psychotherapy: Continuation of Contact by Telephone and Correspondence. *Amer. J. Psychiat.,* 134:200–202.
SAUL, L. (1951). A Note on the Telephone as a Technical Aid. *Psychoanal. Quart.,* 20:287–290.
SHENGOLD, L. (1982). The Symbol of Telephoning. *J. Amer. Psychoanal. Assn.,* 30: 461–470.
SILVERMAN, M. (1982a). A Nine Year Old's Use of the Telephone: Symbolism in Statu Nascendi. *Psychoanal. Quart.,* 51:598–611.
―――― (1982b). The Voice of Conscience and the Sounds of the Analytic Hour. *Psychoanal. Quart.,* 51:196–217.

Author Index

Subject Index

$5- Gen 8/16 K